The World Cup

The World Cup

The **Ultimate** Guide to the **Greatest** Sports **Spectacle** in the **World**

Fernando Fiore

Translated from the Spanish by Ezra E. Fitz

rayo

An Imprint of HarperCollinsPublishers

THE WORLD CUP. Copyright © 2006 by Fernando Fiore. Translation
copyright © 2006 by Ezra E. Fitz. All rights reserved. Printed in the United
States of America. No part of this book may be used or reproduced in any
manner whatsoever without written permission except in the case of brief
quotations embodied in critical articles and reviews. For information, address
HarperCollins Publishers, 10 East 53rd Street, New York, NY 10022.

HarperCollins books may be purchased for educational, business, or sales
promotional use. For information, please write: Special Markets Department,
HarperCollins Publishers, 10 East 53rd Street, New York, NY 10022.

FIRST EDITION

Designed by Timothy J. Shaner/Night & Day Design
Photo research by David E. Franck / Franckfotos, Inc.

Library of Congress Cataloging-in-Publication Data has been applied for.

ISBN-10: 0-06-082089-6   ISBN-13: 978-0-06-082089-3

06 07 08 09 10 ❖ / RRD 10 9 8 7 6 5 4 3 2

For my son,

Gianluca, and for

the orange tree I planted in my yard,

because, in life, every man ought to have

a son, plant a tree, and write a book.

"Goals Are True Loves."

(I don't know who coined that expression, but it is my favorite soccer saying!)

Contents

Opening Whistle

If you're holding this guide in your hands (whether you've bought it or were given it as a gift), then chances are you're planning on enjoying the 2006 FIFA World Cup on television; or maybe you're even planning on traveling to Germany to see it firsthand.

In either case, just like this book, you are in good hands. These pages contain everything you need to know in order to enjoy the greatest sporting event in the world. I probably don't have to tell *you* how important it is; I'm sure you already know. Still, maybe I should ask for a show of hands: Is there anybody out there who does not grasp the magnitude, transcendence, significance, impact, and influence—economic, social, political, and cultural—of the World Cup?

If you've got your arm in the air, don't feel bad. Welcome. You're still in good hands.

What I present here ranges from the history and profiles of the thirty-two teams that will compete in the eighteenth FIFA World Cup, Germany 2006 (the official name of the event), to the can't-miss sights in each of the twelve host cities, passing through (of course!) the stars and the stories of the seventeen previous World Cups, the protagonists, the great goals, the electric parties, and all the final matches.

"MY PEOPLE"

Particular attention will be paid to the participating Latin American nations and their outstanding figures, not to mention their past successes. In general, the history of the World Cup is the story of the

soccer powers and their accomplishments. We will see that here, but we will also see much, much more.

For example, how Chile made it to the World Cup after the fall of Allende; the war between Honduras and El Salvador leading up to Mexico '70; the first Brazilian "Pelé"; why Maradona was not on the roster for Argentina '78; the drama of the "Padre" for Chile '62; the amazing goal scored by Colombia against the greatest keeper on earth; how the Jules Rimet Trophy was stolen in London *and* in Rio; the Latino players on the U.S. team; why Amadeo Carrizo only played in one World Cup; the expulsion of Rattín in England; the Peruvian referee who ejected Garrincha; Cuba and the only Cup they ever attended; how Costa Rica and Bolivia reached their first Cups; Pelé's first goal; the debuts of "El Pibe" Valderrama and of "Nene" Cubillas; and more. Much more.

MEXICO IN THE WORLD CUP

The Mexican national team will receive special attention. After Brazil, Mexico is the Latin American country with the most World Cup appearances, and the history of its team is filled with warm anecdotes and dramatic, little-known episodes that illustrate the evolution of a soccer power that now ranks among the ten best in the world.

We will be learning about the five World Cups of "La Tota" Carbajal; the Tegucigalpa fiasco; the first Mexican goal scored in a World Cup; the "Tri" by Trellez; the goals scored by "Güero" Cárdenas; the soap opera of *Los Cachirules*; the debut of "Chava" Reyes and other Chivas players in the Cup; the score Borja notched in London; the great goal by Negrete in the Azteca; what happened in the qualifying match with Haiti; the first draw and the first win; the arrival of "Bora"; the day they had to wear borrowed jerseys; the debut of Hugo Sánchez, and why he didn't want to take a penalty kick at U.S.A. '94.

MY ANECDOTES

I will also take the liberty of humbly sharing with you my own personal anecdotes, both as a fan and as a journalist. I am eternally grateful to have been able to enjoy so many World Cup matches, and to have had the honor of meeting and befriending many stars, including "O Rei" Pelé, Maradona, Valderrama, Cubillas, Carrizo, Perfumo, Francescoli, Chilavert, Stoichkov, Clavijo, Carbajal, and Hugo Sánchez.

FORMAT

All of this will be presented in the form of a World Cup match, complete with overtime and penalty kicks.

The "First Half" will be a presentation of the beauty of Germany and its principal characteristics. The "Second Half" is a tour through the history of the various World Cup finals. Then we'll move into "Overtime" and get to know the thirty-two participating nations and their stars. That's where you'll also find the official event calendar, called "Follow the Cup," so that you can follow along with the events and results of each game, and make your own notes and commentaries. Finally, the game will conclude and the champion will take his "Victory lap," which, in our case, is a loop through the twelve host cities of Germany '06.

And just for fun, all throughout the book you'll find facts and trivia with which to stump your friends during this summer's Cup.

But enough talking!

Find your favorite chair, make yourself comfortable, and allow me to take you on the most extraordinary adventure in the history of sports: that of the World Cup.

Fernando Fiore
Miami, 2006

Welcome to Deutschland!

As they say in German: *Wilkommen in Deutschland!* By way of introduction—and for those who don't know—the home of the 2006 World Cup is one of the most enchanting and picturesque countries on earth. It is a place of beautiful landscapes, fascinating cities, and its people are marvelous, industrious, and intelligent, often brilliant. It has a complex, extensive history that is, at times, dark and controversial, but in any event it is inextricably linked to the history of the Western world.

Germany's cultural contributions have been inestimable and incomparable, especially when it comes to classical music. It should be enough just to say that this was the birthplace of Bach and Beethoven. And scientists of such caliber and importance as Humboldt and Einstein were also born here.

But don't worry, it's not all men. Germany is also the land of such beautiful and enigmatic ladies as Marlene Dietrich and Nastassja Kinski, and—of course—Claudia Schiffer and Heidi Klum. And let's not forget the sports stars, like the tennis player Steffi Graf and the figure skater Katerina Witt. (I'm sure there are many other worthy examples, but these are the first ones that come to mind.)

Soccer-wise, we have Beckenbauer, Rummenigge, Seeler, Klinsman, and Muller. It is certainly a land of good soccer.

And good beer!

For many, it's the best on earth, with a range of varieties that exists nowhere else. And cars, you ask? Simply put, they're the best on the

market. Elegant, solidly built, and powerful. (And quite expensive as well!)

I have to admit that the language is not easy, but the non-Germans who speak it attest to its wealth and poetry.

Compared with countries like France and England, Germany is not a homogenous, centralized nation. Here there is no single city dominating the rest of the country, as is the case with Paris and London. In this way, it is more like the United States, with its many great independent metropolises.

In Germany, the north, around Hamburg, is much different from the south, where you'll find Munich. The same holds true for Berlin in the east, which bears little resemblance to Frankfurt in the west. These differences are readily apparent in the landscape, the food, and in the regional accents (though, not being a German speaker myself, I couldn't hope to distinguish them).

GERMANY'S FIRST WORLD CUP

The year 2006 will be the second time Germany has hosted a World Cup. (Mexico and France have already had the honor of repeating.) The first of the German Cups was in 1974, and it gave us much to talk about. It had it all: controversies, surprises, good soccer, bad matches, stunning revelations, and a couple of exceptional stars whom we'll devote some space to below.

Back then, only sixteen countries representing five continents participated. Thirty-eight matches were played in six different cities. Ninety-seven goals were tallied, for an average of 2.5 per game. It wasn't the most productive Cup in history, but it was in the top three.

Germany '74 also saw the debut of some future greats. Some players became stars on the international soccer scene, while others became some of the greatest of all time. Names like Johan Cruyff, Dino Zoff, Grzegorz Lato, and Mario Kempes emerged during this Cup as world conquerors.

It was also the Cup of the two Germanys, the Dutch "Clockwork Orange," the new trophy, the "Telstar" ball, the mascots "Tip and Tap," extreme security, and it was the first to be televised around the globe in color.

Notable absences included Spain, England, and Mexico.

In the final match, in Munich, the host side, West Germany, downed the pretournament favorites, Holland, 2–1. It was the first time in history that the final was decided by penalty kicks, and also the first time that the host nation was crowned world champion.

Today, thirty-two years later, Germany is ready to repeat the show, but this time as a single, united nation, with more experience, more participants, more stars, better stadiums, and much more money.

Let's go to Deutschland!

THE TWELVE SITES

Each city is unforgettable, filled with beauty and history. Who hasn't heard tales of Berlin, Hamburg, Frankfurt, Cologne, Nuremberg, or Munich?

But there's more.

Stuttgart, Dortmund, Leipzig, Hanover, Gelsenkirchen, and Kaiserslautern. The Cup will occupy every corner of the country, and every region. Each of these twelve cities will be the scene of at least five matches. (Berlin, Munich, Stuttgart, and Dortmund will see six each.)

The matches will be played in spectacular stadiums, some of them historic in their own right, like the Olympic stadium in Berlin, which Adolf Hitler commissioned for the 1936 Olympics. It is there that the final match will be played on the ninth of July.

Other stadiums have been majestically remodeled, like the one in Cologne, and the old Waldstadion in Frankfurt, where the 2005 Confederations Cup was played. The new ones stand in Hamburg and

Munich, where the Cup will kick off on June 9th. Both of them are pure architectural joy. And all of them are anxiously waiting for things to get under way, so that they might begin to write their own new chapters in soccer history.

Furthermore, the people of these twelve cities are eager to offer the best of everything to the players, the journalists, the volunteers, and—of course—the thousands of fans from across the globe who are coming to enjoy the competition.

Airports, hotels, shops and stores, museums, restaurants, bars and pubs, clubs and discotheques are ready for action, as are the famous German biergartens.

So if you're heading to Germany this summer, you can forget about your diet. Here's why:

"GUTEN APPETIT!"

Let's talk a bit about German cuisine. (If you're German or a vegetarian, please feel free to skip ahead to the next section!) First, let's get this out of the way: Germany is not famous for its food. This isn't Italy. Or France. But, surprisingly enough to my own Latin tastes, there are some very interesting, and even delicious, dishes to be found there.

For example, sausages.

If you're not sure whether you like sausages, don't be afraid. Take a chance. It's the most common item in German cuisine, and the variety is such that surely you can find something to suit your tastes. Approach them with open mouth and open mind. Chances are you'll return home both surprised and satisfied— and with your cholesterol through the roof!

As with beer, each German city and region boasts its own type of sausage, or *wurst*, as they are

called. The most famous one of all is the frankfurter, which is made of beef, and—as the name implies—originated in the city of Frankfurt.

Another well-known sausage is the brockwurst, the popular red hot dog that is made from pork and eaten the world over. Throw it on a bun with some mustard and enjoy it like the natives!

My favorite is bratwurst, also known as weisswurst, which originated in Munich. It's a white sausage, made with veal, and steamed—never boiled. I prefer them without any condiments, but many people enjoy a bit of mustard and a slather of sauerkraut to give them added flavor.

Sausage, however, isn't a complete meal in and of itself; it's more of a light lunch or a snack between meals. While in the rest of the world everyone stops working at 11 a.m. for a coffee break, the Germans do the same with a wurst and mustard.

HOW DO YOU SAY "PORK" IN GERMAN?

The most typical German foods, regardless of region, consist of pork and the two most important crops of Central Europe, potatoes and cabbage. It might not sound very appetizing, but believe me, it has its flavor. Everything is matched with good, hearty breads and washed down, of course, with beer.

Pork, or *schwein*, is prepared in a number of different ways, the most common of which is roasted. The Germans also eat a good amount of ham. Potatoes (in German they are known as *kartoffeln*) are never missing from a German table. They come steamed, roasted, boiled, stewed, mashed, and—like everywhere else in the world—fried. In this last case, they're called *pommes frites*, and work on your pronunciation, because I'm sure you're going to want to order some.

Cabbage is known as *kraut*. Like potatoes, no German plate is complete without it. *Kraut* comes in red and white forms, but the most popular form of all is the famous, bitter sauerkraut, that international accompaniment to hot dogs.

Next comes the world-famous *wiener schnitzel*, which is made of veal, breaded, and fried. Popular throughout Germany, it is even sold in the stadiums, where it's served with bread, like a sandwich, and it's delicious with mustard. In restaurants, it's typically served with—you guessed it—*kartoffeln* or *kraut*.

Now, when German chefs (yes, they do exist, and they're quite good) decide to get creative, they look to the two other unofficial national foodstuffs: the onion and the apple. It's then that you'll see

exotic plates of roast pork with potatoes, cabbage, and some sort of onion salsa with apples.

And, last but not least, if you don't like pork, Germany also offers beef, chicken, fish, and other seafood, though in somewhat limited variety. The chicken is either roasted or grilled and comes, needless to say, with potatoes, cabbage, onion, and apples. It's most often served in biergartens.

Fish is found in the north of the country, in Hamburg and its neighboring towns. Herring is the most popular of all. In the south, in Munich and Bavaria, trout are raised in lakes and fish farms. Both varieties are delicious, and present tasty alternatives to all the sausage and pork.

LET'S TALK ABOUT "BIER"

Germany's most notable export is, of course, beer. Or *bier*, if you want to be more proper. It's pronounced just as it is in English, and it's usually consumed in a biergarten, which is a sort of open-air establishment where folks gather to drink and chat. Biergartens are also a place for picnicking, with everyone bringing their own food, which is permitted. Of all the many things you have to experience while in Germany, the biergarten has to be tops on the list.

Germany boasts over a thousand years of experience in the brewing and drinking of beer. It began in the Middle Ages, when Bavarian monks would brew it in their monasteries to help quell their hunger pangs during days of fasting. Those monks sure knew how to live, right?!

There are so many brands and varieties of German beer that it's tough to find the single one you like the best. To help you in that quest, let me start you off with a few simple observations. There are regular beers, which are golden in color, and dark beers, which are closer to black. Of the golden varieties, the lighter ones are known as Pils, and the heavier ones are called Weissbier. That's all you need to know to get started. Where you'll run into trouble is with the fact that each variety is represented by *thousands* of brands.

Figuring out which ones you like is one of the real pleasures of drinking beer in the greatest beer land in the world. Every city and every region has its own variety, as does every bar and restaurant. And the best place for finding yourself a wide selection is the biergarten.

According to the "experts," the best beer of all comes from Munich. But they also recommend the brews that hail from the area around the Rhine, where Frankfurt and Cologne are located. As for me, I like them all. Choosing is just too difficult.

Let me also say this: if you aren't a beer drinker, don't let that stop you from trying a few sips. This is *real beer* through and through, the kind that puts hair on your chest, heavy and bitter.

And of course, be sure to say *Prost* instead of *Salud*!

BREAD AND "KUCHEN"

The million brands of beer in Germany are eclipsed only by the millions of types of bread they bake. This is a country of bakers and bread lovers of all sorts.

Actually, it's not millions, it's closer to three hundred types of bread, or *brot* in German. German bakeries are fabulous, and not unlike the ones I so prize in Latin America. Loaves and rolls of bread both sweet and salty abound, and they are made with every sort of flour imaginable, from wheat to barley to rye.

And if you have a yen for something dessert-like, then it's *kuchen* you're after: cakes, pies, torts, tarts, pastries . . . any sweet, oven-baked delicacy. The variety of German confections is as broad as it is delicious.

One of my favorite German customs is the afternoon snack of *kaffe und kuchen*, which takes place daily at four o'clock. And if your *kuchen* is topped with sweet cream or vanilla frosting, then . . . mmmm! Your afternoon is looking all right.

INTERNATIONAL COOKING

If nothing we've discussed so far catches your attention, don't worry. You're not going to go hungry in Germany. In every city in which games will be played, you'll find a multitude of international restaurants, offering Italian, Chinese, Japanese, Thai, Indian, and French (the most expensive, of course) food to quell your appetite. You'll also find restaurants offering Mexican, Argentine, Cuban, and Spanish cuisine, and I'll talk more about them in the chapter on the host cities. Finally, if you're really in a hurry, McDonald's franchises are popping up all over the German map.

So, now, with food in our bellies and happiness in our hearts, we're ready to embark on our tour of the twelve host cities, but first . . . let's do a bit of time traveling, from the distant past where the first World Cup was held—in Uruguay in 1930—up to the present day. Because, as the saying goes, "There is no future without a past."

SEC
+

OND
IALF

The History of
the World Cup

One:
The Birth of the World Cup

If there is a story that does justice to the famous expression "He who perseveres, triumphs," it's the story of the birth of the World Cup. All great human endeavors require the vision of one and the sacrifices of many, and the creation of the most important sporting event on the planet was no exception.

The birth of the World Cup was (and allow me a bit of inspiration here) the natural culmination of a series of events, personalities, and historic circumstances that, over eighty years ago, converged harmoniously thanks to the influence and charisma of one of the most visionary men of his time, a man who was a dedicated lover of a most passionate sport.

Now I will calm down and tell his story as simply as I can.

THE BIRTH OF AN IDEA

It started with a French lawyer, one Jules Rimet, who, like myself, was also a *"presidente,"* though not of the *República Deportiva* show, but rather the French Football Federation, and then, years later, of the fledgling Fédération Internationale de Football Association, the world-famous FIFA.

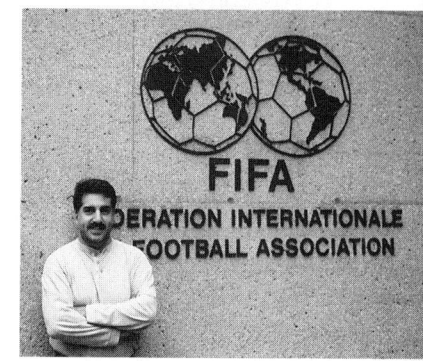

The First World War was at an end, and the decade of the 1920s was about to get under way. Soccer was turning fifty, after having been invented by the British, and it was already being played in countries across the globe, and especially in Latin America.

Teams had sprung up everywhere, like River in Argentina, Peñarol in Uruguay, Colo-Colo in Chile, Guadalajara in Mexico, and Millonarios in Bogotá, and they were filling stadiums.

JULES HITS THE SCENE

FIFA already existed, but not as the powerful and influential force it is today. Sixteen years after it was founded, in 1904, the majority of its twenty member nations were European, and the hiatus imposed by the Great War had weakened it greatly. But in 1921 the election of the forty-eight-year-old Rimet as FIFA's president changed everything.

TRIVIA

Who is considered the father of the World Cup?

Monsieur Jules didn't simply recruit new member nations; he standardized the rules of the game, he organized the Olympic soccer competitions, and, finally—less than ten years later—he created the World Cup.

He served for thirty-three years, and when he finally retired, in 1954, the organization had no fewer than eighty-five member nations, and five World Cups had been staged! Without his passion and perseverance, the history of world soccer would have been something quite different, and this book might never have been written. (I shudder at the thought.)

But here we are, and the World Cup is a reality.

The next competition is gearing up in Germany, and it is all thanks to that exceptional Frenchman who both loved the game of footie and understood its economic potential.

Now let's get back to the story of how it all came about.

FIRST THERE WAS THE OLYMPICS

Thanks to Jules Rimet's organizational abilities, 1921 saw soccer propagated throughout the world, even to the point where it had become one of the principal attractions at the Olympic Games.

In the 1924 Paris games, followed by Amsterdam '28, twenty-four nations competed, with the Europeans marveling at the advances made by the South Americans in the sport. Especially the Uruguayans. In those two Olympic competitions, *los charrúas* outscored every opponent they faced, winning the gold on both occasions.

And how!

In Paris, for example, they downed Yugoslavia 7–0, the hosts 5–1, and the United States by a margin of 3–0. Four years later, in Amsterdam, they doled out similar beatings en route to defending their gold medal. Every reputable newspaper on the planet reported the feat, and soccer received an unprecedented and unexpected shot of publicity.

FIFA was establishing itself as a true international organization, and the game was growing ever more popular.

THE BIRTH OF THE CUP

It was just after the Amsterdam games that Jules Rimet took advantage of FIFA's annual meeting to propose a grand idea: *Why don't we organize an international competition—like the Olympics—to be held every four years, but only of soccer? What do you say?*

The assembled members went berserk.

They immediately approved the proposal and created a trophy, called the FIFA Cup, which would be awarded to the winner. Thus was born the World Cup of Soccer, just like that, on May 28, 1928.

The rest is history.

BUT WHERE THE HELL IS URUGUAY?

It was decided that the inaugural event would be held in 1930, and six countries, including Italy, Spain, Hungary, Sweden, and Holland, offered to act as host.

But the sixth, Uruguay, was the one that Rimet favored.

Uruguay possessed the best team on earth, they were decisive two-time Olympic champions, and, in 1930, the country would be celebrating the centennial of its independence. The honor of hosting an event of such magnitude was a perfect tribute, and Don Jules was intent on giving it to Uruguay.

"Uru-*what*?!?" was the collective reaction.

"It's too far," said some. "The travel costs will be much too high," claimed others. "It will take two months coming and going, and the club teams won't be willing to release their players for that long," was another of the complaints.

Further, what sort of player would be allowed to participate? Would it be a strictly amateur competition like the Olympics? Or would professionals be allowed to participate, given that more and more players were turning pro?

The debate was heated and intense.

But soon it was over. When all the votes were counted, Rimet had prevailed: the World Cup would be held in Uruguay. And if you didn't like the decision, then you didn't need to go! As simple as that.

The Italians were the first nation to decline their invitation. Then Spain, Holland, Sweden, and Yugoslavia followed suit. They claimed that you couldn't have a "World" Cup in Uruguay. Political squabbles, you see, were nothing new to soccer. Only the players had changed.

THE ENGLISH DISPUTE

England was the most offended, and not over the aforementioned issues. They were still up in arms against FIFA over the "professional" question. The English league already was professional, but since FIFA had yet to decide what exactly constituted a "professional" athlete, the British players were not allowed to participate in amateur competitions.

TRIVIA

Trivia: Why didn't England play in the first World Cup?

Adding to British disgust was the fact that much of the rest of Europe was operating under a camouflaged professional system that had gained the tacit approval of FIFA.

As such, England decided that not only would they boycott the inaugural World Cup competition, but they would also renounce their membership in FIFA! This dispute would last eighteen years and prevented the British from competing in the first four World Cups.

But that wasn't all . . .

THE STOCK MARKET CRASH

As we all know, in late 1929 the U.S. economy plunged with the crash of the New York Stock Exchange, and the decade of the 1930s began with the entire globe mired in a devastating economic depression.

This prompted even more countries to decline to attend the inaugural competition, despite the fact that the host nation had promised to cover the travel and lodging expenses of the participants.

"Will there be a Cup?" wondered many.

Yes, though it would be a boycotted one.

A BIT OF HISTORY

Before we go to Montevideo to relive the fascinating story of the first World Cup, let me ask you a few questions: How many Cups have there been? Who won the first? Which was the greatest of all? How many did the great Pelé play in? And Maradona? Who is the all-time top goalscorer? How many Cups did Mexico play in? When did

Colombia make her debut? Has Honduras ever participated?

The questions abound, and the answers beg for footnotes upon footnotes.

The history of World Cups past is extensive and marvelous. It is the most fascinating volume in the great encyclopedia of world soccer. And as a friend once said to me, "You can't fully enjoy one Cup without knowing something about what happened in all the others."

I'm not sure if that's true, but it sounds good.

And having a panoramic view—from 1930 to the present day—of the most popular and most successful sporting event on earth is an essential ingredient in any true aficionado's diet.

Plus, there are so many odd and fascinating bits of trivia to throw around—among old friends or new acquaintances, at a sports bar or at home in front of the TV—that will really make you stand out and impress anybody, man or woman.

You never know when names like Puskas and "the Black Spider," or anecdotes like "El Maracanazo" and "The Battle of Bern," are going to come in handy.

Ready?

Permit me to categorize the seventeen World Cup competitions in the following manner:

> The Prehistoric Cups
> The Ancient Cups
> The Modern Cups

The Prehistoric Cups numbered three and comprise Uruguay in 1930, Italy (Part One) in 1934, and France (Part One) in 1938.

The Ancient Cups total four: Brazil in 1950 (the first after World War Two), followed by Switzerland in 1954, Sweden in 1958, and Chile in 1962.

Finally there are the ones we'll call Modern, and which many of us remember watching "live via satellite" on TV. These number ten in all and include England '66, Mexico (Part One) '70, Germany (Part One) '74, Argentina '78, Spain '82, Mexico (Part Two) '86, Italy (Part 2) in 1990, U.S.A. '94, and France (Part Two) '98, culminating in the only World Cup to be jointly hosted by two countries, Japan and South Korea in 2002.

If anyone ever asks you where you found such a list, just tell them you read it in Fernando's book.

Now, if we're all ready . . . ?

Let's dig into the old attic trunk of memories!

Two:
The Prehistoric Cups (1930–38)

The Prehistoric Cups:
Uruguay '30 to France '38

The first three World Cups took place so long ago that it might well seem as if they were held in prehistoric times.

But the fact is that it was less than a hundred years ago.

The sport was the same, and it was played under almost the same rules. The differences lay in the ball (it was much heavier), the jerseys (they had buttons), and the players (they were mainly amateurs).

The number of participating countries was much smaller, perhaps a third of what it is today. The stadiums were quite small, as well. Trips were long and made by boat, as the airplane was still in diapers at the time. Newspapers abounded, and radio was reaching all across the globe. But there was no television. Nor was there nearly as much money tied up in the sport.

In other words, it really was like prehistoric times!

Uruguay 1930: The First World Cup

For me, personally, this first World Cup will always be among my dearest memories.

I know, I know! I wasn't even born in 1930. But the event has been part of my own history and the mythology of my family ever since I had the capacity for thought.

I'll explain.

THE FIORES AND THE CENTENNIAL

I don't know if you know this, but my beloved mother, María Teresa Fiore (rest in peace), was Uruguayan, born in Montevideo in 1922.

In the late 1950s she emigrated to Argentina, where she met my father, Manuel García Díaz. That's where they were married, and where they lived until 1980, when they moved to the United States. I was born in 1960.

Like any good Uruguayan—and under the influence of seven older siblings—my mother grew up loving soccer. And the national team, coupled with the club Nacional in Montevideo, were the twin lights of her fanatic's heart.

To go to the Centenario stadium in the Parque de los Aliados in Montevideo with her brothers and sisters was one of her favorite pastimes and one of her most fond childhood memories.

For as long as I can remember I have been listening to her speak with nostalgia and eloquence about those soccer afternoons: the classic matches between Nacional and Peñarol, the World Cup qualifiers, the "friendlies" with the Argentine and Italian teams, the Copa América tournaments in '42 and '56 . . . She even remembers what sorts of treats they sold at the concession stands!

But of all the anecdotes she told of her visits to the Centenario with her family, there is one in particular that always stands out. Today, as I write these lines, it all comes rushing back to me as an essential part of World Cup history.

UNCLE "NEGRO"

It happens that one of my mother's brothers, Luis "El Negro" Fiore, was one of the hundreds of masons who, with a patriotic conscience, worked tirelessly on the construction of the Centenario.

In and of itself, this fact is no big thing, but—as you will see— the construction of the stadium was such a difficult task, and filled with so many setbacks, that everyone who was a part of it would tell the story for the rest of their lives!

And Uncle Luis was no exception. I grew up listening to it!

Which is why, when I visited the Centenario for the first time in my life, in the summer of 1967 when I was only seven years old, I felt as if I already knew the place. It was a sort of déjà vu. And throughout all my childhood summers, which I spent in Uruguay, I would return to the stadium many times, and I learned to love it as if it were my own.

THE CENTENARIO IS NOT READY

That was the bad news that greeted the teams as they arrived in Uruguay for the first World Cup.

As I've said, practically all of Europe was boycotting, and the worldwide depression had complicated things for those countries who did choose to attend. And to make matters worse, the construction of the signature stadium was running perilously behind schedule.

For starters, ground was not broken until barely six months before the first games were to be played; and, secondly, just days before the inauguration of play, Uruguay was inundated with rains that flooded the field and prevented the concrete rostrums from drying properly.

And this is where "El Negro" chimes in with his stories.

He tells how, under immense plastic awnings, he and his mason *compañeros* would pour the concrete for the stands and then aim blowtorches and giant fans at them to help them dry. The rain was incessant and the pressure on the workers was intense—and growing every day.

Nevertheless, according to my uncle, there was a profound sense of patriotism involved. They were working for Uruguay and for its international reputation. The stadium simply *had* to be ready, and the World Cup *had* to be celebrated as it would anywhere else in the world. They weren't about to give the boycotting countries the satisfaction of seeing Uruguay hold anything less than a first-rate international competition.

"Will there be a Cup?" was still the question.

Yes, there would be—though it would not open in the Centenario.

"FIND ANOTHER FIELD"

This was the sad message of exhaustion and frustration handed down by the chief of the whole operation, the architect Juan Antonio Scasso.

Despite working around the clock in three shifts (one of which took place at night under giant banks of floodlights) and after having spent over a million dollars ("big bucks," my uncle called it), July 13th arrived—the date of the opening ceremonies—and the Centenario was not ready.

My mother, María Teresa Fiore, next to my uncle Luis "El Negro" Fiore.

As a last-minute contingency plan, it was decided that the first few games would be played at the Peñarol field in the Pocitos neighborhood, and at the Parque Central de Nacional. It ended up being the first eight games in all, and it wasn't until the following week—on July 18th, to be exact—that they could finally unveil the Centenario.

> **TRIVIA**
> In which stadium was the first World Cup match played?

Mamá recalled how some of the papers called it "sheer madness" to put so many people (70,000!) in a concrete stadium that hadn't finished drying. Some predicted that the structure would completely collapse, but fortunately nothing of the sort came to pass, and the Centenario welcomed the World Cup with open arms.

Only five days late.

THE GROUPS

So it was that on July 13, 1930, the wheels of the World Cup began to turn . . . wheels that, seventy-six years later, bring us now to Germany 2006.

> **TRIVIA**
> Which World Cup saw the greatest number of American nations participate?

In the end, only four European nations traveled to Montevideo: France (how could the FIFA president's own country decline to attend?), Belgium (which had hosted the Olympics in 1920 and had no interest in hosting again), and the two tiny countries of Romania and Yugoslavia.

The four nations traveled as people did in those days: by boat. As promised, Uruguay sent ships to pick them up. The French, Belgian, and Romanian contingents spent two weeks on board the *Conte Verde*, arriving at the port of Montevideo—along with Monsieur Rimet and the Brazilian team, which they had picked up in Rio de Janeiro, on the way—on July 5th, a week before the championship began. Yugoslavia arrived three days later on board another ship, *El Florida*.

Nine American nations were added to these four European ones. Along with the host country, Mexico, the United States, Argentina, Brazil, Bolivia, Chile, Peru, and Paraguay were represented. (Owing to the European boycott, this first World Cup had the largest number of participating American nations ever.)

Once all the teams had arrived (not before, as is the case nowadays), the groups were selected. Here is how it all broke down:

Group A: Argentina, Chile, France, and Mexico
Group B: Yugoslavia, Brazil, and Bolivia
Group C: Romania, Peru, and Uruguay
Group D: Belgium, United States, and Paraguay

The winners of each group would advance to the semifinal round.

THE STARS

There weren't many. The most well-known players were the Uruguayan veterans of the '24 and '28 Olympics, almost all of whom were over thirty years of age.

Among them, the most famous and admired was the defender José Nasazzi, captain of the team and better known as "El Mariscal" (The Marshal) for his leadership on the field. He had captained his team in the two Olympic competitions and for Uruguay's three Copa América titles in '23, '24, and '26.

The big goalscorers on the team were Pedro Cea (who had five in this Cup) and the two Héctors: Héctor "El Mago" (The Wizard) Scarone, and Héctor "El Manco" (The One-Armed) Castro.

The Argentines counted among their ranks the man who would end up top scorer of the tournament with eight goals: Guillermo Stábile, star player for Huracán of Buenos Aires and, twenty years later, coach of the Argentine national team.

Another standout was the sensational midfielder from San Lorenzo, Luis "Dobleancho" (Doublewide) Monti, who would later take Italian citizenship and go on to play for his adopted nation, becoming the only player in World Cup history to play in two different championships for two different countries. I'm getting ahead of myself, but take note of the trivia!

The youngest member of the Argentine team, of course, was the central defender Francisco "Panchito" Varallo. He was only twenty at the time, and over the course of his illustrious career he would go on to become the top scorer in the history of Boca Juniors, with 181 goals.

WHO WERE THE FAVORITES?

Due to the absence of so many European teams, and by virtue of their being the two-time defending Olympic champions, the Uruguayans were the clear favorites.

Argentina was also strong, having faced Uruguay in the final match of the Amsterdam Olympics two years earlier, with Uruguay

winning 2–1. France and Belgium had experience, but they couldn't compare with the spontaneous, offense-driven soccer played by the Uruguayans and Argentines.

And the Brazilians? I'm here to tell you that they were still in their soccer infancy and weren't even a shadow of what they would become twenty years down the road.

The rest of the teams from the Americas—including Mexico—had little experience, and their players were basically amateurs. The only ones who brought something interesting to the table were the United States team, whose roster included four former Scottish veterans.

And so it was that we come to July 13, 1930, the date when *los charrúas* finally commemorated the centennial of their Constitution, and the most important sporting event on earth got under way on their own soil.

THE MEXICAN DEBUT

Day one saw two games played simultaneously, one at the Parque Central field, which saw the United States defeat Belgium 3–0, and the other at Peñarol's field in Pocitos, where Mexico made its debut against France.

The Mexican selection—*los tricolores*—was made up primarily of amateur players from the club teams América, Atlante, and Necaxa.

Among them were several players who would go on to become stars of Mexican soccer, like the famous "Récord" Rafael Garza, defender for América, Felipe "El Diente" (The Tooth) Rosas, midfielder for Atlante, and Luis, "El Pichojos" (Evil Eyes) Pérez, the striker from Necaxa. Their coach was a Spaniard, Juan Luque de Serra Llonga.

TRIVIA
What was the first World Cup for Mexico? For the United States?

TRIVIA
Who scored Mexico's first World Cup goal?

It was an inauspicious debut for the Mexicans, who fell to the French, 4–1, but Juan "El Trompo" (The Spinning Top) Carreño, striker for Atlante, notched Mexico's lone tally and thus passed into the history books.

As the Cup progressed, the two favorites—Uruguay and Argentina—had no problems and showed no mercy as they handily outscored their opponents. Argentina sank Mexico 6–3 and Chile 3–1 before treating *los gringuitos* to a 6–1 beating.

For their part, the hosts feasted on a banquet of goals at the expense of Romania (4–0) and then against Yugoslavia (6–1) in the semifinal.

THE GRAND FINALE

As everyone expected, the two powerhouses from opposite sides of the Río de la Plata fulfilled their respective obligations, and on July 30th they met in the first-ever World Cup final.

Uruguay and Argentina would be reprising the Olympic final of two years before, in Amsterdam. This first final in the Centenario (they say that there were nearly 30,000 Argentines in the stands!) is where many people say that the myth of the "*charrúa* claw" began—the indomitable force, renowned throughout the soccer-playing world, that Uruguay rallies around when they are behind on the scoreboard.

On this occasion, they were down 2–1 at the break, but the second half became the stuff of legend.

My mother later told me how Uncle Negro (who was able to get tickets through the construction company he worked for) had bet an Argentine friend of his fifty dollars on the game, quite a bit of money in those days. According to him, the halftime scoreboard was making him sweat even more than he did "finishing that stadium, whatever it's called."

TRIVIA

Who squared off in the first-ever World Cup final?

But in the second half, Uruguay brought out the famous claw. Within minutes, Pedro Cea tied the game, and shortly thereafter "El Mago" Scarone put the Uruguayans ahead 3–2. Then, in the 88th minute, with the Argentines looking desperately for the equalizer, "El Manco" Castro dealt the finishing blow, ending the scoring at 4–2. Uruguay was World Champion.

"One for the ages," is how my uncle would describe it for years to come.

Italy 1934: Mussolini's Cup

Since the first World Cup was such a total success, Jules Rimet and FIFA enthusiastically set about to begin preparations for a second.

In 1932 they got together in Zurich, and decided that this time the finals would be held in Europe. And where better than in Italy, which had lobbied so hard to host the first Cup?

"IL DUCE" AND HIS CUP

In those days, Benito Mussolini was both president and dictator of Italy, and he was at the height of his popularity. When he found out

that Italy was to be the next host, the famous "Duce" went crazy . . . with emotion.

He instantly grasped the political implications of the event and decided to involve himself personally in its organization. This was an excellent opportunity for him to show the world the achievements of his government and of the Fascist revolution.

He directed all aspects of the preparation; he chose the venues personally; he allocated money for the construction and refurbishment of stadiums; he offered free train tickets to workers who wanted to attend the games; and he made thousands of game tickets available at low cost.

He even spoke with the national coach, Vittorio Pozzo, to make sure Italy would be fielding the best team possible.

And that's how it was. When the Cup began, on May 27, 1934, the *azzurri* (as they've been called ever since) were the favorites, along with Czechoslovakia and Spain, who were fielding the two best goalkeepers in the world: Frantisek Planicka and Ricardo "El Divino" (The Divine) Zamora.

RADIO AND OTHER INVENTIONS

The first new development of this World Cup was that there were qualifying rounds.

In Uruguay, participation was based on invitation, but in '34 there were so many interested countries that a series of elimination rounds was needed. FIFA had continued to grow, and it now totaled fifty members. Only sixteen of them would be going to Italy.

The second innovation was a direct response to the first Cup: that the host country would have to go through the qualifying rounds just like any other team. The Italians did so against Greece, and they did so without any major difficulty.

Another interesting fact about Italy '34 was that the defending champions did not play. It is the only such case in World Cup history, and it came about because the Uruguayans were still peeved that the

Italians had boycotted their Cup four years earlier—and so they decided to repay the favor in kind.

Plus, FIFA had decided that the first round of the competition would be direct-elimination; in other words, if you lose you go home. Imagine if that were the case today!

Lastly, this Cup went down in history for being the first to be broadcast on radio around the globe. Remember: this is before television!

THE PROTAGONISTS

There were sixteen in all, and here is how the first round broke down:

> Italy eliminates the United States, 7–1
> Czechoslovakia eliminates Romania, 2–1
> Germany eliminates Belgium, 5–2
> Austria eliminates France, 3–2
> Spain eliminates Brazil, 3–1
> Switzerland eliminates Holland, 3–2
> Sweden eliminates Argentina, 3–2
> Hungary eliminates Egypt, 4–2

As you can see, the only representatives from the American continent were Argentina, Brazil, and the United States. Argentina had sent a second-string team, and Brazil still wasn't Brazil.

For their part, the United States played surprisingly well in this, their second Cup. Their roster featured two legitimate stars. One of them, a Boston kid born to Portuguese immigrant parents, was a natural goalscorer by the name of Luis Gonsalves; the other, Warner Nilsen, was a naturalized Dane from St. Louis. Both were shut out in Italy, but both would go on to become two of the brightest stars in U.S. soccer history.

Today, they are both members of the country's Soccer Hall of Fame in Oneonta, New York. When Nilsen was granted the posthumous honor of being inducted, I had the privilege of being present at the ceremony and meeting his family. The emotions that gripped them were contagious. I saw more than a few tears shed during Warner Nilsen Jr.'s acceptance speech.

But getting back to the Cup itself, it's worth noting that all three countries from the Americas were sent packing in the first round. In other words, they had traveled over 6,000 miles to play only a single game, and then turned around and went straight back home.

What a waste of time! Now, of course, FIFA has changed the Cup to include a first round of group play, ensuring every participant of at least three games.

WHAT HAPPENED TO MEXICO?

The same thing that is happening these days: the United States has them in their sights, and they aren't afraid to make fools of them when the opportunity presents itself. Remember the last World Cup?

TRIVIA

Trivia: What country eliminated Mexico in 1934?

For Italy '34, *los aztecas* drew *los estados* in the elimination round, and fell by the wayside 4–2. *Ay!* If this were to happen in the elimination round of Germany 2006, what would Hugo Sánchez have said about Ricardo Lavolpe?

THE FIRST ROME FINAL

On the day of the final, June 10, 1934, "Il Duce" was in the stands at the stadium in Rome . . . the former Stadio Nazionale, which he himself had ordered renamed Stadio del Partito Socialista Nazionale.

On the field, the two best teams of the competition faced off.

On one side of the centerline was Italy, with their two great stars, Giuseppe Meazza (the best Italian player of the day, and whose name now graces the stadium in Milan) and Ángelo Schiavo. Plus, as I mentioned before, Italy also counted among its ranks Luis "Dobleancho" Monti and three other Argentines who had been born to Italian parents.

TRIVIA

Who was the top goalscorer in Italy '34?

The other finalist was Czechoslovakia, led by the tournament's leading scorer, Oldrich Najedly with five goals, and his keeper, Frantisek Planicka, who was considered the best player at his position of the day.

TRIVIA

What was the name of the first player to play in two World Cups for two different countries?

They say the game was very evenly played and very hard fought. It was tied 1–1 after ninety minutes, and went into overtime (which wouldn't happen again until England '66).

Then, finally, five minutes into overtime, Meazza fed Schiavo, who notched the winning goal.

You can imagine Mussolini jumping for joy there in his presidential box, while down on

TRIVIA

Which was the first World Cup final to go into overtime?

the field his team saluted him with their arms raised like obedient Fascists.

But all that notwithstanding, Italy was *il campione del mondo*.

France 1938: The Boycott Cup

For the third Prehistoric Cup, our beloved Jules Rimet returned to his roots.

"Nowhere else but here," he seemed to be saying. "It will be held in my own country, and that's the end of the discussion."

And so it was.

The third installment of the FIFA World Cup was to be in France, despite the fact that the two leading candidates to host were Italy and Argentina. The former was petitioning based on their status as reigning champions, and the latter based on an unwritten assumption that the event should alternate between Europe and Latin America—and once again it was the New World's turn.

But it wasn't to be.

Rimet prevailed by the thinnest of margins (*un dedazo*, as they say in Mexico) and was able to win approval for his native country.

THE LATIN AMERICANS WON'T COME

Argentina, of course, refused to accept the decision; likewise Uruguay, feeling a certain amount of solidarity with her neighbor, and both countries decided not to go.

Most of their Latin American neighbors saw things the same way and aligned themselves with Argentina, declining to attend as well.

These were Mexico, El Salvador, Costa Rica, and Colombia. Only Cuba, the Netherlands Antilles (Aruba and Curaçao), and Brazil agreed to participate. To this day, no one is quite sure why.

Perhaps Cuba participated because it was their first World Cup and they didn't want to miss it. And Brazil . . . who knows? Maybe they had developed an insatiable appetite for *futebol* and just wanted to play.

For whatever reason, Brazil attended France '38—and Argentina did not forgive them for many years. This "difference of opinion" officially marked the beginning of the rivalry between the two great South American powerhouses, which is something we will have a chance to talk more about later.

There were two European teams who also declined to participate: Spain and England. Spain's decision was necessitated by the ongoing civil war in that country, but England was simply holding their grudge against FIFA. Note: the English dispute lasted eighteen years!

THE OTHER PARTICIPANTS

Again there were sixteen countries in all; here are the participants in their first-round matchups:

Switzerland and Germany
France and Belgium
Czechoslovakia and Holland
Italy and Norway
Hungary and the Netherlands Antilles
Sweden and Austria
Brazil and Poland
Cuba and Romania

TRIVIA
Has Cuba ever participated in the World Cup?

These last two countries played a classic match in which they were tied 3–3 after ninety minutes, in the second overtime period Cuba outscored the Romanians 2–1 to advance to the quarterfinals. There they eliminated Sweden 8–0. Ouch!

THE "FIRST PELÉ"

If Brazil had joined the Latin American boycott, the world would have missed the chance to see the first great Brazilian superstar in the history of soccer: "El Diamante Negro" (The Black Diamond).

His name was Leónidas da Silva, a willowy and slippery twenty-six-year-old striker whose renown was without a doubt the precursor to the magic and fame of the great Pelé.

He is credited with having invented the bicycle kick, and he was the first soccer player to endorse a commercial product: a candy bar that was even named "Diamante Negro" in his honor.

His popularity was without precedent in Brazil and helped to make soccer into the national passion that it is today.

Leónidas was the top goalscorer of the tournament, finishing with eight in all, and he was also the first player to score four goals in a single World Cup game. He did it in the best match of the tournament—and one of the best in all the Prehistoric Cups—against Poland.

Brazil fought to a 6–5 overtime victory, thanks largely to the magic of Leónidas, who—as legend has it—played barefoot that day.

TRIVIA

Who was known as "The Black Diamond"?

Leónidas retired from soccer in 1951, after a career with São Paulo, Vasco, Botafogo, and Flamengo. In 2004, at the age of ninety-one, he succumbed to Alzheimer's disease.

THE FIRST PARIS FINAL

The first French final was played on June 19, 1938, in the Colombes stadium, near Paris. Sixty years later, in their *second* hosting, at France '98, the French shocked the defending champions, Brazil, by a score of 3–0. But I'm getting ahead of myself. We'll talk more about that later.

In that first Paris final, Italy, the reigning champions and favorites to defend, squared off against Hungary, the favorite of the French public.

The French, you see, had no love for the Italians, despite the fact that they possessed the best striker in the world at the time, Silvio Piola. The problem was that Italy had defeated the hosts in the quarterfinals 3–1, and then, of course, the French could not bear the thought of a preening Mussolini if the Italian team should be victorious.

Hungary, as we've noted, was the popular favorite, but their popularity didn't do them much good. They hung with the mighty Italians as best they could, but in the end they lost 4–2. Piola scored two of their goals, and Italy became the first two-time champion in World Cup history.

Unfortunately, the Second World War was on the horizon. It erupted a year later, and the World Cup would now endure a twelve-year hiatus, thus bringing the "prehistoric" age to a close.

Three:
The Ancient Cups (1950–62)

The Ancient Cups: Brazil '50 to Chile '62

In 1950, the World Cup resumed its activities in Brazil, and it hasn't stopped since. In fact, it has grown wonderfully, passing into new eras and becoming the most popular sporting event on the planet.

With Brazil '50 we will be leaving behind what I've called the Prehistoric era and moving into Ancient times. I baptized it thus simply because not too many of us have been alive long enough to remember them well. Not even our parents, because there was no television.

The Ancient Cups span sixteen years, and we can only find them in books, articles, and the eyewitness testimony of their surviving protagonists, as well as the films that we've seen over the years. They conclude with the 1962 World Cup in Chile.

So join me in the samba beat of Brazil '50!

Brazil 1950: The Cup Brazil Lost

In 1946, as Europe was catching its breath in the wake of the destruction and death wrought by the war, FIFA was reconvening, with the idea of bringing the World Cup back to life. This time they wanted to do things better, to do things right—with true worldwide participation, with no boycotts or petty political bickering.

Jules Rimet, who already had twenty-four years as president of the organization under his belt, undertook the assignment yet again. He had the presence of mind to return the Cup to the Americas, but he also gave the two subsequent cups to two European nations—Switzerland and Sweden—that had escaped enough of the war's

destruction to be left with the financial resources to stage the event successfully.

And as if that weren't enough, he reconciled with the British, who returned to the competition after their eighteen-year holdout.

In other words, it all was peace and harmony in FIFA. So much so, in fact, that it was decided that Don Jules should be honored by renaming the trophy cup for him.

TRIVIA
In which World Cup did the Jules Rimet Trophy come into play?

The only note of discord was struck by the Argentines, who refused to participate as a slight to the Brazilians. As you'll recall, Brazil did not support the Latin American boycott of the '38 Cup, led by Argentina. As a result, things weren't going too well between the two South American powers, and this only added to what was becoming a historic rivalry.

THE MARACANÃ

The announcement of their selection as host was celebrated throughout Brazil as if it were Carnival itself. They immediately got to work on the preparations, which, among many other things, included the largest stadium on planet Earth. Thus was born the glorious Maracanã, set in the heart of a neighborhood of Rio de Janeiro.

TRIVIA
What is the capacity of Brazil's Maracanã stadium?

Construction took barely two years, and it resulted in a structure with the unimaginable (and to this day unsurpassed) capacity to seat 200,000 spectators!

Soccer was already king in Brazil, and its star production had begun. In other words, a stadium of such magnitude was the most appropriate, most natural thing with which to celebrate an event of this caliber.

THIS TIME IT'S THIRTEEN

There were sixteen teams originally, but only thirteen ended up playing. Argentina, as we've already seen, took a pass on the proceedings, and Austria and Turkey did so as well, though for economic reasons.

So besides the host country, Brazil, and the defending champions, Italy, the participants included: Spain, England, Switzerland, Sweden, and Yugoslavia from Europe; and Mexico, the United States, Bolivia, Chile, Paraguay, and Uruguay from the Americas.

INTRODUCING NUMBERS—A NEW FEATURE

One of the historic novelties of the 1950 Cup was that for the first time the players sported numbers on their jerseys. The reason for this was, interestingly enough, the medium of radio. It was the only way that the broadcast commentators could identify the players from up in the press box in such an immense stadium.

In terms of the competition's format, FIFA did away with the single-elimination format that had been employed in France and returned to a system of "groups." Because of the absences, this is how they broke down:

Group A: Brazil, Yugoslavia, Switzerland, and Mexico
Group B: England, Spain, the United States, and Chile
Group C: Sweden, Italy, and Paraguay
Group D: Bolivia and Uruguay

> **TRIVIA**
> Which was the first World Cup in which the players wore numbers on their jerseys?

For the second round, the winners of each group would square off against the winners of each of the other groups. In the end, whoever had the most points would be crowned as champion.

THE DEBUT OF "LA TOTA"

The Mexican league had turned professional in 1943, and ever since then it had been forging new national idols. Among them was the legendary Horacio Casarín of the Necaxa club, already a well-established veteran, and the best Mexican player of the 1940s. There was also the goalkeeper for León de Guanajuato, a twenty-one-year-old lad by the name of Antonio Carbajal, later to be known as "La Tota." In Brazil '50 he played his first World Cup match.

I had the honor of meeting him on Univision's *República Deportiva* in December of 1999. We invited him to be a panelist on a program dedicated to the greatest soccer players of the twentieth century. Many experts worldwide include him on their lists of soccer greats, and never before had I been in the presence of a player so filled with history.

> **TRIVIA**
> Which World Cup saw the debut of "La Tota" Carbajal?

He became the only player to compete in five World Cups (a record that stood until 1994, when it was broken by Lothar Matthaeus of Germany), and he is the only keeper in history to face down all the greatest strikers of his era.

For Don Antonio, his first World Cup hangs with a bittersweet taste. On the one hand, it was sweet because Mexico had returned to the grand stage after a twenty-year absence. But then again, it was "sad and bitter," as he told me, "because the team was thrown together so quickly." The coach was switched at the last minute, Antonio "La Pulga" (The Flea) Vial stepping in for Rafael "Récord" Garza; they only trained together for fifteen days before leaving for Brazil, and in a pair of tune-up matches they were thrashed by Real Madrid (7–1) and Atlético de Bilbao (6–3).

"To make matters worse," he added, "our debut was a disaster."

They spent a week in transit on board a ship, and had to open the Cup on June 24th against the man of the house and in his brand-new stadium. They fell 4–0, and it would have been worse if not for several sensational saves by "La Tota."

Next they traveled to Pôrto Allegre—almost a full day's drive—only to bow 4–1 before Yugoslavia. In this game as well, the contrast between Carbajal's magnificent performance and the unwieldy defense was as remarkable as it was inexplicable.

TRIVIA
What team did Mexico face while wearing borrowed jerseys in Brazil '50?

The farewell match was bitter as well.

Not only did they fall 2–1 to Switzerland (Mexico's lone goal was notched by Casarín), but they had to play wearing jerseys borrowed from the Pôrto Alegre team. The color of the jerseys the Mexicans wore at the time (red) resembled

From left to right: *"La Tota Carbajal, Luís Blanco, Alfredo Dominguez Muro, Manuel Negrete, and Oscar Restrepo.*

those of the Swiss team, and someone decided that they had to change.

"You could say," Carbajal recalls, "that we were behind from the start."

THE SHOCK OF THE CENTURY

And it happened in English.

To the English, I should say, on June 29, 1950, in Belo Horizonte (about 200 miles north of Rio), and it is considered the greatest and most important victory in the history of Team U.S.A.

It was the third World Cup for the United States, whose team was composed mainly of amateur players hailing from Boston, New York, Philadelphia, and St. Louis—players with scant international experience. They occupied a spot in Group B, along with Spain, England, and Chile. Their first game was unremarkable; Spain defeated them by a score of 3–1.

The only memorable moment was the U.S.A.'s lone goal, notched by the star of the team and one of the greatest players in that country's history: John Souza, the Boston-raised son of Portuguese immigrants and, later, an inductee in U.S. soccer's Hall of Fame.

But the shock I'm speaking of came in the second match.

Los gringuitos were in Belo Horizonte to square off against England, one of the pretournament favorites and, as we've noted, a country making its debut after an eighteen-year-long standoff with FIFA. Their roster included three of the best players in the history of English soccer: the great Billy Wright, Tom Finney, and—perhaps the best of the bunch—the legendary Stanley Matthews, already thirty-five years of age and considered by many to be the greatest British footballer of all time, just ahead of Bobby Charlton, according to those who saw him play.

The U.S. players feared the game might be a repeat of their inauspicious debut, or even worse. One of them, Harry Keough of St. Louis, described the team's mood leading up to the game this way: "If Spain scored three on us, then England was going to run right over us."

With Harry Keough.

Keough has been telling this story for fifty-five years. He's quite the character, a man still full of joy and life at the age of eighty-two. He's married to a Mexican woman, and they spend their winters in Guadalajara. I met him at the Hall of Fame, at the induction of Marcelo Balboa and my great friend Fernando Clavijo.

"I remember that day like it was yesterday," Don Harry says when I ask him about the match. "We had packed the box, trying anything to keep them from scoring. The only reason we didn't hang from the crossbar was because it was illegal," he recalls with a burst of laughter.

And that's how the game played out. The English dominated play, but they couldn't punch one across. Team U.S.A. had set up an impenetrable wall in their own penalty area, and every once in a while they would venture a counterattack in the direction of the English goal, but without any major consequences.

One of these attacks came in the 37th minute. Walter Bahr lofted a diagonal cross in front of the English keeper, Bert Williams, and toward the U.S. striker of Haitian origin Joe Gaetjens.

The cross came in at a tangent, and just when it seemed that Williams was about to come off his line to intercept it, Gaetjens leaped from his spot at the post and just barely got his head on the ball.

It was "by a millimeter," as Don Harry puts it, but that millimeter was enough to deflect the flight of the ball past the astonished English keeper and into the net.

"If Joe were alive and with us today, he'd tell you he has no idea how the hell he got to that ball," says Keough. "To say nothing of what part of his head it came off of!"

But the fact of the matter is that the ball found its way past the keeper Williams and into the back of the net. Goal! Goal United States!

Harry recalls that after celebrating with his teammates, one of them, Joe Maca, looked to him and said, "Now we've got their attention. Hold on to your hat."

The rest of the match resembled a shooting gallery,

TRIVIA
Who scored the U.S. goal that felled England in Brazil '50?

From left to right: *With three American soccer legends: John Souza, Walter Bahr, and Harry Keough.*

with the English players desperately firing away at the U.S. net, minded by Frank Borghi, whose remarkable afternoon maintained the score at 1–0. The final whistle sounded, and the impossible had occurred: the Cinderella of world soccer had toppled the veritable father of the sport.

Unbelievable!

It would be comparable only to, say, Bolivia beating the United States at—what else?—American football!

The following day, very few folks back home in the States heard tell of the feat. Only the *New York Times* included it among its headlines.

"It doesn't matter to me," says Keough. "I just know that I was there, and that I lived through it. Nobody can take that away from me. I'll carry it with me till the day I die."

Their third match, against Chile, was played in Recife, and the boys of U.S. soccer fell 5–2. But the sting of that defeat was hardly felt in comparison with the ecstasy of their historic feat in Belo Horizonte.

THE FINAL ROUND

Four teams had advanced: Brazil, Spain, Sweden, and Uruguay. It was a round-robin affair. Brazil got off to a strong start off by destroying Sweden 7–1 and humiliating Spain 6–1. Their third and final match was against Uruguay, who had drawn with Spain and struggled mightily to defeat Sweden.

So Brazil had four points to their name, and Uruguay three, when they squared off. It was the last match of the competition, and the winner of it would be World Cup champions. In other words, this was the final. Brazil would lift the Jules Rimet Trophy with a tie or better, whereas *los charrúas* would need to win outright in order to be crowned champions.

You might be able to guess what happened next.

THE "MARACANAZO"

In order to fully appreciate the magnitude of the so-called Maracanazo, try to mentally transport yourself back to that Brazilian Sunday of July 6, 1950.

The country was about to successfully put the finishing touches on an event of supreme magnitude; soccer fever was spreading across the country like wildfire, the home team had been scoring mercilessly, almost at will, with twenty-one tallies in only five games, and, as you might expect, their stars were shining bright. Ademir, the center forward, was leading all scorers with nine goals.

Logic said, "Poor Uruguay! It's going to be a massacre!"

But as we all know . . . there is often no logic in soccer.

Brazil took the field at the majestic Maracanã, filled to bursting with some 205,000 fans. Packing fireworks, horns, and drums, they were absolutely convinced that, ninety minutes hence, they would be the new Champions of the World.

And the game begins.

The noise in the stands is deafening. Chanting, whistling, and drumming. Brazil dominates with ease. Uruguay plays a game of defense and counterattack. A shot by Oscar Omar Míguez hits the post. Brazil reacts. Short touches here. Long balls played there. Nobody can find a weakness to exploit. The minutes tick by. The Brazilians start to take long-range shots on the Uruguayan keeper. Roque Máspoli is brilliant. The fans hoot madly. But Brazil's goal does not come. *Los charrúas* continue to counter. Ruben Morán shoots. It's just off target. The first half ends. Nil–nil.

"In forty-five minutes we'll be champions," the Brazilians say to themselves.

The match restarts. Brazil comes out in full force. The concrete the very stadium is built from is shaking. The 47th minute, Zizinho and Jair string together some great plays. Once. Twice. But Uruguay seems to be weathering the storm. Then Jair passes to Franca. He shoots. He scores.

Brazil 1, Uruguay 0.

The crowd erupts. "We're as good as champions," thinks Brazil.

The game goes on. The minutes pass. Uruguay remains calm. Their captain, Obdulio Varela, "El Negro Jefe" ("The Black Boss"), directs the defense. The 67th minute. Another counterattack. Uruguay advances up the right flank. A long pass from Varela to number 7, Alcides Ghiggia. Just before he reaches the touchline, he places a cross. Enter "Pepe" Schiafino. Volley. The ball rockets off his instep. The keeper Barboza is helpless. Goal. Tie game.

A sepulchral silence.

But Brazil would still be triumphant with a tie. The chanting strikes up again. More firecrackers are shot off. More horns and drums. All of Brazil watches expectantly. Máspoli saves again. The 30th minute. "Fifteen minutes to the championship." Not long now. The 34th minute. Only eleven to go. Another Uruguayan attack up the right-hand side; Julio Pérez and Ghiggia play the ball back and forth between them. Once, twice, three times. Ghiggia breaks toward the touchline with the ball at his feet. It looks like a repeat of the first goal. Bigode is all over him. You can see Barboza come off his line. But this time Ghiggia doesn't cut it back. He shoots. It skips down off the crossbar. Barboza dives for it. But he doesn't reach it in time. Goal.

Uruguay 2, Brazil 1.

The only celebrating now is being done by the Uruguayans on the field. The stadium falls silent. The drums are mute. Throats tighten up. Eyes well up with tears. Total disbelief. The heart of an entire nation has been split in two. Crushed.

Time runs out. Brazil wants to fight on, but they cannot. Ridel, the English referee, sounds the final three whistles. It's over. Uruguay has made history. They walked into the "Maracanazo" and emerged the second two-time champion in World Cup history.

TRIVIA

Who scored the winning goal in the famous match known as the "Maracanazo"?

A great Carnival broke out, only not in Brazil. This parade ran along Avenida 18 de Julio in Montevideo. According to my old man's stories, he and his brothers were among the first ones out there in the street. It was a tremendous celebration, and it lasted throughout the night. Hundreds of thousands of Uruguayans were embracing each other, singing, dancing, crying, drinking. A few people collapsed in the streets, while others were found in their homes next to their radios, the victims of heart attacks.

All of Brazil, on the other hand, lapsed into a period of national mourning the likes of which had never been seen before in the country's history. There were deaths recorded there, too, but they were suicides.

They would have to wait eight more years to relieve the pain.

GHIGGIA SPEAKS

I was surprised when I first met Alcides Ghiggia. He has a small, slight frame, though he is in excellent physical health for a man of seventy-nine. It seems that fame and glory have served him quite well.

We met one September afternoon at the Museo del Fútbol del Uruguay in Montevideo. It's a spectacular museum, and it's located in the best of all possible places in Uruguay, the Estadio Centenario. There, surrounded by dozens of photos of himself and one immense mural detailing the famous goal, we talk about that final match.

"Only three people have ever quieted the Maracanã," he tells me with seriousness and full measure of pride. "The Pope, Frank Sinatra, and Alcides Ghiggia."

He is referring, of course, to the deathly silence that gripped the famous stadium on that fateful afternoon more than fifty years ago.

The same silence that Brazilians observed years later at a mass led by John Paul II—and during a Sinatra concert in the 1970s.

"The only thing you could hear was our own team celebrating," Ghiggia affirms as I picture the scene: he and his teammates frantically embracing one another at midfield, shouting with joy, almost in tears.

His is a privileged memory. I don't know whether it's because the story has been told so many times over, or because such feats are never forgotten. He remembers everything down to the last detail, including the names of the Uruguayan photographers situated behind Barboza's net when he scored that famous goal.

"Barboza made the logical play, and I made the illogical one," Don Alcides explains with regard to the Brazilian keeper's reactions during that play. Barboza was thinking that Ghiggia was going to turn it back toward the center, as was the case with the first Uruguayan goal. But this time was different.

"Barboza was waiting for me to cross it, and he came off his line a little bit, which makes sense. But I defied logic and—with almost no room at all—I shot at the near post." Here a slight smile breaks through the seriousness of his tale.

As he speaks, I look behind him at the immense, sepia photograph of the goal, which covers an entire wall of the museum. Barboza lies sprawled out on the ground, Bigode has raised his right hand to his head, while Ghiggia—with that great number 7 on his back—has

With Alcides Ghiggia, the Uruguayan Maracanazo hero.

already started running off in celebration. Everyone in Uruguay knows this photo.

But it's not the only image of the "Goal of the Century" that they have there in the museum. They have numerous photos, taken from all different angles, both before, during, and after Ghiggia's shot. They also have the boots and jerseys worn by *los charrúas*, along with posters, programs, other souvenirs, and more photos of that and other World Cups.

Ghiggia tells how, after the final whistle, he leaped into the arms of the captain of the team, Obdulio Varela, who had delivered the pass, and said, "We're champions, Negro, we're champions!"

Then came the confusion. The players didn't know what to do; whether to wait for the presentation of the Cup there on the field or to head back into the locker rooms.

"We were completely clueless," Ghiggia recalls. "We ended up just sitting in the tunnel, because nobody came out to present us with the Cup."

Actually, the Cup was being brought all the way down from the president's box up in the stadium by Jules Rimet himself. It took him several minutes to reach ground level. In fact, he'd left his seat with the game still tied at one apiece, and he never even saw Uruguay's second goal. When he reached the field, all he found was a mob of people without passes, without guards, and without joy. He looked for the Brazilian team, but couldn't find them. He couldn't understand what was going on.

Ghiggia tells how, when Varela saw Rimet emerge with the Cup in hand, he walked up to him and said simply, "Are you going to give us the Cup or not?"

That was their coronation: a solemn celebration, sans speeches and festivities, surrounded by photographers and curious onlookers.

"He presented us with the Cup, and we went into the locker room," says Don Alcides. There they began a proper celebration, complete with popping champagne bottles. Then they hit the showers. The game had ended at five in the afternoon. They waited for the stadium to clear.

"Around eight o'clock, we looked out, saw that the place was empty, and we tiptoed out to our bus. The streets were completely bare."

The following day, Montevideo gave them a hero's welcome.

Switzerland 1954:
The Cup that Hungary Lost

By 1954 Jules Rimet was ready to retire. He had just turned eighty, and FIFA itself was fifty years old.

To be sure, he could retire a happy man because the World Cup, his magnum opus and lifework, was preparing for a fifth installment in charming Switzerland. And the stage could not have been set any better: Switzerland, which was the new seat of FIFA, was a beautiful country with spectacular cities such as Bern, Geneva, Zurich, and Basel; and what's more, it had been spared the destruction of World War II.

This would be Don Jules' last Cup. As soon as the final whistle sounded, he would hand his eponymous trophy to the winner and retire from FIFA. Perhaps that is why destiny paid him such a tribute. Switzerland '54 turned out to be the best World Cup to date, but not because of organization. It was because of goals.

They scored 140! An average of five per match. It was easily the most productive Cup, and I doubt that such a goals-per-game average will ever be broken.

THE APPEARANCE OF TELEVISION

Switzerland '54 also went down in history thanks to television. It was the first World Cup to make use of it. Nevertheless—just as happens today in the era of "high definition"—the new technology existed, but relatively few people actually had it in their homes.

It was, however, an experiment of limited scope. Swiss state television broadcast only nine live matches, and the signal extended only to Switzerland and a few neighboring countries. In the rest of the poor world, like Latin America, the new medium had yet to arrive, or people simply didn't have TV sets yet.

TRIVIA
What was the first World Cup to be broadcast on television?

Only Mexico, Brazil, and Cuba enjoyed the new technology. It had been introduced in 1950, but worldwide live broadcasts were as yet unknown.

Compared with the astronomical numbers of viewers today, the TV audience for Switzerland '54 was insignificant. It's been estimated that a total of eight million people in all watched the games on the small screen—which, all things considered, was not a bad start.

FIRST ROUND—WHAT NERVE!

The only thing to dull the memory of this Cup was the format of the competition.

For whatever reason (maybe it was Rimet's age, who knows?) FIFA went back to their first-round experiment and decided to form four groups of teams, with a "one seed" and a "two seed" in each group who would not have to face each other in the first round.

Huh? I'll explain.

In Group A, for example, Brazil and France would not have to face each other. In Group B it was Hungary and Turkey who wouldn't square off. The same with Uruguay and Austria in Group C, and Italy and England in Group D. FIFA's audacious idea was to facilitate the advance of the pretournament favorites. Few liked the idea, and many protested. But it was applied just the same.

TRIVIA
In what year did South Korea make their World Cup debut?

In all, sixteen countries participated: twelve European nations, three Latin American ones, and South Korea, which was making its World Cup debut.

THE LATIN AMERICANS

The representatives from the Americas were: Uruguay, twice champions and still the best team in the world; Brazil, whose roster had been completely revamped since the Maracanazo; and Mexico, representing North and Central America and the Caribbean, and featuring "La Tota" in his second World Cup.

THE EUROPEANS

Among the twelve European nations were England, competing in their second Cup, and the hosts, Switzerland, who were tabbed as pretournament favorites by many.

And there was a "new" country making its appearance in the wake of World War II, West Germany, which had been banned by FIFA from participating in Brazil on account of atrocities committed during the war.

Also returning to the fray were the twice-winning Italians, who were seasoned and ready.

Last but not least was another of the favorites—and the latest sensation—Hungary, which was known throughout the civilized world variously as "The Hungarian Machine," "The Marvelous Magyars," or "The Magical Magyars."

THE UNFORGETTABLE MAGYARS

The team was simply sensational. The best team on the planet. Their roster featured several exceptional players, and they were going through their best stretch in history, having won an Olympic gold two years earlier in Helsinki and carrying a four-year, thirty-one-game unbeaten streak into the finals.

What's more, a few months before the Cup, in November of the previous year, they visited the English at Wembley and dealt them a historic 6–3 defeat. It was England's first loss in their flagship stadium, and news of the feat circled the globe.

Among all their stars, two shone brightest. One was their captain, Ferenc Puskas, an out-of-this-world lefty who came into his own with Real Madrid a few years earlier and who would go on to become one of the greatest of all time.

The other great one was Sandor Kocsis, a true goalscoring machine. He started off the Cup by notching three against South Korea, four against Germany, and two against Brazil. He finished up as the Cup's top scorer with eleven tallies in only five games.

TRIVIA

Who was Puskas?

Barbaric!

Hungary entered the Cup as the absolute favorite in everyone's eyes, from the press to the experts to the public. And, as was expected, they reached the final.

But the story doesn't end there. That final match will never be forgotten . . . especially not in Hungary.

"LA TOTA" AND "EL GÜERO"

This was Mexico's third World Cup, and also the first in which they played in their now-famous green jerseys and white shorts.

This Cup also marked another big first for Mexico: the appearance of someone who would go on to participate in three Cups as a player and two more as a coach, Raúl Cárdenas.

Mexico had no problem qualifying for Switzerland '54. With "La Tota" between the sticks, they easily eliminated the United States (4–0 and 3–1) and Haiti (8–0 and 4–0).

TRIVIA

In which World Cup did Mexico first wear the famous green jersey?

But just before the Cup began, there was a change at the helm. Horacio Casarín resigned after a disastrous international tour, and was replaced by the Spaniard Antonio López Herranz.

The Mexicans' experience in Switzerland '54 wasn't as bitter as it was in Brazil '50. They played two

TRIVIA
In which World Cup did Raúl Cárdenas make his debut as a player?

matches and, by chance, they found they would make their debut against Brazil yet again. This time they lost 5–0 in Geneva, on June 16th. But "La Tota" was not in the lineup that day; the *penta* of goals were scored on his backup, Salvador Mota, the keeper for Club Atlante.

Their second match, also in Geneva, was played three days later, and it turned out to be the best single match Mexico had played in a World Cup to that day. Carbajal emerged as the headliner, and—according to him—they deserved to win.

"The referee awarded a penalty to the French," he explained when I first met him.

The Mexicans had mounted a surprising comeback from a 0–2 deficit with goals by José Luis Lamadrid, a teammate of Carbajal's at León, and Tomas Balcázar of Chivas. But then, when everybody thought the scoring was done and the game was headed for a draw, the Spanish referee saw a hand ball by Jorge Romo of Toluca, and assigned the maximum penalty.

The man who stepped up to take it was no less than the legendary French striker Raymond Kopa, who would go on to star for Real Madrid years later. "La Tota" dove to his right, but Kopa drove the ball high into the opposite side of the net. Goal.

France wins 3–2, and Mexico goes home with yet another loss.

"The referee's name was Asensi," Carbajal remarked. "Manuel Asensi. I'm never going to forget that name."

A HISTORIC SECOND ROUND

If the first round was controversial in its format, the second round erased any lingering bad taste.

It will forever be etched in history as one of the most electrifying and spectacular stretches of any World Cup. It includes three classic matches that—thanks to the proliferation of televisions around the world by 1954—we're still talking about to this day.

The three matchups were Austria–Switzerland, Hungary–Brazil, and Hungary–Uruguay. The first two were quarterfinal matches, while the last one was in the semis.

THE SHOOT-OUT OF THE CENTURY

The shoot-out of the century was between two evenly matched teams, and to this day the record they set remains unsurpassed.

First, let me just say that the score was 5–4 … at the end of the first half! The protagonists were Austria and Switzerland, and the match took place on June 26th in Lausanne. Switzerland opened the scoring in the 15th minute, and after that the match became a Ping-Pong game of goals. One for you, one for me. One over here, one over there. With five minutes left in the first half and the scoreboard reading 4–4, Switzerland notched their fifth goal.

And when play resumed, the pattern continued.

Austria scored eight minutes into the second half, tying the match at 5–5. Three minutes later, they pulled ahead with another goal, and they were able to maintain this advantage until the Swiss avalanche that came toward the end of the match. The scoring finally ended in the 85th minute, with the hosts on top by a score of 7–5, and from there the match went straight into the history books.

Austria's Wagner scored four times that afternoon, equaling Leónidas's record from Italy '34.

THE BATTLE OF BERN

What started out as a highly anticipated match ended up an embarrassment.

It was the first—and last—brawl in World Cup history, and one that many (especially FIFA) would prefer to forget. It took place on June 27, 1954, in Bern's Wankdorf stadium, at a match between Hungary and Brazil (who, starting with this Cup, wore their famous green-and-gold jerseys).

Brazil had begun to heat up in the games leading up to the Cup, and their roster included a new figure and future star of the team, Didi. They pounded Mexico and drew with Yugoslavia, which was enough to get them into the second round. But in their minds they still harbored the bitter memory of the Maracanazo.

"What better opponent than the Hungarian Machine for demonstrating what we can do?" the Brazilians thought.

Hungary, as I mentioned, was all the rage. Their mouths were watering at the prospect of a match of this caliber. "If we're really this good, we'll have to prove it against these South Americans," they thought (according to me!).

The Magyars were playing without Puskas, who was sidelined due to injury. Nevertheless, the first half ended 2–1 in their favor. But at the start of the second half, the Brazilians came out determined to make up the deficit.

TRIVIA

At which World Cup did Didi make his debut?

Perhaps a bit too determined.

They began to play hard. Less than fifteen minutes had elapsed and already there were two expulsions. A minute later, Hungary accounted for the third. This opened up the Brazilians, who began to play even harder, in search of the equalizer. They got it in twenty minutes later, and didn't let their guard down. They continued to shove and kick their way to the end, and—in the 88th minute—when Hungary marked the fourth goal, another Brazilian was sent off.

The actual battle commenced after the final whistle.

The Hungarian coach was punched in the face. A Brazilian was hit with a bottle (they say it was Puskas who threw it from the bench). Kicks for Kocsis. Photographers and police rushed the field. More shoving and punching. Coaches and substitutes joined in the melee, and people from the stands did too. The Hungarians made a dash for the locker rooms, but the Brazilians chased after them. The brawl continued. Officials arrived. So did the police.

Calm was finally restored.

FIFA never quite knew what to do about this embarrassing episode. One small measure of comfort was that it hadn't been widely broadcast, so not too many people had seen it on television. Their only conclusion was to publicly condemn the Brazilians, but without fines or other punishments.

> **TRIVIA**
> Which World Cup match became known as "The Battle of Bern"?

And that was it. No fines, no punishments.

Brazil packed their bags for home, and Hungary packed theirs for the semifinals.

Years later, the English referee Arthur Ellis recalled the match in an interview. "They behaved like beasts. It was a disgrace," he recalled.

It was never made clear whether he was referring to the Brazilians specifically or to all of the players involved.

URUGUAY'S STREAK COMES TO AN END

And what a streak it was. They hadn't lost in thirty matches. In fifty, actually. In Switzerland, playing with many veterans of the Maracanazo, they downed Yugoslavia 2–0 before thrashing Scotland 7–0 to close out the first round. Then they dispatched England 4–2 in the quarterfinals.

Hungary was waiting in the semis. The match, which took place on June 30th in Lausanne, had all the trappings of a classic. With Brazil and England neatly out of the way, the two best teams on the planet were left to face each other.

And it fulfilled all expectations; it was a classic indeed.

The two sides played back-and-forth for ninety minutes. Hungary started strong, jumping out to a 2–0 lead, but the *"charrúa* claw" refused to give in and climbed their way back into the game. On the strength of two goals by Juan Eduardo Hohberg (the star of Peñarol and, years later, the coach of Colombia's Cúcuta and Mexico's San Luis), Uruguay tied the match, forcing an overtime.

But to their great dismay, that was when the magic of Sandor Kocsis began to shine, eclipsing even Hohberg's brilliance. He scored twice in a twenty-minute span, and the game ended with the score of 4–2.

Hungary was in the final.

Not only had Uruguay been defeated for the first time in a World Cup match, but they had also lost their crown.

THE GRAND FINALE IN BERN ("THE WANKDORFAZO")

The final was played on a cold and rainy Sunday, July 4, 1954, at the Wankdorf in Bern.

The Hungarians were returning to the scene of "The Battle of Bern" to face the Germans, who were fresh off a 6–1 drubbing of their Austrian cousins. That was the first of six finals that they've participated in to this day.

The Germans, for their part, were also motivated by revenge, as Hungary had beaten them shamelessly in the first round by an 8–3 margin. But the invincible Hungarians hadn't just demonstrated their abilities against the Germans; they had also defeated the two great South American teams, Brazil and Uruguay. And with Puskas back in the lineup, they were feeling more confident than ever.

TRIVIA
What was the first World Cup Final that Germany participated in?

The match proved worthy of a final, and it was the first final ever to be broadcast on television. Hungary had, throughout the tournament, solidified their status as favorites. Puskas opened the scoring in the 5th minute, and two minutes later Zoltan Czibor scored the second.

Like the Brazilians in the Maracanã, the Hungarians felt as if the Cup was already theirs.

But, just like the 1950 Uruguay team, Germany refused to break. They fought hard, determined to prove that the earlier 8–3 match was a fluke, and got on the board in the 10th minute. And in the 20th, they equalized.

They went into overtime tied at two goals apiece. "We pick back

up with the action," as the commentators famously say, with Hungary running all over the German defense, firing off shots. They hit the woodwork on no less than three separate occasions, and perhaps it is from this game that the rather unscientific theory, held by a friend of mine, comes that says: "The team that hits the posts loses." According to him, it's a sign of bad luck to come. I'll leave it to you to decide!

But whatever the reason, luck was not on the side of "The Magical Magyars."

After dominating the entire second half, during which the Swiss referee disallowed a questionable Hungarian goal, the Germans launched what would prove to be a fatal counterattack. Their right forward, Helmut Rahn—who was known throughout Germany as "The Boss," and who had also fired home the equalizer in the first half—broke the deadlock with barely five minutes to go before the final whistle.

Germany 3, Hungary 2. Who could have predicted that?

The "Wandorfazo" became to Hungary what the "Maracanazo" was to Brazil. But in Germany it's remembered as "The Miracle of Bern," which gave rise to the theory (much more scientific than my friend's dictum) that "The favorite does not always win."

For Hungary, it was the end of a dream. The blame fell to Puskas for playing hurt. The entire team shunned him on the long trip home.

THE END OF AN ERA

That loss in Switzerland was an unfortunate sign of things to come for Hungary. Two years later they would be invaded by the Soviets, thus beginning thirty years of Communist rule.

Many of their star players ended up in exile, where some of them found success. Puskas, for example, went to Spain and spent a number of triumphant years with Real Madrid alongside Alfredo Di Stéfano. Kocsis went to Barcelona.

In terms of soccer, Hungary never recovered. Four years later, in Sweden, they failed to make it out of the first round, and in England '66 they were eliminated by the Soviets themselves. They missed Mexico '70 and Germany '74. They reappeared in Argentina '78, but they lost every game.

They didn't have another success until Spain '82, where they thrashed El Salvador 10–1. But that impressive showing wasn't worth much, as they failed to advance to the second round.

They didn't even qualify for Germany '06. Still . . . the Hungarian Cavalry rides on.

Sweden 1958:
Pelé's World Cup

The sixth World Cup was also the first without Jules Rimet's stewardship.

Don Jules had retired as the head of FIFA in 1954, barely having handed over the cup that bore his name to the Germans. He was eighty years old, and he passed away two years later, in October of 1956.

With him in mind, the Swedes set about organizing what would turn out to be one of the most memorable Cups in history. Sweden '58 stood out for three specific reasons: the occasion's impeccable preparation, a Frenchman named Just Fontaine, and a Brazilian known simply as Pelé.

THE GROUPS

The Swedish organizers rejected the controversial system of elimination used by the Swiss, applying instead a brand-new system that would last for several Cups thereafter: four groups of four teams each, wherein each team plays against every other, the top two from each group advancing to the second round of single-elimination play.

The number of participating nations was back up to sixteen, and the breakdown was as follows:

Group A: West Germany, Czechoslovakia, Northern Ireland, and Argentina
Group B: France, Yugoslavia, Scotland, and Paraguay
Group C: Sweden, Hungary, Wales, and Mexico
Group D: Austria, Brazil, England, and the U.S.S.R.

GRAND OPENINGS

Before I tell you who made their debuts here, I'd like to call your attention to two glaring absences in the field at this Cup—namely, both of the two-time world champions, Italy and Uruguay. The former having been eliminated by Northern Ireland, the latter by Paraguay.

Fortunately, their absences were barely felt, for the list of newcomers proved to be, to this day, the most extensive and distinguished list in World Cup history. A dozen young stars would debut here, and each would go on to loom large for their respective countries and for world soccer in general.

TRIVIA

In which World Cup did Lev Yashin, Amadeo Carrizo, and Bobby Charlton all make their first appearances?

SUÉDE · SWEDEN · SUECIA · SCHWEDEN 8-29.6. 1958

FOOTBALL
FUTBOL
FUSSBALL

Besides the Russian goalkeeper Lev Yashin, also known as the "Black Spider," a couple of other legendary goalkeepers emerged here, specifically Amadeo Carrizo of Argentina and Gilmar of Brazil. Argentina also introduced Néstor "Pipo" Rossi, and Mexico unveiled the top goalscorer in the history of Chivas de Guadalajara, Salvador "El Chava" Reyes.

England brought along someone who would go on to become one of their greatest players of all time, the Manchester United star Bobby Charlton, though he didn't appear in a match. Germany presented the world with one of its own future superstars, Uwe Seeler; and France featured the highest-scoring striker in World Cup history, Just Fontaine.

But it was Brazil that had the most impressive list of future stars: Garrincha, Zagalo, Vavá, and—the best of the bunch—a seventeen-year-old kid named Edson.

"O REI" IS BORN

His full name is Edson Arantes do Nascimento, but as a child, and for reasons even he doesn't quite understand, he acquired the nickname Pelé.

And that's what it's been ever since.

He was born in a little town called Tres Corações, in the state of Minas Gerais, on October 23, 1940. And his dream was always to be a *futebolista* like his father, who had played for Fluminense.

When Edson was six, his family moved to the town of Bauru, in the state of São Paulo, and that is where he spent his formative years—poor, shining shoes, and playing soccer with balls made of knotted-up rags.

At sixteen, he was discovered by a former national team player, Waldemir de Brito, who invited him to a tryout with the local professional team, the famous Santos of São Paulo. And, as they say, the rest was history.

TRIVIA

What was the name of the coach who gave Pelé his first cap with the national team?

The team liked what they saw and offered the youngster a contract worth ten dollars a month. In a match on September 7, 1956, Pelé made his debut, coming on as a substitute: scoring a goal, he solidified his spot on the roster. Bit by bit, and match by match, the kid began to capture the attention of the Paulistas. He started winning praise from the press (which in Brazil can be very demanding of its athletes), and people started to recognize and talk about him. Throughout all of 1957, the national press wrote articles on the miraculous kid from Santos. The name Pelé was on everybody's lips.

A stout man with thick glasses, Vicente Feola, who had been made the new coach of the national team right in the thick of the qualifying stretch, took note of the hype and went to see the youngster play.

He went, he saw, and he was convinced.

Pelé got his first cap in a friendly against Argentina in late 1957. Pelé didn't come on until the second half, but it was more than enough time for him to showcase his many talents: speed, intelligence, and a special sort of cool calmness that was quite unusual for a boy of his age.

Feola saw him as a diamond in the rough with a tremendously bright future. However, he didn't think he was quite ready for the rigors of a World Cup. Pelé's time, he thought, would come four years down the line, in Chile '62, not in Sweden '58. And he decided to leave him off the roster.

Enter João Havelange.

ENTER DON JOÃO

João Havelange was the new president of the Confederación Brasileña de Deportes (CBD), and he was a visionary.

He made it his goal to modernize Brazilian soccer, and his strategy was to put the ugly memory of Bern behind them, to remove the thorn that was the Maracanazo, and win a World Cup.

To do that, he would have to choose his players carefully, develop new talent, give them the support they needed, and, especially, instill a sense of discipline. In Havelange's estimation, a player must not only prepare physically, he must do so mentally as well.

He was the first sports figure in history to hire an official doctor, dentist, and nutritionist for a national team. He even brought in a psychologist.

Feola agreed with his boss on every point but one: Pelé. João thought the lad needed to go to Sweden, but the coach said no. "He's still developing," he said. João insisted and Feola resisted. The president pushed, and the corpulent coach pushed back.

But we already know who won the fight.

Pelé would travel to Sweden.

But Feola stuck to his guns as much as he could. The youngster didn't see a minute of playing time against either Austria or England.

In steps Havelange once again.

We don't quite know what he said to the coach, but we do know that Pelé was in the starting lineup for their third match, against the U.S.S.R.

THE NEW "SCRATCH"

The *"Scratch do Oro"* of 1958 included four players who, along with the "Black Pearl," seemed destined to make history for Brazil.

They were the goalkeeper Gilmar, the center forward Izidio Neto, (better known as Vavá), and the two wingers, Mario "O Lobo" (The Wolf) Zagallo on the left, and Manoel Dos Santos, better known as the sensational Garrincha, on the right.

The only holdovers from the previous World Cup were the two Santoses—Nilton and Djalma (no relation)—and Valdir Pereira, the engine of the team, affectionately known as Didi.

Only Gilmar and Zagalo were permanent starters. They both played against Austria, which Brazil shut down 3–0. Vavá made his debut against England, and the result was an unimpressive 0–0 draw.

Thanks to Havelange, Pelé finally appeared in the third match of the first round, against the Soviets, on June 15, 1958. He played quite well and received much attention from the international press. Brazil won 2–0, on the strength of two goals by Vavá. They were headed for the second round.

"Did you see that?" I picture Havelange asking Feola after the match.

And speaking of first appearances, another Brazilian who made his World Cup debut against the Soviets was Garrincha. He also garnered some considerable praise from the press. Thus began the careers of the two greatest players Brazil has ever given the world . . . and I'm saying this with the hope that Romario and Ronaldo will forgive me!

In the quarterfinals, Brazil was to face Wales. Feola returned Pelé to the lineup, and the young king did not disappoint, scoring his first World Cup goal—which also proved to be the only goal of the match. And what a goal it was! It's been preserved on video, so you can see how, in the 70th minute of a tight game, Pelé plays the ball off his chest, just inside the Welsh penalty area, makes half a turn, eludes his marker, and fires a low shot just inside the post and to the left of the keeper, Jack Kelsey. Simply spectacular.

TRIVIA

What team did Pelé first appear against in a World Cup? And what team did he score his first goal against? Extra credit if you can name the keeper!

The lad had given Brazil both the win and a spot in the semifinals. Their next opponent would present them with a historic matchup: Pelé face-to-face with the other sensation of the tournament, Just Fontaine.

JUST FONTAINE

That's the name of the man who, to this day, holds the title of "Most Goals in Any World Cup." Thirteen in all. And forty-eight years and eleven tournaments later, the record has yet to be broken.

It hasn't even been threatened.

When he arrived in Sweden that summer for his first World Cup, Fontaine was twenty-seven years old and the star of the French club Reims. His inclusion on the team alone made France one of the favorites—and, thanks to him, they went very far indeed.

In their first match, Fontaine had himself a hat trick in the midst of a 7–3 win over Paraguay. In their second, they fell 3–2 to Yugoslavia, but Fontaine scored both times for his side. In the final match of the first round, they defeated Scotland 2–1, and Fontaine had scored yet again.

Six goals in three games!

In the quarterfinals, Fontaine continued on his blistering pace, and scored two more in a 4–0 win over Northern Ireland. Then, in the semifinal, he found himself facing a man—a boy, actually—who stole the show from him.

THE REEMERGENCE OF ARGENTINA—WHAT A DISASTER!

In Sweden, Argentina played in their first World Cup since 1934. Remember that they had boycotted in '38 and '50, and that Brazil had eliminated them on the road to Switzerland '54.

This new Argentine squad was coming off a Copa América victory the year before, and their roster was filled with players from *La Máquina* (The Machine), my beloved River Plate Club of Buenos Aires. That top club in all of Argentina was going through the best years in their history, having won titles in 1952, '53, '55, '56, and '57.

They were a veritable phenomenon!

The coach of the Argentine side was Guillermo Stábile, who also happened to be the top goalscorer from the inaugural World Cup. He called up no fewer than thirteen players from River—including nine of their starters—which was absolutely unheard of.

Among them were Néstor "Pipo" Rossi, "El Negro" José Ramos Delgado, Roberto Zárate, "El Feo" (Ugly) Ángel Labruna, Enrique "El Cabezón" (Big Head) Sívori, and the keeper (the hero of my youth) Amadeo Raúl Carrizo.

Unfortunately, this side was met with the same fate as the 2002 team in Japan and South Korea. They entered the tournament among the favorites, and yet they bowed out after the first round.

The only difference is that the circumstances in Sweden were even more humiliating.

Argentina opened against Germany on June 8th in the city of Malmö, losing 3–1 to the defending world champions. But they were able to regroup and win their next match in Halmstad, 3–0 over Northern Ireland.

For their third match that week, they traveled to Helsingborg to face Czechoslovakia. Despite needing only a tie to advance, Argentina inexplicably forgot everything they knew about soccer that day and walked straight into a catastrophic and disgraceful defeat, losing to Czechoslovakia 6–1!

It was 3–0 at the break. Argentina opened the scoring in the second half, but soon thereafter gave up the next three. It was the worst defeat in the history of Argentine soccer, with the possible exception of the 5–0 loss to Colombia back in '93.

Nobody in Argentina saw the match because nobody in Argentina had television, but they did follow the game on the radio, and they read all the papers the next day. The reporters were merciless, and their criticisms were crude and hurtful. Nobody was spared, from the coach on down.

The most chastised of all was my idol himself. Everyone seemed to agree that he was the most at fault.

"The journalists were ruthless with me," Don Amadeo said last year in Buenos Aires when I was interviewing him for this book. "It was very difficult for me. I usually turned in very solid performances. I admit that I made my share of mistakes, but I wasn't the only reason we lost."

Carrizo admitted to me that the Czechs were younger and better prepared physically. "They really ran us over," he said.

Coach Labruna summed it up this way: "We went into the match blindfolded. We were completely blind." Amadeo agreed.

The trip home was even worse. The fans threw coins at them in the airport, and then—every time River would play—the opposing fans would taunt them with memories of Sweden.

"Many players let it get to them and became lethargic and depressed," says Carrizo. "In fact, River didn't win another championship for eighteen years!"

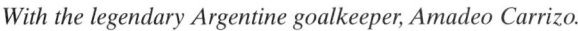

With the legendary Argentine goalkeeper, Amadeo Carrizo.

But the first victim of the fallout was Coach Stábile, who resigned after nine years at the helm. "We would have to change our strategy if we wanted to beat the Europeans," he concluded.

And it would take twenty years.

In 1978 they won their first Cup, thus erasing Argentina's bitter memory—for everyone, that is, except Manuel García Díaz, my father.

MY "FIRST" WORLD CUP

Papá is the one who first made me into a River fan, as well as a fan of his favorite player, the great Amadeo.

My bedroom at home in Buenos Aires was adorned with photos of the legendary keeper in action, and thanks to his inspiration my first steps on the field were taken in front of the goal. Like millions of other kids my age, I wanted to be the next Amadeo! (Though destiny, of course, had other plans for me.)

Like any good Argentine and soccer fanatic, Papá never forgot the failure in Sweden. I remember how when I was very young—long before moving to Uruguay and hearing Uncle Negro's stories about the construction of the Centenario—I would listen to my father talk about Sweden.

He talked about it often, and with anger and frustration. But not out of the shame that you might expect; rather, his anger was directed at the critics who berated his idol.

"Leave him alone!" he would say staunchly, sticking up for the guy every time the topic came up, and especially if it was among his friends who were aficionados of Boca. I heard all these heated discussions, but I had no idea what they were all about.

According to my old man, the keeper was not to blame. This was the conclusion he'd come to even after seeing each one of the six Czech goals replayed on film.

"Only one goal was his fault!" he would exclaim. "If it weren't for Amadeo, they would have hung twenty on us!"

The anecdote made Carrizo laugh. "Fortunately your father isn't the only one. There were lots of people who supported me, who always

With my father at the zoo.

stuck by me. Send him my thanks," he said with an honest smile. I replied that my father had passed away in 1982, and that he was resting peacefully with the knowledge that his hero was innocent of the charges occasioned by that humiliating 6–1 defeat.

So that's how I came to meet the great Amadeo, and how, thanks to him, I had my first encounter with a place called Sweden and a thing called the World Cup. Which is why I always say that, technically, Sweden was my first.

MEXICO'S FIRST POINT

In Sweden '58, Mexico ran into the same sort of luck as did Argentina. They were also drummed out in the first round, but at least they could take one good memory with them, all thanks to Wales.

Los tricolores had got their ticket punched to Sweden, leaving first Canada and the United States and Costa Rica in their qualifying wake.

The foundation of the team was set on the Chivas del Club Guadalajara, which in those days was the class of the Mexican league. They had just won the first championship in their history the year before, and—not unlike my River—they would go on to win five more . . . in a row! Thus they earned the nickname *"Campeonísmo."*

In all, there were seven *chiverío* players on the roster: Héctor "Chale" Hernández, José "Jamaicón" Villegas, "El Niño" Paco Flores, Crescenico "Mellone" Gutiérrez, "El Tigre" Guillermo Sepúlveda, and a striker who would go on to become the top goalscorer in Chivas history, the marvelous "Chava" Reyes.

The legendary Guadalajara goalkeeper, Jaime "Tubo" Gómez, was also called up, but he didn't play. The post still belonged to "La Tota," who was playing in his third World Cup.

Roster spots were also occupied by some other favorites of the day, including Jesús del Muro from Atlas, and "El Güero" Raúl Cárdenas from Zacatepec, who was playing in his second Cup.

The coach was once again the Spaniard Antonio López Herranz, but both the public and the press were clamoring for "Nacho" Trellez, who was the best Mexican coach at the time.

The Mexican Federation's solution was to name him the team's "trainer" and send him to

Sweden alongside the Spaniard, who was given the title of "technical director." Imagine if they had tried to do the same thing with Hugo and Lavolpe . . . *¡Mama mía!*

Just as it happened in Brazil '50, *los aztecas* would play their first match against the hosts, this time Sweden, in the Solna stadium in Stockholm. The date was the eighth of June. They played well but lost 3–0.

Three days later, for their second appearance on that same stage, Mexico showed their teeth. In the final minute they salvaged a tie against Wales, thanks to the head of Jaime "El Flaco" (Slim) Belmonte of Irapuato. With the 1–1 tie, Mexico had its first point in World Cup history, and Belmonte has been known ever since as "The Hero of Solna." (Take note of this for trivia purposes!)

For their third game, this time against Hungary in the city of Sandviken, Mexico looked more like a hospital ward than a soccer team. Because substitutions were still not allowed, they were forced to play with injuries to "Chava," "La Tota," "El Tigre," and Jesús del Muro. They played as well as they could, but still fell 4–0.

But that wasn't the important thing, for they had scored an unforgettable point.

Granted, they would have to wait another four years before getting their first win, but I'll tell you about that one later.

PELÉ vs. FONTAINE

Now let's get to the duel between the great Pelé and the Frenchman with the thirteen goals.

Brazil had advanced through to the semifinals on the strength of Pelé's goal against Wales, and France got in with a 4–0 win over Ireland that included two by Fontaine. He had eight in only four matches!

Inevitably, the press and all the world were focusing their attention on the impending head-to-head matchup. Everyone was as excited as they would have been were it the final itself. It was all about France, the best offensive team, which had fifteen goals in four matches against Brazil and its impenetrable defense.

They played in Göteborg on June 24, 1958. Thirty-five thousand people were watching from the stands, and a million more in front of their televisions.

Here is how things played out: Vavá opened the scoring in only the 1st minute, but Fontaine bounced back in the 8th. The score remained tied—and the two sides were evenly matched—until six minutes before the half, when Didi knocked home Brazil's second goal.

I don't know what Feola said to Pelé there in the locker room, but after the break the kid came out on fire. He scored in the 52nd, the 64th, and the 75th minutes.

Wow!

Pelé 3, Fontaine 1.

It was as if poor Just had simply vanished from the pitch. France managed to score only one more goal near the end, and the game went into the books 5–2 in favor of the Brazilian *"Scratch."*

Brazil had reached the final for the second time in their history.

FONTAINE BREAKS THE RECORD

Having been eliminated in the semis, France would have to settle for an appearance in the third-place match. Their opponent was Germany, who had lost their champion's crown in the other semifinal against the Swedes, 3–1.

TRIVIA
Who is the top goalscorer in World Cup history?

At the time, the record for most goals in a single World Cup was held by the Hungarian Sandor Kocsis, who had scored eleven times four years earlier. Fontaine was coming into this match with nine. It was his chance to break the record—and rinse the bad taste from his mouth left by Brazil.

And Germany paid the price.

Fontaine was champing at the bit, and he scored once, twice, three times, and then—*boom!*—his fourth goal of the game. France massacred them 6–3, and Just concluded the tournament with thirteen goals, breaking the record and setting the bar at a new height that to this day has yet to be threatened.

Five decades and eleven Cups later, the record remains his. The only one to come close was the German Gerd Muller, who scored ten at Mexico '70. But we'll get to him later.

Will someone break the record this summer? Might it be. . . Adriano? Ronaldo? Ronaldinho? Borgetti? Crespo?

Place your bets!

GRAND FINALE IN STOCKHOLM: THE RASUNDAZO

Brazil had an account to settle. With themselves.

In Italy '38, they lost in the semifinals. In 1950, Uruguay beat them in their own house. In 1954, they fell to Hungary in the quarter finals. They weren't about to let Sweden perpetuate this sad history.

(Havelange had already returned home to Brazil, "to attend to matters of the Confederation," but they say it was really to avoid the pain of watching yet another defeat!)

How does the expression go—"the third time's the charm"? Well, in this case, it was the fourth.

With this as their motivation, Feola's *"Scratch"* took the rain-spotted field that Sunday, June 29th, the new promises of Pelé, Vavá, and Garrincha among them. For Sweden, the goal was to win their first World Cup on their own turf in front of their king, Gustav VI, and to avoid a sort of Scandinavian Maracanazo.

And they quietly took the lead, opening the scoring in the 4th minute!

But it didn't last long. From that point on, Brazil took the bull by the horns and went about obliterating their curse.

Vavá tied it up in the 9th, and then put Brazil in the lead in the 32nd minute. Both goals came off devilish passes by Garrincha. Then, ten minutes into the second half, Pelé pushed the difference to 3–1 with the prettiest goal of the tournament: from inside the penalty area, and with a defender all over him, Pelé chests the ball down and eludes his marker with a half-turn. A second one immediately closes, and Pelé puts the ball past him with perfect touch on the header. As the ball is coming back down—but before it reaches the turf—Pelé volleys with his right. *Wham!* A spectacular goal!

Thirteen minutes later, Zagallo knocks home Brazil's fourth, before Sweden finally responds in the 80th minute.

But Pelé wasn't quite finished yet.

With just one minute left to play, when everyone thought the final score was destined to be 4–2, the youngster capped it all with one more. If you'll indulge me, I'll describe this one, as well: Pelé had planted himself outside the area when he received the ball from Didi. He trapped it softly before passing it back to Zagallo on the left side. Then he raced to the penalty spot and called for the cross. It arrived, and— as John Motson would later put it—"This time Pelé used his head to outfox the keeper Svensson!"

Four is good, but a fifth is better still.

A journalist for *Paris-Match* wrote that a king had been born— *"Le Roi de Football."* Of course, in Portuguese they said *"O Rei . . ."* The nickname stuck, and the rest is history.

Brazil would raise the Jules Rimet Trophy for the first time, thus founding a soccer dynasty that, today, remains unrivaled.

But now I'm going to dance a little *cueca*, because we're moving on to Chile!

CAMPEONATO MUNDIAL DE FUTBOL
WORLD FOOTBALL CHAMPIONSHIP
CHAMPIONNAT MONDIAL DE FOOTBALL
COUPE JULES RIMET

CHILE
1962

Chile 1962: Garrincha's Cup

FIFA had no choice. Having held two consecutive World Cups in Europe, the next event would have to be somewhere in the Americas. It was June of 1956, two years before Sweden '58, and FIFA representatives were meeting in Lisbon to make the decision.

Once again—just as in 1938 and 1950—Argentina petitioned for the right to host, but it was given to another candidate. At the end of the day, thirty-two votes were cast in favor of Chile versus only ten for Argentina. Fourteen countries abstained from the vote, which is interesting.

But why Chile?

Credit is due to a man who dedicated his life to bringing the World Cup to Chile. He started off his speech to the delegation in Lisbon—which was conducted in four languages, mind you—with an impassioned plea that still resonates in the Chilean psyche: "Because we have nothing, we want to do everything."

His name was Carlos Dittborn, and he was president of the Comité Organizor del Chile '62.

His famous phrase was an expression of the fact that his country—though poor, underdeveloped, lacking communication technology, and with few athletic facilities—was ready to throw all its heart and soul into the undertaking if it could have the honor of hosting.

It worked.

Dittborn returned to Santiago a hero, and immediately began the tireless work of preparing for the seventh World Cup, 1962. The Jules Rimet Trophy would travel from one pole of the globe to the other, from Sweden to Chile, from Scandinavia to Patagonia.

And the Chileans really did put heart and soul into it.

From highways and hotels to airports, customs checks, and even stadiums. They built a new stadium in Arica and expanded the Estadio Nacional in Santiago, as well as the Sausalito in Viña and the one in Rancagua, near the capital. The project was slated to last six years, and just when they were entering the home stretch, two years before the Cup, they were hit by an act of God: an earthquake that ravaged the entire southern part of the country, from Chiloé to Concepción.

FIFA feared the Chile Cup would never be.

They considered a last-minute change of venue, but neither Dittborn nor the Chilean people would hear of it. President Alessandri's government intervened, work continued, and the Cup was open for business on May 30, 1962.

Dittborn, however, was not in attendance.

One month earlier, on April 28, he fell victim to a heart attack. He was only thirty-eight years old, and his wife was nine months pregnant at the time. His two sons, Carlos and Juan Pablo, took his place at the emotional opening ceremonies, hoisting the flag while the band from the Escuela Militar played the national anthem.

Their father was surely up in heaven, next to Jules Rimet, looking down upon them.

SIXTEEN AGAIN

It was another sixteen-team field, with ten European teams and six from Latin America. No Asian or African nations were represented.

They also kept the system of four round-robin groups with the top two in each group advancing to the elimination rounds. But to keep down the travel requirements for the teams (remember, there weren't many highways), they decided that each group would play their games in just one city. Note the parity and the difficulty level of each group; here's how they broke down:

> **Group A** (Arica): Soviet Union, Yugoslavia, Uruguay,
> Colombia
> **Group B** (Santiago): Chile, Switzerland, Italy, West Germany
> **Group C** (Viña del Mar): Brazil, Mexico, Spain,
> Czechoslovakia
> **Group D** (Rancagua): Argentina, Hungary, Bulgaria,
> England

"LA ROJA" DEBUTS

Once they had finished preparations to host the Cup, the next step for Chile was to assemble their national team, the famous *"Roja,"* so called because of the color of their jerseys.

The Chilean Federation chose the veteran Fernando "Tata" Riera for their coach and called him home from Portugal, where he was coaching Belenense. The process of putting together the roster was long and tedious, but it yielded the hoped-for result: the best *Selección Nacional* of all time.

The pillars of the team were the goalkeeper Misael "Gato" Escuti, the defender Lucho Eyzaguirre, midfielders Jorge "Chino" Toro and Eladio Rojas, the strikers Jaime Ramírez, Alberto "Tito" Fouilloux, and the team's brightest star and one of the greatest players ever produced by Chile, Leonel Sánchez.

On the day of their debut in Santiago against Switzerland, May 30th, Chile was a happy place. It was the most democratic country on the continent; the poet and native son Pablo Neruda was internationally famous; Pinochet was no more; and Salvador Allende was a politician with a future.

And all of this happiness was echoed in their victory over the Swiss. *"La Roja,"* wearing white jerseys this time, fell behind early but rallied for a 3–1 win on two goals by Leonel and one by Jaime Rodríguez. They had started off on the right foot.

Their second match was against Italy, and the political atmosphere with regard to these two national teams was tense and charged. Leading up to the Cup, the Italian press had published a pair of arti-

cles that was rather unflattering of Chile, emphasizing the country's poverty and other social problems. Nobody likes to see their dirty laundry aired internationally, and the Chileans were deeply offended.

And—as always happens in such cases—those national antagonisms got played out on the soccer field.

It was a hard-tackling and heavy-hitting match, and sometimes openly violent. There was a fair amount of pushing and shoving, and it almost became "The Battle of Santiago." In the end it was the Italians who bore the brunt of the punishment. Leonel Sánchez openly threw a punch at one of them, but the English referee saw fit to send off the Italian. Later he ejected another.

Italy ended up with only nine players on the field. Chile did not squander their advantage, and downed the *azurri* 2–0, thanks to Jaime Ramírez (again) and "Chino" Toro, who scored a rocket of a goal from outside the area.

Italy went home early, and Chile moved on to the quarterfinals, but not without leaving a measure of resentment in their wake.

COLOMBIA'S DEBUT

Chile '62 has the peculiar distinction of being the first and only World Cup where two Latin American teams had automatic berths: Chile, as the host, and Brazil, as the defending champion. This worked to Colombia's advantage, which they exploited by winning a spot for themselves.

And it was worth it!

The Colombians, coached by the renowned Argentine Adolfo Pedernera, made World Cup history with a sensational tie and a shocking goal . . . against the best goalkeeper in the world!

"How did it happen?" you're sure to ask, and in your best Colombian accent.

"Be careful," I'll warn, "Gather round and I'll tell you."

They played on the first day of competition—May 30, 1962—in the stadium in Arica, which had been recently renamed the Estadio Carlos Dittborn in honor of the father of Chile's Cup. Their opponent was Uruguay, twice world champions, who featured two young Peñarol players and future *charrúa* stars Pedro Virgilio Rocha and Luis Cubilla (who also played for my beloved River).

Colombia lost the match after going up 1–0 on a penalty converted by Francisco "Cobo" Zuluaga. But just after the break, Cubilla tied it up for Uruguay, and

TRIVIA

Who was the coach of Colombia in Chile '62?

"El Pepe" José Sasia put the finishing touch on a 2–1 scoreboard.

The "sensational tie" would come in the *cafeteros'* second match.

It also took place in Arica, on June 3rd, against the U.S.S.R. The Soviets were competing in their second World Cup, and they came to Chile as both Olympic and European Champions. What's more, they boasted the best keeper on earth, "The Black Spider," Lev Yashin of Moscow's Dynamo.

Nobody was surprised by the halftime score: 3–1 in favor of the Communists.

The Soviets continued to dominate the game at the start of the second half, and knocked home a fourth goal in the 57th minute. That was it; the game was as good as over.

Ah, but here is where the soccer gods looked down, shining a ray of hope on Colombia; and it reached Marcos Coll, the twenty-seven-year-old midfielder from Barranquilla. In the 68th minute, he struck a devilish (or miraculous, you might say) corner and shocked none other than Yashin himself with a goal!

"Tómele Compadre!" my beloved Rosana Franco would say.

It was the first time in World Cup history that anyone had scored such a goal. And it was also the first time that a team would come from three goals down to earn a tie.

The *"golazononón"* by "Olímpico Coll" (as he was subsequently dubbed by the Colombians) brought the score to 4–2, and the Colombian side roared to life and began an all-out assault on Yashin's net.

José Antonio Rada scored Chile's third just five minutes later, and—much to the dismay of the Soviets and their keeper—Marino Klinger tied things up only two minutes after that.

What a way to make your debut!

Unfortunately for the Colombians, the joy would only last four days. On June 7th they faced Yugoslavia, to whom they bowed 5–0, thus ending the first chapter of their World Cup history.

The second would be written twenty-eight years later, in Italy. And what a chapter it was. You'll see . . .

THE OLD LADY DOESN'T GO

My beloved mother wanted to be there for the debut of *la celeste* against Colombia, but thanks to me she wasn't able to. Here's what happened.

I was barely two years old when her siblings in Uruguay invited her to Chile, via bus from Montevideo. But when she told Papá about

her plans, he really hit the roof and put a stop to the trip right there.

"And who's going to take care of the kid? Me? Are you crazy!" he exclaimed.

Mamá, who never took orders from him, or anybody, was suddenly and surprisingly speechless. Since she didn't have any intentions of missing a World Cup—especially one so close by—she began to scour all of Buenos Aires for a babysitter so she would be able to meet up with her brothers and sisters for the second round of the tournament.

You can imagine the rest.

After beating Colombia, Uruguay fell to Yugoslavia 3–1, and then to the Soviets 2–1. They were eliminated in the first round and headed back to Montevideo. Her siblings did, too. And so my mother, who had ended up finding a babysitter, was left with her wishes *and* her baby.

The only good to come out of the whole experience? Uncle Negro got to see his second World Cup; and I didn't have to stay with a babysitter.

LA TOTA'S FOURTH

To reach Chile, Mexico had to endure a long and winding qualifying road. First they won the CONCACAF region by eliminating the Netherlands Antilles and Costa Rica (again!), and then they survived a playoff with Paraguay.

They arrived in Chile with a new attitude, thanks to the strong leadership of the new *presidente de la federación*, a man who had modernized Mexican soccer, the great Guillermo Cañedo.

One of his first decisions was to prepare *los tricolores* with plenty of time and lots of international friendlies. To direct it all he hired as coach the man from the *cachucas*, "Nacho" Trellez. It was then that the expression *"Sí se puede"* (roughly: "Yes, we can") began to be heard in Mexico.

Players from *"Campioncillo"* Chivas again dominated the roster, with six in all. Necaxa had four; América, Atlas, Toluca, and Oro had two apiece; while Monterrey, Irapuato, Zacatepec, and León each had one.

Playing in their second World Cup were "Chava" Reyes, "Chale"

With my mother, María Teresa.

Hernández, and "El Tubo" Gómez, still the backup to Carbajal, who for his part was playing in his fourth Cup, a new record. "El Güero" Raúl Cárdenas was making his third appearance.

Once again they had the unfortunate luck to share a group with the Brazilians, who, this time, were the defending world champions.

All right!

And not only that, but they had to face them in their opening match, just as they did in Rio in 1950 and in Geneva in 1954, games they lost by the combined score of 9–0. This time the site was Viña del Mar, the date May 30th, the opening day of the Cup.

They lost, but not by so much.

They played the champions hard, and only fell 2–0, the second goal a classic take by Pelé. It's the goal that Don Antonio remembers most clearly of the ones he's given up in his career. And why not? It's an honor—well, something of an honor—to have been scored on by "O Rei."

Holding Brazil to a low-scoring game inspired *los tricolores*. They very nearly eked out a goalless draw with Spain, and would have, too, if Joaquín Peiró hadn't found a chink in Carbajal's defense…in the 89th minute, no less!

Incredible!

THE FIRST VICTORY FOR LOS AZTECAS

For their third match, Mexico entered the confines of Viña, hoping to change their luck. Their opponents were the Czechs, who had opened their campaign by holding Pelé & Co. to a scoreless draw. (They would meet again in the finals . . .)

Don't blink!

This record would last all the way until South Korea/Japan 2002, when the Turkish player Hakan Sukur opened the scoring against the latter of the two hosts only eleven seconds after the opening whistle.

TRIVIA

In which match was the quickest goal ever scored against "La Tota"?

But the Mexicans were not shaken. They rallied together and began to play a back-and-forth game against the Europeans. And their efforts paid off.

In the 13th minute, "El Chololo" Isidoro Díaz (of Irapuato) tied things up. At the 30-minute mark, "El Negro" Alfredo del Águila (of Toluca), who played a brilliant game that was heavily praised by the Chilean press, gave Mexico the lead. They reached the second half in Viña with the score 2–1.

It was the first time that Mexico went into the locker room ahead on the scoreboard.

In the second half, the Mexicans decided to play the best defense they possibly could. The clock was winding down, and the Czechs began desperately to unleash cannon-like shots. "La Tota" made majestic saves on at least three separate occasions. Czechoslovakia's rally never materialized. In fact, an *azteca* counterattack resulted in a goal for Héctor "Chale" Hernández, and Mexico's first-ever World Cup win went into the books, a 3–1 victory.

TRIVIA

What was Mexico's first-ever World Cup victory?

The boys of *los tricolores* didn't continue on into the elimination rounds, but for the first time they would be returning home from a World Cup with their heads held high. After five appearances, they had finally emerged as a credible threat to any competitor.

And why not?

For his efforts in Chile, "La Tota" was selected by an Italian newspaper as one of the best players in the world at the time, and when he returned home to Mexico he was offered an endorsement deal by Coco Milk and began to appear on television commercials.

Nice going, *compadre*!

CARRIZO SAYS "NO THANKS"

After their failure in Sweden, many veteran players did not want to participate in the next World Cup for fear of being browbeaten again by their own press and fans. One of them was my beloved Amadeo Carrizo.

The task of convincing him otherwise fell to the new *albiceleste* coach, Juan Carlos "Toto" Lorenzo. He begged, he pleaded, he did everything possible to convince him otherwise, but Amadeo was unmoved. He simply didn't want anything to do with the World Cup.

The team flew to Chile without him.

The only veteran whom Lorenzo was able to convince was Néstor Rossi. Everyone else was a new face, including Silvio Marzolini, Vladislao Cap, José Sanfilippo, and Antonio Ubaldo Rattín. The goalkeeper was Antonio Roma (of Boca).

Had Argentina improved?

Maybe so, because they were not humiliated, but they didn't exactly have a resounding success, either. They drew Group D (Rancagua), along with Bulgaria, England, and Hungary. They defeated

the Bulgarians 1–0 but fell to the English 1–3. Against Hungary they managed only a 0–0 draw.

They had conquered their fear, but still they returned home without glory. Their appearance in that tournament was nothing more than that: an appearance.

And Carrizo?

That year, his run and that of River remained intact: runners-up yet again, a mere two points behind Boca (grrr!).

"THE UNITED NATIONS OF SPAIN"

That's how the Chilean press described the Spanish selection. They had more international personnel on their roster than any other team—five, to be exact.

From Argentina came their coach, the legendary Helenio Herrera, who united the great Hungarian now playing his second (if uneventful) World Cup with his second country, Ferenc Puskas, with the Uruguayan José Santamaría, the Paraguayan Eulogio Martínez, and the great absentee of these finals, the Argentine Alfredo Di Stéfano, who went down with an injury just days before the competition began and missed out on his chance to play.

TRIVIA

For which country did Ferenc Puskas play in his second World Cup? Why didn't Alfredo Di Stéfano participate?

PELÉ IS ALSO INJURED

The defending world champions reached Chile as favorites once again. The core of the team remained intact, and Pelé, now twenty-one years of age, was coming into his own as the best player on earth.

As we've already seen, they opened their campaign in Viña del Mar against Mexico. Pelé had a goal for the ages, and the Brazilians won 2–0. Their second match was against Czechoslovakia (whom they would meet again in the final), and it ended in a scoreless draw. But in one shot on the Czech goal, Pelé strained a muscle in his left thigh and was forced to the sidelines.

Panic for Brazil!

"O que é que vamos fazer agora?" they asked themselves. What were they going to do? Indeed, everyone wanted to see what they would be able to do.

One thing they didn't do was lose hope—after all, they still had Amarildo and Garrincha.

Amarildo started in place of the injured Pelé in Brazil's final match of the first round, and he scored both goals in the win. They came midway through the second half, when Brazil was down 1–0 and struggling. But the playmaker behind each of the goals was his teammate from Botafogo, Garrincha, who had no problem shouldering the bulk of the load while "O Rei" was sidelined.

In the quarterfinals, Garrincha single-handedly defeated the English. Steering the team for ninety minutes, he assisted Vavá on one goal and scored two others himself (the latter of which was a beautiful strike from outside the area) to seal a 3–1 victory. And the world rejoiced.

Brazil was through to the semifinals, and the press—both Chilean and international—searched for words of praise for the Brazilians whose performance made them all but forget about the absence of Pelé.

CHILE BIDS FAREWELL TO "THE SPIDER"

They didn't say it with flowers but with goals.

Chile and the U.S.S.R. played in the Arica desert, and expectations were running high. First of all, never before had Chile advanced to the elimination stage of a World Cup. But, secondly—and perhaps more important—they were facing the European champions and the best keeper in the world, Lev Yashin, "The Black Spider."

But *black*? Leonel Sánchez had him seeing red!

Sánchez opened the scoring in the 10th minute with a spectacular free kick, his third goal of the finals, and he very nearly knocked in two more in the first half alone. The Soviets tied things up in the 27th, but Eladio Rojas immediately answered with a booming shot from outside the area that gave a one-goal advantage back to the *sureños*.

And that was how the match ended, 2–1, Chile, and a national celebration broke out all across the country. The Chileans couldn't believe it. They were in the semifinals, and Yashin was on his way home.

But the celebration was dampened somewhat when they learned that they would be facing Brazil.

Gulp!

CHILE AND BRAZIL IN THE SEMIFINAL

What a shame that one of these two teams would have to be eliminated!

An all–Latin American final between the hosts and the defending champions would have been the perfect conclusion to this World Cup, but it wasn't to be. Chile was to face the *"Scratch"* in the semis, and they would prepare for the worst while hoping for the best.

The match had been slated to be played in Viña, but the organizers moved it to the Estadio Nacional in Santiago, which had a greater seating capacity. And on that thirteenth of June, 1962, 70,000 people packed the stands while four million more tuned in their TVs to watch the show put on by Garrincha and friends.

And what a show it was!

The scoring began early, in the 9th minute. Amarildo tackled a Chilean player inside the box, and the rebound squired over to the feet of Garrincha, who knew what to do with it. Brazil 1, Chile 0.

Twenty minutes later, Garrincha swept into the six-yard box and got his head to a corner by Zagallo, notching his second goal.

Things were looking bad for Chile, but they did not give in. Toward the end of the first half, "El Chino" Toro scored on a perfectly placed free kick (his second goal of the competition) and opened things up for the hosts. There was still hope.

But as the second half opened, Brazil scored again off a corner. This time it was Garrincha who played the ball in and Vavá who rose to the occasion to bring it home. Brazil 3, Chile 1.

Chile was on the ropes, but they would not go down quietly.

Leonel Sánchez converted a penalty kick in the 75th minute for his fourth goal of the Cup, but Brazil answered back only two minutes later, again off the head of Vavá.

Brazil was sweeping its way to the final match—their second in a row—but the win would be bittersweet. With five minutes left in the match, Garrincha, who had been driving the Chilean defense mad, apparently became frustrated at being hacked all afternoon and lashed out against Toro. Referee Arturo Yamazaki, a Peruvian of Japanese ethnicity (and the same Yamazaki who today owns Mexican citizenship and directs their Comisión de Árbitros de la Federación), ejected him.

> **TRIVIA**
> Where was the referee who sent off Garrincha from?

Garrincha would be out of the final match! Well, we shall see . . .

CHILE: THIRD IN THE WORLD

The ugly episode would be quickly forgotten. The country's attention was focused on the third-place match between their beloved *Roja* and Yugoslavia, who had fallen 3–1 to the Czechs in the other semifinal.

They played in Santiago, on the sixteenth of June—the very same day the son of Carlos Dittborn was born in a nearby hospital.

The event was evenly matched and surprisingly without emotion, but all that changed when Eladio Rojas opened the scoring for Chile with his second goal of the tournament and the stands awoke. Suddenly the crowd began to like the idea of being the third-best team in the world and got behind their selection. With their help, *La Roja* held that slimmest of advantages throughout, to win the match 1–0.

TRIVIA

Where did Chile finish in their own home World Cup?

It wasn't the ideal result for Chile, but it was quite memorable nonetheless. Against all odds, and even the most optimistic of predictions, Chile was third in the world— not bad at all for a nation competing in only its third World Cup.

THE FINAL IN SANTIAGO

The great unanswered question leading up to the final match was whether or not Garrincha would play.

Rumors abounded: phone calls by the Brazilian government offering money, similar actions by the Chilean government, a mythical suitcase full of money that arrived in Santiago from Brasilia, and talk that FIFA itself was trying to get Yamazaki to change his match report . . . any and all manner of speculation.

In the end, all we know is that for some reason FIFA reconsidered Garrincha's expulsion and reinstated him for the match. (The poor guy had been playing with a fever of 104!)

So let's get to the match itself!

Brazil, playing in the third championship in their country's history, was facing Czechoslovakia, which was appearing in their second, the first having been the final of Italy '34, where they lost 2–1 in overtime to the hosts.

With Chile's run at an end, the spectators filling the seats of the Estadio Nacional were solidly behind *os filhos do samba*. Feeling quite at home, the world champions took the field that seventeenth of June, 1962, with Garrincha leading the team in place of Pelé, who was still injured, and ready to reprise the success they enjoyed in Sweden four years before.

And just as happened in Sweden, Brazil fell behind at first, after a goal by Josef Masopust, who was universally regarded as the best European player of the day.

But also as happened in Sweden, the Brazilians, undaunted, quickly found the equalizer. In the 14th minute, Amarildo broke free along the left flank and raced toward the touchline, where, instead of crossing, he threaded the ball between the Czech keeper and the near post. Goal Brazil.

After the break—this time in the 69th minute—Amarildo escaped up the left-hand side and ran for the touchline again, but this time he did play the ball up and across the mouth of the goal, where it glanced off the head of the defender Zito and into the net. Brazil had their second goal of the match, but there was one more yet to come.

Djalma Santos received a throw-in, and sent a soaring cross into the Czech penalty area. The goalkeeper, Willy Schrojv, came off his line for what looked like an easy save, but he became tangled up with another player and lost the ball, which landed at the feet of Amarildo, who mercilessly fired into the back of the net for this fourth goal of the Cup.

Brazil had won the Jules Rimet Trophy for the second time, and they had done so without Pelé. It was their other stars who had imbued them with a sense of success.

England '66 would be the trial by fire.

Pelé went on to pluck out the thorn of his Chilean experience by winning the Copa Libertadores and the Copa Intercontinental with his club, Santos, as if saying to the world, "You *see!*"

Four:
The Modern
Cups (1966–78)

The Modern Cups:
England '66 to Argentina '78

Finally we have come to the World Cups that many of us have lived through and know personally. That's why I call it the "Modern" World Cup era. It was born of the most transforming invention of the twentieth century, an invention that changed society, economics, and, inevitably, soccer, as well.

Can you guess?

I'm referring of course, to television, good old TV.

Switzerland experimented with the new medium in 1954. Eight years later it was used on a limited basis in Chile, but it was England '66 that fully embraced the new technology and shot it around the globe via another, even newer, technology: satellite transmission.

The first communications satellite, the *Early Bird*, was launched in early 1965. When the World Cup came to England, the pioneering BBC was equipped to transmit—live via satellite (though in black and white)—the first truly "universal" sporting event.

So pass me the remote control and let's head for London!

England '66: Eusebio's Cup

In addition to the novelty of TV, England '66 was the World Cup of odd officiating, disputed expulsions, a most shocking robbery, an African boycott, an Asian surprise, another injury to Pelé, the first mascot, the introduction of ball boys, and the debut of extraordinary players such as Beckenbauer, Perfumo, Tostão, Jairzinho, Figueroa, Mazzola, and a sensational Portuguese striker named Eusebio Ferreira da Silva, better known simply as Eusebio, "The Black Panther."

WORLD CUP

JULY 11 to 30
1966
ENGLAND

We'll see how the eighth World Cup looked alongside the music of the Beatles and the Carnaby Street miniskirts that were so popular with women all over the world—and men, too!

THE AFRICAN BOYCOTT

Ironically, the blood brothers of Eusebio (who was born in Mozambique) did not participate in this World Cup. And the reason was quite simple: Africa wanted a permanent spot in the finals, without having to play off against teams from Asia or Oceania.

So, as a means of protest, the sixteen African member nations of FIFA formed an alliance and declined to participate unless they were granted permanent representation not dependent upon defeating any other nations. FIFA, for some unknown reason, refused to give ground on this point, and the African nations said "Sorry" to England, and opted to stay at home.

TRIVIA
Which World Cup was boycotted by the entire African continent?

It would be another four years before FIFA recognized the error of their position, and granted the African nations what they already deserved.

WHERE'S THE CUP?

Stolen!

People were dumbstruck. Nobody had any clue as to who would have the audacity to do such a thing. But the fact is that England awoke on March 20, 1966, to the news that the famous Jules Rimet Trophy, which was made of solid gold, had been stolen from Westminster's Central Hall during the night.

How embarrassing!

TRIVIA
Who found the Jules Rimet Trophy after it had been robbed?

Scotland Yard was immediately mobilized and began to scour London and the rest of Great Britain. The World Cup organizers offered a reward of 6,000 pounds for information leading to its recovery. But even with all these resources, who do you think it was who found the thing?

A dog!

It's true. His name was Pickles, and he was a black-and-white terrier. A week after the robbery, he was walking with his owner through a south London neighborhood when all of a sudden he smelled something odd in someone's garden. Upon further inspection, it was a paper bag containing the Jules Rimet Trophy itself.

TRIVIA
During which World Cup was the Jules Rimet Trophy stolen?

Pickles was instantly a national hero!

An entire nation went mad with gratitude and infatuation with that little pup. Photo ops, movies, TV and radio appearances, and more movies. The English—and the rest of the world, as well—were fascinated by the whole ordeal, especially with the emergence of such an unlikely hero. FIFA, on the other hand, simply breathed a deep sigh of relief.

"WILLIE" THE MASCOT

The only animal to compete with Pickles for England's heart in 1966 was a lion. His name was Willie, and he was a very furry and very friendly little cub who made World Cup history by being the first official mascot.

The idea, according to the organizing committee, was to choose something that would represent "the lineage and nobility of the United Kingdom." In other words, they were so proud of the fact that they were hosting a World Cup that they wanted to shout it to the world. And what better way to do it than with a plush toy!

TRIVIA
What was the first official World Cup mascot? In which Cup did he appear?

Hundreds of thousands of Willie toys of all shapes and sizes were manufactured, and all sorts of posters and other graphics were printed with his image prominently displayed. Willy was a hit.

Not only did the English promote their "lineage" and "nobility," but they also cleared several million pounds in sales. When FIFA saw the figures for itself, they immediately decided that from that point on, every World Cup would have its own mascot.

Yes sir!

STILL SIXTEEN

We still aren't at the age of the thirty-two-team finals. In 1966, the World Cup was still a rather exclusive club, with only sixteen participants. Here are the privileged few, divided into four groups in seven cities:

Group A (London): England, Uruguay, France, Mexico

Group B (Sheffield and Birmingham): West Germany, Argentina, Spain, Switzerland

Group C (Liverpool and Manchester): Brazil, Bulgaria, Portugal, Hungary
Group D (Middlesbrough and Sunderland): Chile, the U.S.S.R., North Korea, Italy

"ADIÓS," TOTA

England's World Cup opened for business on July 11, 1966, only four days after my beloved Antonio Carbajal turned thirty-seven.

His birthday gift from the Federación Mexicana de Fútbol was a trip to yet another World Cup, though this time as the backup to "Nacho" Calderón (from the Chivas club), who was the new starting goalkeeper.

"La Tota" was honored to accept, which made him the founding member of the Five World Cups Club. And for years, he would be the only member of that prestigious group.

The downside of competing in so many World Cups was that he also became the most scored-upon keeper of all—and among those goals given up was, at the time, the quickest: only fifteen seconds into play. But neither of these two dubious distinctions took anything away from his glory and his grandeur. That's why they erected a statue of him in León, in the Mexican state of Guanajuato.

He only played one match in England, but he bid farewell contentedly. The team did, too. They had prepared themselves assiduously for six months, once again under the watchful eye of "Nacho" Trellez and with the total support of the head of the Federation, Guillermo Cañedo. They didn't make it through to the second round, but they did drastically reduce the number of goals scored against them, taking only three in all. Finally, Mexico had its most successful showing to date, with only one defeat.

They started off well, tying the French 1–1 in Wembley Stadium on July 13th (Enrique Borja of Club América scored their lone goal in the 3rd minute of play). After falling 2–0 to the hosts, they fought to a goalless draw with Uruguay. It was in this contest that "La Tota" played his farewell World Cup match.

That night, back at their London hotel, his teammates threw him a proper Mexican *fiesta*, and Carbajal sang at the tops of his lungs *"Cucurrucucú, Paloma."*

I can almost hear him now!

THE DEBUT OF DON ELÍAS

Following their successful third-place showing in the previous World Cup, Chile maintained their high caliber of soccer and, with a new coach, Don Lucho Alamos, qualified for England '66. They joined Argentina, Brazil, Mexico, and Uruguay as the representatives of the continent of South America.

The new *Roja* included a few veterans from the previous Cup, including Leonel Sánchez, Fouilloux, and Landa, but they had a rising star in the form of a nineteen-year-old boy possessed of uncanny class and elegance, especially for a defender. Eventually he would go on to become the greatest Chilean defender of all time and be recognized internationally as one of the world's one hundred greatest footballers of all time.

I'm referring, of course, to the sensational Elías Figueroa.

TRIVIA
In which World Cup did the Chilean defender Elías Figueroa make his debut?

England '66 catapulted him to fame. After the Cup, Peñarol brought him over to Uruguay, and after that he found his way to Brazil's Internacional club, in Pôrto Alegre, which is where Don Elías spent the prime of his playing career. He took "Inter" (Internacional) to its first Brazilian championship, he was selected three times by the Latin American press as best soccer player of the continent (more times than Zico, Cubillas, Rivelino, Valderrama, and even Pelé himself), and he was named the best defender in the history of the Brazilian league.

La Roja opened their England '66 campaign in Sunderland—up on the North Sea coast—on the thirteenth of July, facing Italy. Remember, they had defeated the *azzurri* four years earlier, in Santiago, in an ugly match full of pushing, shoving, and ejections. In other words, this had all the makings of a grudge match.

Italy arrived with a completely renovated roster, full of new and flashy players. The English press had tabbed them as favorites, and among them were future legends like the goalkeeper Enrico Albertosi, the defender Giacinto Facchetti, and the midfielders Gianni Rivera and Sandro Mazzola.

Neither Figueroa nor his teammates could quite keep up with the Italians that afternoon, who opened the scoring in the 8th minute (goal by Mazzola) and consistently frustrated all Chilean attempts to get the equalizer. With two minutes left in the match, the Italians got an insurance goal, and their account with *La Roja* was finally settled.

TRIVIA
When did Mazzola, Facchetti, and Rivera make their World Cup debuts?

In their second Group D match, Chile faced World Cup newcomers North Korea in Middlesbrough. Here there were no surprises with the Koreans (still!) and the match ended in a 1–1 tie.

Their final opponent of the first round presented Chile with yet another rematch, this time against Lev "Black Spider" Yashin and the U.S.S.R., whom they had eliminated 2–1 in the quarterfinals of the previous World Cup. Yashin was not playing that day; he was the backup keeper, and would retire after this, his third Cup.

At the final whistle, the scoreboard read the same as it had been in Santiago, but this time it was not in Chile's favor. The Soviets were advancing on to the quarterfinals, while Figueroa and his teammates were heading home.

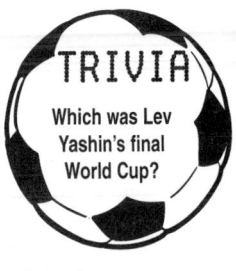

TRIVIA

Which was Lev Yashin's final World Cup?

ANOTHER DEBUT: BECKENBAUER

Even at the tender age of twenty, Beckenbauer's class was readily apparent.

That's why Franz Beckenbauer was named as a defender to the West German national team, although in reality he was not a defender in any sense of the word. He was what they called a "sweeper," or a player who backed up the defenders but also had free rein to venture forward on offense, depending on the requirements of the match. Today, nobody plays this position—except for the occasional wing back—because the players have so many matches that this sort of multiple responsibility is simply too much!

When he arrived in England, Beckenbauer had been playing professionally for Bayern Munich for only two seasons, and he'd made his first cap a mere nine months before.

But his debut in this World Cup couldn't have been more auspicious. West Germany started off with a 5–0 win over Switzerland, with young Franz accounting for two of the goals! As we have seen before in these tournaments, the interna-

In Germany with Franz Beckenbauer.

tional press is always on the lookout for an exciting new spark plug to focus their attention on, and this elegant young German stood out among the crowd.

Thus, a legend was born.

I had the pleasure of interviewing him during the 2005 Confederations Cup. I asked the then-president of the Germany 2006 Organizing Committee if he ever thought about one day running for president, given the amount of love that Germans of all sorts have for him. He laughed and said no. "I'm not interested in politics. I'd rather rest for a good long while than be president." And with that, he shook my hand and then boarded his private helicopter, to be whisked off to yet another soccer game.

A helicopter!

Such are the advantages of being president of the Organizing Committee, let alone president of the nation!

EUSEBIO AND THE FABULOUS PORTUGUESE

Eusebio arrived in England as one of the main attractions, only twenty-four years old and with many victories to his name. He had been named 1965's European Footballer of the Year, and his team, Lisbon's Benfico, was the continental champion.

Here was an impeccably classy player. Besides strength and speed, he could unleash cannon-like shots from either leg, and he could score from even the tightest of corners. The international press made the inevitable comparisons to Pelé.

Portugal's World Cup roster featured many great players besides Eusebio; indeed, some consider it their greatest generation of players ever, as it included such names as Morais, Hilario, José Augusto, Torres, and Simões.

Their first match was simply sensational, and it fulfilled all expectations, despite the fact that Eusebio himself did not score. It was in Manchester, on July 13th, and Portugal steamrolled Hungary 3–1. Their second match was against Bulgaria, whom they blasted 3–0, and the game saw Eusebio's first of nine goals in that World Cup.

Their third match would be one for the ages. The Black Panther would be facing the Black Pearl. We'll look at that match soon.

TRIVIA
In which World Cup did Eusebio play, and against whom did he score his first goal?

ARGENTINA—ANOTHER POWERHOUSE

Maybe nobody realized it at the time, but the Argentine selection included a group of players who, as was the case with Italy, would go on to become prominent names in the pantheon of world soccer.

I'm referring to legends of Argentine soccer lore like Roberto Perfumo, Luis Artime, Ermindo Onega, and Oscar Mas, the four of whom made their collective World Cup debut in England alongside a few veterans of Chile '62: Antonio Roma, Silvio Marzolini, and Antonio Rattín.

And things weren't bad at all, until they got quite bad indeed. Ugly, I should say.

They started off in Birmingham against Spain (which was fielding Gento, Luisito, Suárez, del Sol, and Pirri), whom they defeated 2–1 on a pair of goals by Luis Artime.

After that (again in Birmingham), they faced the West Germans, whom they fought to a scoreless draw. Their third and final match of the first round was played in Sheffield, and their opponents were the Swiss. Artime scored again, and Onega added one of his own, to lead the *albiceleste* to a 2–0 win and a spot in the second round—for the first time since 1930.

So far, so good.

But the worst was yet to come, in the quarterfinals, against the host, England, which was responsible for bringing the sport to Argentina a century before. The match is still talked about to this day, and FIFA is still accused of shady dealings and unfair play.

I'll tell you what happened and you can decide for yourself.

THE SHOCK OF THE CENTURY

The Maracanazo was historic; the United States' 1–0 victory over England in 1950 was unexpected, and the '54 final was incredible. But who would ever dream of imagining that a team from a small, obscure, Communist country composed largely of amateurs could defeat the mighty Italians, one of the favorites to win it all?

It was an impossibility. But that's exactly what happened.

July 19, 2006, will mark the fortieth anniversary of what happened that fateful day in Middlesbrough. At match time, the Italians stood second in their group and needed only a draw to advance. North Korea, on the other hand, needed a win to stay alive.

It's a long story, and it's still told, in both Italy and North Korea. Suffice it to say that, for the first few minutes of the match, it seemed as if the Italians would have no problem handling the quick and elusive *chinitos*. They dominated play at will, and had a few near-miss goal opportunities.

But, as they say, he who does not score is often scored upon.

North Korea struck first, in the 42nd minute, with a powerful, sweeping, glancing shot by Pak Doo Ik. And the scoreboard still read 1–0 when the final whistle blew, sending North Korea on their way into the second round, something no Asian team had ever done before. (Trivia alert! And here's some more: Pak Doo Ik was a thirty-one-year-old dentist who played soccer in his free time.)

Italy returned home with its tail between its legs. Headlines like *"Vergogna Nazionale"* (National Shame) and *"Il nostro calico e'morto"* (Our soccer is dead) were emblazoned across the Italian papers the next day. In an attempt to avoid an ugly scene at the Rome airport, the team changed their travel plans and flew into Genoa, but hundreds of angry fans found out and showed up to welcome them back with a barrage of tomatoes.

TRIVIA

What match is known as "The Shock of the Century"?

The only good thing about the whole situation was that Mussolini was no longer alive. If he had been, who knows what he would have done to the poor *azzurri!*

BRAZIL ALSO SAYS "CIAO"

At least the Italians weren't the only favorites to bow out in the first round. Two-time world champions Brazil were also sent home early. In fact, it may have been worse for them, because they were beaten so soundly: by six goals in the first two matches. Even with Pelé and Garrincha on the field!

The slide began in Liverpool, on July 15th, in the second match of Group C, against the Hungarians. Brazil had opened strong, as expected, beating Bulgaria 2–0 on goals by Pelé and Garrincha, but it came at a cost: O Rei was injured by a Bulgarian kick.

Nevertheless, Brazil still hoped for a similar victory over Hungary, which had looked quite poor in a 3–1 loss to the fabulous Portuguese.

The Magyars were seeking to revive their glory of 1954, and took full advantage of Pelé's absence to roll to a 3–1 victory over the *"Scratch."* Tostão, who—like Gerson and Jairzinho—was making his World Cup debut, scored Brazil's lone goal.

After that came the final match of the first round, the hand-to-hand combat in Liverpool between "The Black Panther" of Portugal and "The Black Pearl" of Brazil, who seemed to have recovered enough from his injury to return to the starting lineup.

Yes, Pelé played, but he was still not one hundred percent, and he proved a nonfactor in the match. It was Eusebio who would shine.

He scored twice, including a sensational strike from inside the area that sealed a historic 3–1 victory. Portugal eliminated the two-time champions *do mundo*, and had done so in spectacular fashion. They were through to the second round.

TRIVIA

Which country eliminated Brazil in England '66?

When he limped back to Brazil in defeat, Pelé swore that he would never again play in a World Cup. The violent play had left a sickening feeling in his gut.

Luckily for us, he didn't keep his word, otherwise we would have all been deprived of the magic he worked four years later!

DUBIOUS OFFICIATING

In the quarterfinals, Argentina faced England, and West Germany faced Uruguay. For England's match, FIFA had assigned a German referee; and, correspondingly, an Englishman would be officiating West Germany's match.

Coincidence?

Possibly. But when you consider what occurred in each match, you can't help but wonder.

The Latin American press—especially those from around the River Plate region—maintain to this day that there was a conspiracy to favor the Europeans. For their part, the Europeans—especially the English—still chuckle at the South Americans' paranoia. Whatever the case may be, neither Argentina nor Uruguay would be playing in the World Cup title match.

THE RATTÍN SHOW

Everything appeared to be going well in London on July 23, 1966. Argentina was facing England for the second consecutive time in a World Cup. Four years earlier, in Chile, the English had won 3–1.

The match opened well and promised good things to come, with Argentina having the upper hand. Bit by bit, the game grew rough, with fouls committed by both teams that were ignored by the referee Rudolph Kreitlein.

In the 34th minute, Perfumo committed a foul outside the area, and Kreitlein awarded a free kick. The Argentine captain, Antonio Ubaldo Rattín, began to protest the call, but the official paid him no heed and motioned for play to resume. Rattín, however, continued to press the issue, until Kreitlein suddenly turned around and ejected him from the match.

And the show began.

Rattín refused to leave the field, and the game was at a standstill. Some of his teammates tried to convince him to go, while others insisted that if he were sent off, they would be leaving as well. The standoff lasted for ten minutes. Finally, Rattín left the field, but he didn't get far: he sat down on a strip of red carpet that ran from field level up to the luxury box of Queen Elizabeth. The spectators began to boo him loudly, pelting him with candy and cups of beer. The police came, and the Argentine captain retired to the locker rooms, but not before he furiously tore down the corner flag, which was painted in the colors of the Union Jack.

TRIVIA

Who was Rattín, and why was he sent off?

And the whole world was watching on television!

Argentina played on, and, though dispirited and with a numerical disadvantage, they managed to keep the scoreboard clean until thirty-two minutes remaining in the second half, when Hurst put one home for the English. They went on to win by that 1–0 score, and advanced to the semifinals. Argentina was going home, bitter and ashamed.

RATTÍN SPEAKS

Much has been written about this incident, and everyone on earth seems to have an opinion. Nevertheless, it's the protagonists who should have the final say. In a statement released after the match, the referee Herr Kreitlein said that Rattín had shot him an angry look, which he interpreted as an insult, and for that reason he expelled him.

To get the other side of the story, I flew to Buenos Aires to interview Rattín himself, who is now active in politics and still in excellent physical condition. He graciously agreed to meet with me, and invited me to his home. As he has always maintained, Rattín said he was simply trying "to cool things down" because things were getting tense and the English were starting to dominate the game.

With respect to the ten minutes that it took him to leave the field, Rattín told me that he had asked for a translator because "I didn't understand what the referee was telling me. I didn't speak English or German, and the guy didn't speak any Spanish. And I didn't want to leave the field until I had a translator."

And why camp out on the red carpet?

Rattín explained, "I didn't understand its significance," and he spoke so plainly and with such conviction that it's hard not to believe him. He also said that he just sat down "to rest" and to watch the rest of the match. Then his voice took on a certain amount of youthful impudence as he recalled picking up the candy that the crowd was pelting him with and eating it. "They were calling me 'animal, animal,' but I just laughed and helped myself to some chocolate."

Regarding the corner flag, Don Antonio admitted doing it just to rile up the 70,000 partisan fans who were booing and shouting at him.

So, looking back on things, does he think he might have overdone it just a bit?

The former national team captain simply chalks everything up to the immense pressure of the match. "The ref was a disgrace," he said. "The English were doing anything to win."

He also told me that the organizers had asked for representatives from each team to meet in a London hotel before the match in order to select the referees. But when the Argentine representatives showed up at the designated time, "they had already chosen!"

Forty years later, Rattín still regrets what happened, but not because of his own conduct. It's the English behavior he laments. His resentment is palpable: "I think they were stronger than us, yes, but they did everything they could to guarantee victory. They did everything they could to make sure Argentina would be eliminated."

And that's how it stands. What do you think?

URUGUAY VS. WEST GERMANY: MORE EJECTIONS

Uruguay was also victimized, though they didn't raise quite so much of a row. They played their quarterfinal match that same day, July 23rd, in Sheffield, with the English referee James Finney in charge of the field of play.

The first half ended 1–0 in favor of the Germans, but the opening moments of the second half saw an Uruguayan attack that resulted in a goal of their own . . . well, a near goal, I should say, because just as the ball was about to cross the goal line, the West German center back Schnellinger reached out to block it with his hand.

The whole world saw it. That is, everyone except for the official.

The Uruguayans were beside themselves. They complained desperately, and raised their voices in protest, but Mr. Finney refused to award a penalty kick and instead ejected two of the South Americans: Horacio Troche and Héctor Silva. Left with only nine players on the field, they were picked apart by the West German machine.

Within minutes after play resumed, Beckenbauer scored their second, Uwe Seeler got the third, and Haller notched the fourth. The final Latin American team had been eliminated, leaving three European squads and the surprising North Koreans.

MY GLORIOUS TRANSISTOR

England was my second World Cup. I was six years old in 1966, and that was when I began playing soccer in the park with my fellow first-graders from Escuela Esteban Echeverria, in the Belgrano district of Buenos Aires.

I didn't know much about the game—let alone about the World Cup—save for what I've already told you about my old man and about Amadeo Carrizo, whom I worshiped and tried to imitate in our games in the park.

But suddenly, thanks to the magic of radio, I learned about the beauty of the World Cup.

My parents were able to follow any and all developments over the airwaves. I still remember that contraption: it was a small, portable, transistor radio—the latest fad—encased in leather and made by Spica.

Thanks to that Spica, I'll never forget those World Cup days. First, because of the exciting cries of *"¡gol!"* and because of the serious commentary on the events happening on English fields, commentaries that grew in both color and tone with the expulsion of Rattín and the elimination of both Argentina and Uruguay. But also because of that unmistakable sound that filled our tiny apartment at 1372 Calle Luis María Campos in Belgrano.

Whenever Argentina, Uruguay, or Italy would be on, the emotional voice of the commentators surging from distant shores would mix with the shouts from Papá and his friends, and with the racket of the Singer sewing machine belonging to my mother, who worked in the home as a seamstress. The incessant machine-gun *ratatatat* of that sewing machine blended in amid the radio broadcasts and the emotional voices of all the listeners, including that of Mamá, who expressed her own thoughts on the matches without looking up from her work.

Everything returned to normal when Argentina and Uruguay were eliminated. That day, the World Cup was as good as over for our family, and the Spica was turned back to music stations.

I remember it like it was yesterday!

PORTUGAL'S SCARE

Liverpool, July 23rd, the quarterfinals. The match was between two nations making their World Cup debuts: Portugal and North Korea. The former had eliminated Brazil, while the latter had unexpectedly vanquished the Italians. It was shaping up to be a highly anticipated match.

And a mere sixty seconds into the match the surprises commenced. North Korea scored. Twenty minutes later, they scored again. Two minutes after that, a third. North Korea 3, Portugal 0. And they were only in the 24th minute.

Incredible! Nobody could believe what was happening.

Where was Eusebio?

"Um momentinho," said the Panther. *"Estou aqui."* And indeed he was there and he was just awakening.

He scored his first goal in the 27th minute and the second in the 43rd, before hitting home with penalty shots in the 57th and 59th minutes. He had single-handedly brought the score to 4–3, and had set the North Koreans reeling. Before the final whistle blew, José Augusto made the score 5–3, and that's how Portugal would advance to the semifinals.

But the Koreans returned to Pyongyang awash in glory. To this day, they are the greatest heroes in the history of North Korea.

THE FINAL IN WEMBLEY

The soccer cathedral was all decked out on Sunday, July 30, 1966, and ready to host a World Cup final for the first time. On the field, the proud hosts were graciously wearing their red jerseys so that the West Germans could play in their traditional white uniforms. In the stands, 70,000 souls accompanied Queen Elizabeth II, the English prime minister Harold Wilson, the West German chancellor Ludwig Erhard, and the president of FIFA, the Briton Stanley Rous, who was surely happy to see his compatriots in the final match.

Throughout the world, twenty million people were watching on television.

The English would have to play the match of their lives in order to erase all doubts that this, their own World Cup, had been manipulated, organized, and scripted from the very beginning with the intent of making them champions. If they didn't win, it would be an embarrassment for the entire kingdom!

Fortunately, Alf Ramsey's team was able to put its best foot forward and play a great game. They were led by their captain, the great midfielder Bobby Moore, as well as their great striker Geoff Hurst and the keeper Gordon Banks. But the very soul of the team was the greatest English player of all time, and their career goals leader as well: the legendary Bobby Charlton.

It was, without a doubt, the best English team of all time.

The West Germans, however, weren't far behind. In addition to their sensational newcomer Beckenbauer, they had Karl-Heinz Schnellinger, who had also proven to be one of the best defenders of that Cup, despite the infamous play where he saved a sure goal by Uruguay off the line with his hand. They also featured the ever-dangerous striker Uwe Seeler, as well as their team leader in goals, Helmut Haller, who would win the coveted Silver Boot as the tournament's second-highest goalscorer.

It was a hotly contested match: fast-paced, intense, and, at times, controversial. The two teams reached the half time tied, with goals each by Haller and Hurst. In the 58th minute, Peters broke the deadlock, and the English saw their dream on the verge of becoming a reality.

But with exactly one minute left to play—and the English struggling to contain their emotions, feeling so close to the trophy—Weber swept in to tie the game once again.

"Bloody hell!" exclaimed the English, but it was true: the World Cup final was headed for overtime, for only the second time ever.

And that's where Geoff Hurst made history—doubly.

First, he scored one of the most controversial goals in World Cup history: the infamous, much-discussed and -analyzed shot that ricocheted off the crossbar and down onto the goal line below. There is no video evidence that it ever crossed that line; however, the Swiss referee Gottfried Dienst consulted with his linesman and awarded a goal.

Later, as if to erase any doubts and reconfirm the English triumph, Hurst notched another, putting the scoreboard at 4–2 and becoming in the process the first player to achieve a hat trick in a World Cup final. It's thanks to him that England was able to lift the Jules Rimet Trophy for the first—and so far only—time.

THE ARGENTINE CONSOLATION

London wasn't a complete loss. The news wasn't very widespread at the time, but during that summer, the Executive Committee of FIFA decided to award Argentina—finally!—the right to host the World Cup twelve years hence, in 1978.

I don't know for a fact whether it did much to calm the Argentines' frustrations; somehow I doubt it.

But now let's break out the tacos and mariachis, because we're heading for Mexico!

Mexico 1970: Pelé's Other World Cup

The traveling, the travails, and the persistence of Guillermo Cañedo all came to fruition during the 1964 Tokyo Olympics.

That was where FIFA gathered together to choose the host nation for the 1970 World Cup. It came down to Mexico and Argentina (the eternal candidate). Many Europeans thought that playing Cup matches at the high altitudes of some Mexican cities was a recipe for disaster. But we already know what the decision turned out to be. Don Guille returned to Mexico City with the rights to host the ninth Jules Rimet World Cup. It was the second World Cup with an official mascot—this time a short little Mexican named "Juanito."

FIFA's decision was particularly influenced by Mexico's preparations for the 1968 Olympics. The Executive Committee assumed

that the Aztec nation's experience just two years before the 1970 Cup—not to mention all the new Olympic infrastructure—would prepare them ideally to host a World Cup.

TRIVIA

What was the name of the mascot for Mexico '70?

They were right. For its quality of play as well as its excellent organization, the first World Cup in Mexico will be remembered as one of the best of all time, and the newly built Estadio Azteca in Mexico City—"The Colossus of Santa Ursula"—as the scene of one of the greatest finals ever.

CARDS AND SUBSTITUTIONS

Mexico '70 will also be remembered for being the first World Cup to feature the use of red and yellow cards, and for permitting the use of in-game substitutions.

And it was about time! Up until then, injured players had to suffer there on the field unless they wanted to leave their team undermanned. This is what happened to Pelé in Chile against

Czechoslovakia, and in England against Portugal. At the same time, the violent play that emerged in those two Cups led FIFA to establish an explicit system of cautions and ejections. And thus was born the "yellow card," which could be followed by the infamous "red," meaning you were done for the day!

In the 1970 Cup there were no expulsions, and the first-ever substitution took place in the very first match, between Mexico and the U.S.S.R. In the second half, the Soviets subbed Anatoli Puzarch for Victor Serebrianickov, and minutes later the Mexicans swapped Mario Velarde for Antonio Munguía.

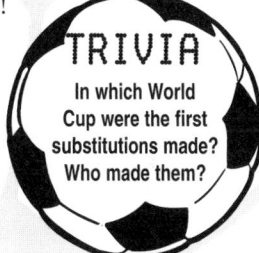

TRIVIA

In which World Cup were the first substitutions made? Who made them?

A NEW BALL

Beginning with 1970, FIFA signed a contract, still in effect today, with the German sporting goods company Adidas to provide the official World Cup ball.

FIFA's mind was squarely on Europe when they decided to schedule Mexico '70 kickoffs for twelve noon. The objective was to satisfy European TV viewers, who wanted to watch the live broadcasts in prime time. However, it was detrimental to the players, who would have to labor under the harsh Mexican sun at midday.

Protests were lodged, but television won out. In order to counteract the effects, most teams arrived in Mexico three to four weeks before their opening matches in order to better acclimate themselves.

"MI CASA ES SU CASA"

The teams arrived at the Mexico City airport to the sounds of mariachi music and the welcoming smiles, kisses, flowers, and souvenirs of the beautiful Lupita dolls in their traditional dress. It was a grand Mexican *fiesta*, attentively watched by curious fans and reporters, and captured by television cameras for the rest of the world to see.

¡Bienvenidos a México!

The reception was just a hint of things to come, and proof positive that the expression *"mi casa es su casa"* truly does describe Mexican hospitality. Which is partly why they were so offended to learn that the English team had brought their own supply of water with them, hoping to avoid "Montezuma's revenge."

What a lack of respect!

STILL ONLY SIXTEEN

The number of participating countries had not changed. It was still only sixteen, and the standard 1958 format—four groups of four teams, with the top two teams from each group advancing to the elimination rounds—remained intact as well.

The draw was held at the Salón Independencia del Hotel Maria Isabel on Avenida Reforma in the capital city, directly across from the Ángel de la Independencia. Here's how the groups fell out:

> **Group A** (Mexico City): Mexico, U.S.S.R., Belgium, El Salvador
>
> **Group B** (Puebla and Toluca): Italy, Uruguay, Sweden, Israel
>
> **Group C** (Guadalajara): Brazil, England, Sweden, Romania (the very first "Group of Death" in the history of World Cup draws)
>
> **Group D** (León): West Germany, Peru, Bulgaria, Morocco

WELCOME, AFRICA!

Another World Cup first for Mexico '70 was that FIFA finally acceded to African demands for direct representation in the World Cup finals without having to work their way through Asia and Oceania first.

And the honor went to Morocco, who were attending this, their first World Cup. They drew into Group D, along with West Germany, Peru, and Bulgaria, and they played quite well for first-timers. They lost their first two matches, but in their third they tied Bulgaria 1–1. They didn't win a spot in the second round, but they won a good deal of respect.

The representative from Asia and Oceania was Israel, also making their World Cup debut. They played in Group B, along with Italy, Uruguay, and Sweden, and they met with even more success than the Moroccans, finishing with two draws. Their only defeat was 2–0 against Uruguay.

They also headed home after the first round, but with quite a few Mexican souvenirs.

THE "SOCCER WAR"

Since Mexico was guaranteed a spot as host, El Salvador saw an extraordinary opportunity to participate in their own first World Cup. But Honduras did as well. And so they went to war.

In reality it wasn't quite that simple, but the myth perpetrated by the international press made it seem like that. The so-called Soccer

War actually had nothing to do with sports. It was a long-drawn-out border conflict that had existed for fifty years between two countries that now faced each other in the World Cup qualifiers—and, sadly, an athletic competition turned into a military conflict.

It's important to mention that in the years leading up to the World Cup in Mexico, relations between Honduras and El Salvador were tense and strained. In 1969, Honduras had initiated a program of deportation for thousands of Salvadorans, who took it as both an insult and a violation of their human rights.

Things only continued to escalate with the news that the two countries would face off in an elimination series on the road to the World Cup.

The first match was to be played at the Estadio Morazán in Tegucigalpa on June 8, 1969, and it's not hard to imagine the tension in the air. The night before, the Honduran fans refused to let the Salvadoran team sleep by making noise and throwing stones at the windows of their hotel.

The following day, Honduras won 1–0.

A week later, at Flor Blanca in San Salvador, the Salvadoran fans repaid their visitors in kind, welcoming the Honduran team with insulting chants and death threats. This time the match went to El Salvador 3–0, and the Hondurans had to leave the stadium under the protection of a military escort.

Since each side had won once, the berth in the World Cup would have to be decided on neutral ground. FIFA selected the Azteca in Mexico City, and it was there that they met for a third time, on June 27th. El Salvador went on to win by a score of 3–2, and Honduras was eliminated from the World Cup.

But the political tension between the two countries did not wane with this resolution. On July 14th, the Salvadoran army invaded Honduras and war broke out between the two countries. It lasted a hundred hours and left 2,000 people dead and countless other victims wounded before the Organization of American States intervened and orchestrated a cease-fire.

So, soccer did not *cause* the war, but the two events will be forever linked.

EL SALVADOR'S DEBUT

The fact of the matter is that El Salvador was appearing in their first ever World Cup, and because they were a neighboring country their fans didn't have far to travel. In fact, they were sharing Group A with their neighbor Mexico, as well as with Belgium and Italy.

We celebrate "El Mágico" Jorge González as the best Salvadoran player of all time—but he was only eleven years old in 1970, and so, clearly, he was not on the roster in Mexico. But his predecessors were, and among them were the likes of Raúl Magaña, Mauricio "Pipo" Rodríguez, Saturnino Osorio, and the two Salvadors: Salvador Mariona and Salvador Cabezas.

Unfortunately, this World Cup debut wasn't quite what the Salvadoran fans—or the players—were hoping for. They lost all three of their first-round games, and were outscored by a total of nine to nil.

Eventually, relations between Honduras and El Salvador began to thaw, and in 1980 they signed a new peace treaty. Today, their national teams face each other regularly, and without the threat of war.

THE PRESSURE ON "LOS TRI"

For many people, 1970 was do-or-die time for *los tricolores*. It was "their" World Cup, and they had to compete well to avoid messing up, or *embarrarla*, as they say in Mexico.

Under the tutelage of the head of their federation, Guillermo Cañedo, the team set about their preparations with time and care. In a friendly in late 1968, they defeated Brazil at the Azteca. But after that, things didn't go quite so well. In May of the following year, they embarked on a seven-nation European tour, and the Mexican team could muster only one win and two draws against four defeats. As a result, "Nacho" Trellez either resigned or was forced from his spot as technical director, to be replaced by his own assistant and former national team star and veteran of three World Cups, "El Güero" Raúl Cárdenas.

After much experimentation and tweaking of the roster, the final squad comprised five players from Cruz Azul, four from América, three from Pumas, two each from Chivas and Necaxa, and one apiece from Veracruz, Toluca, Atlante, and León.

The prominent figures were: "Nacho" Calderón, the Chivas keeper; "El Halcón" Gustavo Peña and "El Negro" Antonio Munguía, both from Cruz Azul; Aaron Padilla and José Luis "La Calaca" González, both from Pumas; Javier "El Cabo" Valdivia from Chivas; and the great striker from Club América, Enrique Borja.

MEXICO KICKS OFF THEIR CUP

Mexico got things started on May 31, 1970, with their match against the Soviet Union. The match was a rather boring one that ended in a nil–nil draw, but it is notable for trivia buffs in that it

was the first World Cup match to see in-game substitutions, and also the first appearance of a yellow card, which was shown to "El Halcón" Peña.

In their second match, Mexico did what they had been doing in recent years, which was to thrash El Salvador 4–0. But their third game, against Belgium, would be crucial, because nothing short of a win would allow them to advance to the second round. Early on in that June 11th match, Mexico took the lead on a penalty impeccably struck by their captain, "El Halcón" Peña, in the 16th minute. For the rest of the match, *los tri* were content to hang back and defend their advantage. Which they did, successfully. With a 1–0 final score, they were through to the second round for the first time in their history.

Every street, home, and bar broke out in song and dance: a grand national *fiesta*. But the joy lasted only three days. It was all extinguished during the bombing in Toluca that became known as "La Bombonera." It was the match where they faced Italy, who had struggled to advance, scoring only once in three matches.

This fact likely emboldened the Mexicans, and the hopes of *los tri* were lifted even higher still when "La Calaca" González scored the first goal of the match in the 13th minute of play. But Italy picked themselves up, dusted themselves off, and rolled right over the Mexicans, who ended up playing their worst game of the Cup. Mario Bertini tied things up, Gigi Riva gave Italy the lead, and Gianni Rivera notched a third goal before Riva scored again to finish it off.

Italy 4, Mexico 1.

The miracle never materialized: what might have been, was not. They just couldn't do it. *Los tri* had bowed out of their own World Cup, and all Mexico could do was throw their support to Brazil for the remainder of the tournament.

CAÑEDO GOES

Three days after the conclusion of the World Cup, Guillermo Cañedo surprised everyone by resigning as head of Mexican soccer, giving the national Federation what he called "the freedom to act" and reorganize. It was the end of an era.

"We have to change the mentality of Mexican soccer," he declared in his parting statement.

But things didn't change immediately, and Mexican soccer fell into the worst decade of its history. However, the seed of Cañedo's suggestion had taken root, and eventually the Mexicans did manage to change their attitude and emerge from the pit into which they'd fallen.

Today they are ranked among the ten best teams in the world, thanks largely to the work and leadership of "Don Guille."

PELÉ GETS HIS WAY

Because he didn't get injured, he could show the world what he was capable of.

And that's exactly what he did. With class and elegance, "O Rei" offered us the best sports spectacle of all time. The only single performance to approach his was that of Maradona—sixteen years later, on the same stage. There must be something in that Mexican air!

The selection that accompanied Pelé to Mexico would help him to forget the failure of London and the sting of Santiago. And there were several newcomers among them: Felix on goal; Wilson Piazza and the captain Carlos Alberto on defense; the midfielders Clodoaldo and Gerson; and the powerful lefty Rivelino up front. In addition, the veterans Jairzinho and Tostão were each competing in their second World Cup.

TRIVIA

Who was Brazil's coach in 1970?

At the head of the squad—and making his debut as coach—was Pelé's old teammate from Sweden and Chile, "O Lobo" Mario Zagallo.

If there is one team that has been written about more than any other, it is, without a doubt, the 1970 Brazilian squad. It was a symphony of soccer, a ballet on grass, a poem of goals, a tribute to creativity in all its forms . . . and you know the rest.

They started off at the Jalisco in Guadalajara, defeating the Czechs 4–1, the win featuring a beautiful goal by Pelé; they beat the defending world champions, England, 1–0, on a brilliant strike by Jairzinho off a Pelé pass; and they eliminated Romania 3–2, this time with two by "O Rei" and the third by Jairzinho. In the second round they downed Peru 4–2, and then in the semis they beat Uruguay 3–1 on the feet of Clodoaldo, Rivelino, and Jairzinho again, who would go into the record books for being the only player in World Cup history to score in every match. (For purposes of trivia, please note: seven goals in six games.)

PERU'S "NENE"

The Peruvians knew he was good, but the rest of the world had yet to find out.

He had won Peru's national championship, scored sensational

goals, and his exploits had been well covered in the *Alianza Lima*, but the world at large was not yet privy to his classy play. Mexico '70 was a perfect opportunity to remedy this situation, live via satellite, and in living color.

Teófilo Cubillas was a dark-haired, super-talented, twenty-one-year-old kid who, more than Peruvian, seemed like a Brazilian on the field.

What a player!

He was quick, skillful, intelligent, and baby-faced (hence the nickname: "Nene"). His goals were things of beauty, and his free kicks were powerful and awe-inspiring. Peru had never seen a player of his caliber.

Other than Peruvians themselves, the only people who had witnessed his brilliance were the Argentines, because Nene and his teammates had done the impossible: they eliminated the *albiceleste* from the World Cup finals.

Argentina had needed a win in its last qualifying match—which was played on Boca's home turf—to punch their ticket for Mexico. Unfortunately for my compatriots, neither the efforts nor the enthusiasm of the spectators in the stands were enough. A goal in the 88th minute by Alberto Rendo tied the match at two-all, but a draw was of no value to them, and Argentina was left out of the World Cup.

Which is why my country didn't pay much attention to Mexico '70. Myself included.

I was ten years old at the time and was more interested in my own neighborhood games than in following the Cup on TV. My mamá, on the other hand, was very interested, because her beloved Uruguay had received a favorable draw; but her enthusiasm didn't rub off on me. I was barely even aware that I was living through my third World Cup.

But let's get back to Nene and the Peruvians.

It was the best team ever fielded by Peru, and they were coached by the legendary Brazilian Didi. Cubillas was at the forefront of a generation of exceptional players, which to this day Peru has not been able to replace.

Let's see, there was the goalkeeper Luis Rubiños, the legendary central defender Héctor Chumpitaz, Roberto Challe and Ramón Miflin at midfield, the strikers Julio Baylón and "El Cholo" Hugo Sotíl, and Pedro Pablo Perico León up front.

TRIVIA

Who was Peru's coach at Mexico '70?

Their debut was filled with emotion and pain.

Just days before, an earthquake struck the Peruvian Andes and more than 10,000 lives were lost. Entire towns were wiped off the map. Far from home and with their compatriots in tears, the

Peruvians took the field at Cuauhtemoc in León that second of June, 1970, to face Bulgaria with heavy hearts.

And the Bulgarians didn't spare the grieving Peruvians, opening up a 2–0 lead.

Nene was the first to respond. He hoisted the team squarely on his shoulders and led their play in the second half. Soon, Peru was playing like they knew they could, with deft touches and turns, opening up space, attacking the box, and peppering the Bulgarian goal with shots.

Gallardo was the first to score, followed by Chumpitaz three minutes later. And with ten minutes left to play, Cubillas got his revenge. He scored his first-ever World Cup goal: a rocket of a free kick that closed the match 3–2 in favor of Peru.

Soccer had—at least temporarily—eased the pain of a nation in mourning, and the Peruvians thronged the streets in celebration.

> **TRIVIA**
>
> What was "Nene" Cubillas's first World Cup?

Their second match was against Morocco. Nene played inspiredly. On that day, June 6th, he scored twice himself and assisted on a third by Challe. They were 3–0 winners, and safely through to the second round—a historic debut.

Again, the country was going crazy, forgetting their tragedy at home.

Their final opponent of the first round was West Germany. The machine of Beckenbauer, Seeler, and Schnellinger produced three goals, this time by a World Cup rookie, a twenty-four-year-old named Gerd Müller.

However, Cubillas would not be silenced, and scored one of his own: his fourth goal in three matches. But West Germany would hold on for a 3–1 win.

Unfortunately for the Peruvians, their quarterfinal match was against Brazil, which was universally ranked the best team in the tournament. Their match was played at Guadalajara's Jalisco stadium on June 14. The efforts of Nene and his teammates to contain Pelé and his team came up short. Two goals by Tostão, one by Rivelino, and another by Jairzinho put an end to the Peruvian dream. The match ended 4–2, Brazil, though Cubillas had scored his fifth goal in only his fourth World Cup match.

> **TRIVIA**
>
> How many goals did Cubillas score in Mexico '70?

In Lima they were given a hero's welcome, while back in Mexico they were sorely missed by the Mexican public, who, while they appreciated the spectacle offered by Brazil, would never forget the beautiful soccer displayed by Nene and his red-shirted gang that had descended from Andean heights to astonish the soccer-mad world.

At the conclusion of the World Cup, Didi declined to renew his contract with Peru, turning instead to Buenos Aires to coach my team, River. His Peruvian pupils would not qualify for the 1974 World Cup, though they would reappear four years later in Argentina, where the great Nene would give the world another great performance.

URUGUAY REVIVES HER GLORY

Uruguay did not reach the final because they ran into Brazil in the semis, but if it hadn't been for that . . . *ayayay!* Who knows what might have happened? Another final against the Brazilians?

Perhaps.

But the fact is, this was the best Uruguayan performance in a World Cup since Switzerland '54.

Los charrúas reached Mexico with a solidly rebuilt team. Pedro Virgilio Rocha and Luis Cubilla were veteran leaders playing in their third World Cup. The young newcomers included the defenders Atilio Ancheta and Roberto Matosas, the midfielders Victor Espárrago and Julio Montero Castillo, and the striker Ildo Maneiro. The net was minded by the twenty-five-year-old star of Peñarol, who, after the Cup, would be included in the All World team. His name was Ladislao Mazurkiewicz.

They were scheduled for Puebla's Cuauhtemoc team, and their first match was a 2–0 defeat of Israel on June 2nd. They followed that up with a nil–nil draw against Italy before losing 1–0 to Sweden. But the four points they'd accrued was enough to put them through into the second round.

On June 14th, Uruguay played an extremely tight match in the Azteca against the Soviets, and after ninety minutes the scoreboard was still stuck at 0–0. As the second of two fifteen-minute overtimes drew to a close, everyone was convinced that the result would be decided by penalty kicks, but just then Espárrago came through with an unforgettable goal, and Uruguay was in the semifinals for the first time in sixteen years.

Even though I wasn't exactly paying attention to this World Cup, I couldn't help but hear about *that* goal. I was playing soccer in the streets of Montevideo (where "Tío Negro" lived) when the goal was scored, and immediately I heard cries of joy pour out of every house in the *barrio*. We stopped our own game for a few moments in order to find out the cause of all the celebrating, and that was when I learned that some guy named Espárrago (a name that has always made me laugh) had carried Uruguay through to the semifinals of the World Cup.

But that is where they ran into the *"Scratch,"* and the party soon came to an end. Although Cubilla scored a farewell goal, it wasn't enough to turn the tide. Brazil scored three of their own and sent Uruguay home.

In his frustration, my uncle flatly stated that "FIFA set everything up so that the final would be Europe versus the Americas."

Was he right?

THE REMATCH

What a game!

Once again, the West Germans and the English met in a historic match, one as intense and evenly fought as the final of England '66.

This time, however, the setting was the tiny Nou Camp in León. The English still featured the two Bobbies—Moore and Charlton—as well as Geoff Hurst, who scored the winning goal in Wembley four years earlier. They opened up a 2–0 lead, but Beckenbauer and Seeler ultimately tied the score for the West Germans, and the game went into overtime.

> **TRIVIA**
> Who won the rematch between West Germany and England in Mexico '70?

After 108 minutes of play under the burning Guadalajara sun, both defenses were wearing down, the tournament's top goalscorer, Gerd "The Bomber" Müller, scored his eighth goal of the Cup, giving West Germany the victory.

The English had relinquished their title and were forced to return home—exhausted, but with a decent Mexican tan.

THE GAME OF THE CENTURY

Another great game!

One played between two nations with two World Cup titles each. The West Germans were exhausted after their marathon match, but that did not prevent them from rising to the occasion there in the Azteca against the *azzurri*, who had defeated Mexico in a much less taxing match.

They played ninety minutes of back-and-forth soccer, but at the end of it all the match was tied at one goal apiece, and they were headed for overtime.

Beckenbauer was playing with a dislocated shoulder and his arm was strapped to his chest, but nevertheless the goals suddenly began to materialize, one after the other. Five in twenty-one minutes!

First, Müller scored for West Germany, which was followed by Italy's Roberto Boninsegna. Then the Italians took the lead on a strike by Riva, only to see Müller immediately tie things up again at 3–3. That gave him two tallies for the day, and he ended up as the tournament's top goalscorer. His ten total goals had put him in sight of the record set by Just Fontaine, with his thirteen scores in 1958.

In the end, the West Germans ran out of either gas or luck, and Italy scored again, off the foot of Rivera. The match was finally over: 4–3, in favor of the *azzurri*.

Their unfortunate opponents may have left their hearts on the pitch, but they took with them the unforgettable memory of the greatest semifinal match in history. Which is why it's come to be known as the Match of the Century.

Auf Wiedersehen!

TRIVIA

What became known as the Match of the Century, and in which World Cup did it take place?

THE FIRST AZTECA FINAL

What would be the dominating force—exhaustion or the desire to win?

That was the question dogging the Italians that Sunday, June 21: the day of the final match of Mexico '70. Apparently, desire won out, because they took the Azteca field firmly resolved to face down the Brazilians, who—to the surprise of all—took the first seventeen minutes of the match to find their game.

That's when Pelé appeared.

With a leap that prefigured the best of Michael Jordan, "O Rei" hung in the air long enough to get his head on a cross from Rivelino, and opened the scoring. The Italians understood that their only chance at victory was to shut down those two players. They marked them hard, trying to neutralize them. And they had a bit of luck, too. In the 36th minute, Clodoaldo made a mistake deep in his own end of the field and Boninsegna swept in for the tying strike.

Tutto bene, at least for the moment. As the first half came to a close, Italy still had their legs and lungs.

But then the second half began.

Rivelino unleashed an explosive shot that hit the crossbar, and it was clear that the "*Scratch*" had awoken. The *azzurri* tried to hold on, but the effort winded them. The more Brazil began to shine, the more Italy began to crumble.

"They crushed us," was how Sandro Mazzola described it upon his

return to Rome two days later. When I ran into him, by chance, thirty-two years later in a hotel lobby in Milan, he still looked back fondly on his Mexican experience.

"The ending was the only bad thing about the whole trip," he said with a smile and in perfect Spanish. "The people of Mexico treated us very well, even after what happened in Toluca." He was referring, of course, to the match in which Italy eliminated Mexico from their own World Cup. Then, the great Mazzola asked me if I was Mexican myself and confessed his love for mariachi music and Mexican beer. Without waiting for me to answer, he finished off his thought with a *"¡Que viva México!"* and bid me farewell.

¡Mama mia! Let's get back to the game.

In the 66th minute, Gerson struck from far outside the box, beating the keeper Albertosi. Five minutes later, Pelé appeared once again, feeding Jairzinho, who fired home Brazil's third of the match—his seventh of the Cup.

By then the samba could safely begin.

The Brazilians were toying with the poor Italians as if the match were a scrimmage. Little touches, short passes, long balls, give-and-gos, centering and finishing . . . If you've seen the video, you know what I'm talking about. It was a display never before seen, and never since repeated in World Cup history.

And the final touch again came from Pelé.

In one of those plays that was destined for the history books, he gathered the ball at the edge of the penalty area and faked as if he were going to take on the defenders straightaway and shoot a goal. But suddenly, as if in slow motion, he laid down a no-look pass into the space on the right. From out of nowhere, Carlos Alberto swept in like a hurricane and unleashed an unstoppable shot that clipped the top of the grass on its way to Albertosi's far post.

TRIVIA
When did Brazil win the Jules Rimet Trophy for the third time?

What a goal!

The best Brazilian team of all time had won the World Cup for the third time—and the right to keep the Jules Rimet Trophy forever.

And that is how the Greatest World Championship in History came to an end.

EPILOGUE: WHERE IS THE CUP?

It was stolen—for the second time!

And this time it was never recovered. It had simply vanished.

TRIVIA

Where is the Jules Rimet Trophy that Brazil won in Mexico '70 located?

It happened in Rio de Janeiro in 1983, years after Brazil had brought it home with them from Mexico. The police never had any idea who took it from its case at the Confederación Brasileña de Deportes, nor what they did with it. It was a complete mystery.

Five years later, in December of 1988, a man was found shot dead in a neighborhood in Rio. His name was Antonio Carlos Aranha. The authorities concluded that he had been killed by fellow gang members for refusing to cough up their shares from the sale of the four and a half pounds of melted-down gold that had once been the Jules Rimet Trophy.

A tragic end to a happy story.

Today, the trophy on display at the CBD is a replica of the original.

West Germany 1974:
The World Cup of Cruyff . . . and Lato, Too

Two years after the Munich Olympics, West Germany was preparing for another international sports event. But this time it would be played under a level of security never before seen at a World Cup.

During the Munich games (1972), eleven Israeli athletes were murdered in the Olympic Village by Palestinian terrorists. In order to prevent another such disaster, the World Cup organizers took all necessary precautions.

As a result, this was a Cup of extreme security, with pervasive police presence, guard dogs, gate checks at the stadiums, and hotels that more closely resembled fortresses.

And to make matters worse, there had been threats against Chile's *La Roja*, when, as so often happens in soccer, the players ended up taking the rap for crimes committed by politicians. A few months before the World Cup, a coup had taken place in Santiago, and the Socialist president Salvador Allende had been overthrown and killed. Many people in Europe saw the Chilean selection as representing the new, right-wing government led by General Augusto Pinochet, who had also led the coup. The threats stemmed from there. The wall of security surrounding the Chilean team was supremely tight.

Fortunately, nothing untoward happened. The threats never came to anything, and the tenth FIFA World Cup of Soccer was celebrated peacefully.

But without much fanfare.

WM 74

11.6 - 7.7.1974

Hamburg   Düsseldorf   Frankfurt
West Berlin Gelsenkirchen Stuttgart
Hannover   Dortmund   München

FIFA World Cup 1974

THE NEW TROPHY

When Brazil took home the Jules Rimet Trophy for good, FIFA seemed almost regretful.

In 1971, they got together in Athens to create a new trophy, and while they were there they changed a few rules, as well. They decided that the trophy would no longer bear the name of any one person; rather, it would simply be known as the FIFA World Cup. Nothing more.

They also revised the "three times" rule, which had been on the books since 1930. From now on, every winner would take home a replica of the (new) original trophy.

The new Cup was designed by the Italian sculptor Silvio Gazzaniga, who fashioned it out of eighteen-karat gold. It stands fourteen inches tall and weighs in at slightly over eleven pounds.

I had the privilege of meeting Don Silvio in 2001, in his shop in Milan. There he spoke of the surprising honor of being selected to design and sculpt the new World Cup trophy—although, in reality, as he told us, FIFA hadn't chosen him directly; rather, they had selected the company for which he worked: Bertoni.

The company recommended him, and thus the job was his. And in his workshop he still keeps the original sketches he made, as well as a replica of the actual Cup itself. I (of course!) had to take a photo for posterity's sake.

This new trophy was presented to the soccer world by Pelé on opening day, at Frankfurt's Waldstadion, on June 13, 1974. That same day, the Englishman Stanley Rous retired from his post at FIFA's helm, and announced his successor—that great friend of Pelé, that tireless modernizer of Brazilian soccer, and the man who would soon convert the World Cup into the extraordinary commercial success that it is today. I'm speaking, of course, of João Havelange.

TRIVIA

In what year did nations begin competing for the new FIFA World Cup?

After the speeches came the opening match— between the defending champions, Brazil, and Yugoslavia. And just as happened in Mexico '70, this first game ended in a scoreless draw.

SAME BALL, NEW MASCOT

The contract with Adidas was still in place, and the match balls used in Germany were the same as those used in Mexico: the Telstar.

And the use of official mascots was still in place, as well.

Germany '74 was the third World Cup to feature the use of a mascot. But in this case there wasn't one but two—symbolic of the two Germanys, of course. They were represented by two children, "Tip" and "Tap," though I could never tell them apart.

TRIVIA

How many mascots were used in Germany '74?

A NEW FORMAT

The basic principle of sixteen teams divided into four groups remained intact. The change was that the teams advancing to the second round would be reformatted into two new groups of four teams each. The two winners of each of these latter groups would play for the new FIFA trophy, while the runners-up in each would square off for third place.

Matches were played in nine cities, and here is how the groups broke down:

> **Group A** (West Berlin and Hamburg): Chile, East Germany, West Germany, Australia
> **Group B** (Frankfurt, Gelsenkirchen, and Dortmund): Yugoslavia, Zaire, Brazil, Scotland
> **Group C** (Hanover and Düsseldorf): Holland, Uruguay, Sweden, Bulgaria
> **Group D** (Munich and Stuttgart): Poland, Haiti, Italy, Argentina

ZAIRE, HAITI, AND THE "OTHER" GERMANY

Nineteen seventy-four saw four separate countries appearing in their first-ever World Cup, including Australia (representing Oceania), Zaire (representing Africa), and Haiti (representing North and Central America and the Caribbean). Representing Europe was the host's Communist brother, East Germany, or rather the German Democratic Republic, world famous for its Berlin Wall and athletes on steroids. Could that be why this was the first World Cup to conduct drug testing? Hmm . . .

It was the first time that both Germanys found themselves in the same World Cup, not to mention being in the same group.

Australia bowed out without making any waves, without scoring even a single goal. They lost to both of the Germanys before managing a scoreless draw with Chile.

On the other hand, Zaire had a dramatic debut. First they lost 2–0 to Scotland, before getting steamrolled by Yugoslavia 9–0. In their final match, Brazil defeated them 3–0, giving them a goal differential of negative 14. They have never since returned to the World Cup; indeed, today the country doesn't even exist as such, having been renamed the Congo.

Haiti had better luck.

TRIVIA
What record did Haiti break in Germany '74?

In their first match, against Italy, their striker Emmanuel Sanón notched an early goal, thus ending the keeper Dino Zoff's record of eleven matches (1,142 minutes of play) without conceding a goal. But eventually the Italians woke up and won the match 3–1, and Haiti would also fall to Poland (7–0) and Argentina (4–1).

THE GREAT ABSENCES

As tends to happen in World Cups, some powerful team or other is unexpectedly absent. At Germany '74, there were several notable absences: England, Spain, Peru, and Mexico.

England was going through an extended soccer crisis. They had been eliminated by Poland in the qualifying stages. They also lost in the following event in Argentina. Their comeback, of sorts, wouldn't take place until Spain '82.

The Peru of Cubillas & Co. ended its qualifying series tied with Chile for the final South American slot, and faced a one-game play-off. Chile won that one, and the Peruvians would have to wait another four years to return to the World Cup.

WHAT'S THE DEAL WITH MEXICO?

That's just what Mexicans were asking themselves in 1973.

It all started on November 25th of that year, when their selection arrived in Haiti for the CONCACAF World Cup qualifying tournament. Besides those two, the other competing teams were Honduras, Guatemala, the Netherlands Antilles, and Trinidad.

When the Mexican team showed up in Puerto Principe, they weren't exactly welcomed with open arms. The Haitians were offended because, according to them, a Mexican newspaper had printed a number of racist and otherwise disparaging comments about their country. Word had it that Voodoo priests placed a curse on *los tricolores* so they wouldn't make it to the World Cup.

I don't lend much credence to such things, but it was one of the excuses offered up to rationalize what happened next.

Los tri first faced Guatemala, and came out with a draw, in the course of which Enrique Borja strained a muscle in his thigh and "Nacho" Calderón injured his hand. In their second match, they tied with Honduras, and their backup goalkeeper, Rafael Puente, came down with a fever and was unable to play. They started their third-string keeper, Héctor Brambila, against the Netherlands Antilles, and they won that match easily by an 8–0 margin.

There was still hope, but both Trinidad and Haiti soon put an end to that.

Javier de la Torre's team had been eliminated and returned home with their heads hung in shame.

It was the first great failure of the Mexican team in the qualifying stages. All of Mexico had been hoping to build on their good showings in Chile and England, but they were sadly disappointed instead.

NEW FACES

Besides Havelange as the new president of FIFA, Germany '74 featured a number of other new faces who would define the 1970s.

Among them was a Polish player with world-class skills. His name was Grzegorz Lato, a twenty-four-year-old bald-headed striker who ended up being the tournament's top goalscorer, with seven goals to his credit. He had been Poland's star in the 1972 Munich Olympics as well, leading his country to the gold medal there. And many years later, in 1982–83, he closed out his career in the ranks of my favorite Mexican club team, Atlante.

Nineteen seventy-two also saw the debuts of two exceptional goalkeepers who would go on to compete in several World Cups, even becoming champions. They were Brazil's Emerson Leão and Italy's Dino Zoff, who, as we've mentioned, came into the Cup riding an eleven-match streak of shutouts.

Italy also featured two other grand entrances: Gigi Riva and Giorgio Chinaglia. For Chile, it was two of their greatest players of all time: "El Chino" Carlos Caszely and a crack player who later made history as a player for Mexico's Club América and the coach of San Luis, before joining me in the Univision booth for the 2002 World Cup. I'm talking about my great friend Carlos Reinoso.

Argentina also introduced a number of future

TRIVIA

When did Poland's Lato make his World Cup debut?

stars, such as Ubaldo Fillol, Miguel Brindisi, René Houseman, Carlos Babington, and a twenty-year-old kid who would write a marvelous chapter in the history of Argentine soccer: *el matador de Córdoba*, Mario Kempes.

CRUYFF: HELLO AND GOOD-BYE

None of the aforementioned emerging players can compare with the biggest name from that World Cup: a slim twenty-seven-year-old Dutchman of incomparable class, one of the greatest players of all time, the marvelous Johan Cruyff.

He wore the number 14 across his back, and he was the best European player of the day. He'd won his first all-Holland championship, and later he won European Footballer of the Year on several occasions and three European Cups with his team, the famous Ajax Club of Amsterdam.

Ajax is the team that invented the style of play known as "total football," which combined attacking and defending all at the same time. Holland's "Clockwork Orange" arrived in Germany with their artful style at its highest level, thanks to their coach, Rinus Michel, and the caliber of players like Cruyff and Johan Neeskens.

As was the case with Hungary in 1954, this team was everyone's favorite pick to win it all. The Netherlands hadn't appeared in a World Cup since 1938, and as you'll see, Cruyff & Co. fell flat in the final match and the Dutch missed a wonderful opportunity, not unlike the Magical Magyars had twenty years before.

TRIVIA
What was the name of the coach of Holland's "Clockwork Orange"?

Sadly, it was Cruyff's first and only appearance on the World Cup stage.

ARGENTINA ON MY TELEVISION

If England '66 came to me via radio, Germany '74 was definitely a television experience.

It wasn't very big, and it was a black-and-white, of course, but it was good enough for me to watch my first World Cup, transmitted via satellite.

La albiceleste, led by their captain, Roberto Perfumo, began their campaign in Stuttgart against the Olympic champions, Poland. I'll never forget that game: it was the first time I actually saw my country play in a World Cup.

It was also my first "real" World Cup, meaning that it was live—not on video—and it didn't come to me accompanied by anecdotes and family references. There I was, with my fourteen-year-old passions, sitting in front of the TV with relatives and friends, all gathered together in our new Buenos Aires home on Nuñez Street, eating Argentine *picadas*.

That day, June 15th, got off to a bad start for me and my compatriots: Gregorz Lato came out ready to eat up the pitch. In the 6th minute of play he had already scored his first World Cup goal. Two minutes later, Poland's other star, Andrezej Szarmach, knocked their second past our goalkeeper, Daniel Carnevali.

Down two goals to nothing—and thanks in part to our shouts at the television set—Argentina came to life.

We got one back at the start of the second half, thanks to Ramón Heredia, but the inspiration was short-lived, as Lato notched his second goal of the afternoon a scant two minutes later. Poland 3, Argentina 1. We continued to press, and once again cut the deficit to one after a goal by Carlos Babington, but that was it. All their efforts (and ours!) were spent, and we lost 3–2.

We switched off the television. When my friends and I broke the match down and analyzed it surgically, we came to the conclusion that what had just transpired in Stuttgart was simply due to bad luck. We just knew that things would go better against Italy.

They did go better, but we still didn't win. We tied 1–1, and both of the goals were ours—one of them being an "own goal."

Houseman scored first, in the 18th minute, before Perfumo's own goal in the 34th. Italy didn't have to do much. In our house, it was more of the same: pregame nervousness followed by ninety minutes of yelling at the screen, and wrapping up with the postgame analysis and the shutting off of the TV.

Our final match of the first round was against Haiti. If we didn't win that one, we might as well slit our wrists!

Thankfully, that wasn't necessary.

Houseman opened the scoring once again, followed by Roberto Ayala's goal, as well as two by Héctor Yazalde. We ended up 4–1 winners, and we were through to the second round. The house on Nuñez erupted in celebration. Everyone was embracing, laughing, and shouting. We didn't switch off the TV that evening, as we wanted to hear all the postgame analysis and see replays of the goals. Out in the street, a few cars rolled past, drivers honking their horns and shouting for joy.

That night I dreamed I was in Germany.

CHILE, PINOCHET, AND RED FOR RED

Chile's arrival in Germany was an eventful one. First, on account of the anti-Pinochet protests; and, second, because their very qualification was controversial—also because of Pinochet.

In order to reach Germany, Chile had to play a home-and-away qualifying series against the Soviet Union. The match in Moscow ended in a scoreless draw; and the match in Santiago never occurred.

There were 40,000 spectators in the stands at the Estadio Nacional on that twenty-first of November, 1973. *La Roja* took the field, but the Soviets never appeared. They had simply refused to play in a stadium used by Pinochet as a detention center for leftist political prisoners after the September 11th coup that had overthrown Allende and his government.

Chile scored a symbolic goal at one end of the field, and with that they were on to the World Cup.

They opened their run on June 14th, the second day of the Cup, against the host team at Olympic Stadium in West Berlin, which would also be the site of the final match a few weeks later. The West Germans scored first, with a goal by Breitner in the 15th minute, and they maintained that 1–0 advantage through to the final whistle.

> **TRIVIA**
>
> Who was the first player to be ejected with a red card in a World Cup match?

Caszely was having a bad day, and he was sent off in the second half, thus moving into the record books as the first player to be shown the red card in a World Cup match.

A red card for the man in the red jersey!

Chile's second matchup was on that same field, against the "other host," East Germany. This time they tied, with one goal apiece. Chile's was scored by Sergio Ahumada. A win in their final match of the first round against Australia gave them enough points to advance, but they couldn't pull it off. A goalless tie sent them home with neither pain nor glory.

Chile would miss the following World Cup, returning once, for Spain '82, before enduring an extended hiatus that lasted all the way until France '98, where they had quite a solid showing. But that was their last appearance.

Better luck in 2010!

MAMÁ'S "LA CELESTE"

During that World Cup, I also watched Uruguay's matches on TV. Mamá, however, wasn't as enthusiastic as she had been for previous

Cups, despite the fact that this was her first opportunity to see her beloved *Celeste*, the Uruguayan team, live.

Why, you might ask?

"Those old men aren't going to beat anybody," she said.

The roster was essentially unchanged since Mexico '70, with Cubilla, Rocha, Espárrago, Montero Castillo, and Mazurkiewicz all at least thirty years old. The rest of the players were young, with bright futures, but they weren't of the same caliber as those who had come before them. That's why my mother didn't harbor much hope for success, and their draw certainly didn't help much either: Holland, Bulgaria, and Sweden.

Holland danced circles around them for ninety minutes and won a 2–0 victory. In their second match, they managed to eek out a 1–1 tie, but only by the grace of an 87th-minute goal by Pavoni. But their third match was the worst of all. Mamá didn't even want to watch. They faced Sweden in Düsseldorf, and were shut out 3–0.

What a shame!

It was the end of an era. Uruguay had lost its magic and would not return to a World Cup for twelve years—until Mexico '86.

THE NEW "SCRATCH"

The coach was the same as for Mexico '70—Mario Zagallo—and the team still featured the same two stars, Rivelino and Jairzinho. The rest of the team was new and perhaps not as "fabulous" as it had been in years past.

They started off poorly, and it didn't get any better from there. And they ended the first round with Zaire!

They tied their opening match against Yugoslavia 0–0, which was the same result they managed against Scotland. Struggling heavily, they achieved a 3–0 win over Zaire, but remember that Yugoslavia had thrashed them 9–0. Three teams from that group ended up tied with five points apiece, but Brazil and Yugoslavia advanced based on goal differential.

In the second round, Brazil shared Group A with their archrivals Argentina, as well as East Germany and the favorites, Holland. If they continued to play the way they had been playing they would have no chance of reaching the final.

But Brazil is always Brazil, and suddenly they began to score goals.

They defeated the East Germans in Hanover on a stunning goal by Rivelino. Then, in the same stadium, they downed Argentina 2–1 with goals by Rivelino (again) and Jairzinho. I was watching from

TRIVIA
Who eliminated Brazil in Germany '74?

Buenos Aires, wadding up balls of paper and throwing them at the screen, under the scolding view of my mother.

Finally, the Brazilians faced Holland, needing only a tie to reach the final. But what do you think happened? Cruyff played some inspired soccer. He single-handedly carried the Dutch to victory. He set up Neeskens for their first goal, and notched one of his own at the start of the second half on an unforgettable volley.

Holland was through to the final, and Brazil was left to play a third-place match against Poland, the other great attraction of the tournament. They met the Poles on July 6th and lost 1–0, after giving up a goal to the tournament's top scorer, Grzegorz Lato. Blame for the failure fell to the coach, "Lobo" Zagallo. Fanatical fans marched a funeral cortege past his house in Rio, with his effigy in the coffin. Poor Mario had no other choice but to resign.

TRIVIA
Who was Brazil's coach in Germany '74?

THE SECOND ROUND

The two second-round groups were named, creatively enough, "A" and "B." The winners of each would face each other in the final, while the two runners-up would meet in the third-place match. Here's the breakdown:

> **Group A** (Hanover, Gelsenkirchen, and Dortmund) was another "Group of Death," with: Argentina, East Germany, Brazil, and Holland
>
> **Group B** (Düsseldorf, Frankfurt, and Stuttgart) appeared somewhat less intense, with: Sweden, West Germany, Poland, and Yugoslavia

Argentina started off against none other than the powerful Dutch side, on a rain-laced June 26th in Gelsenkirchen. It was a match for the ages. Cruyff—who, amazingly enough, had yet to score a single World Cup goal—came into his own with not one but two strikes that day!

TRIVIA
Against which team did Cruyff score his first World Cup goal?

His teammates scored two more of their own, while shutting Argentina out. The match ended with the score 4–0, but this time we didn't simply shut off the TV like we had before; no, we wanted to see the replays of Cruyff's goals. To learn.

Then we faced Brazil.

Like I said, it wasn't the Brazil of Cups past, but they were still dangerous. The match in Hanover was highly animated and evenly played . . . perhaps because it was the first time the two neighbors and rivals had ever faced each other in a World Cup.

I shouted as if I were in the stadium myself.

The first half ended with the score deadlocked at one apiece, with the goals coming from Rivelino on a cannon-like shot from outside the area, and from Brindiso on a beautiful free kick. At the start of the second, Jairzinho found some space and scored the second for Brazil. We pushed back insistently, champing at the bit and dominating play, but the goal never materialized. We lost 2–1, and all of us there in the house were left brokenhearted. We deserved at least a tie.

TRIVIA
Which World Cup saw Brazil and Argentina face each other for the first time?

PERÓN AND GOODBYE

Argentina's final match was against the "other" Germans. If Argentina won, and if Brazil defeated Holland, we had a chance to play in the third-place match. Incredible!

But the stars and the planets were not properly aligned that July 3rd.

We at home couldn't even watch on TV. The death of President Juan Domingo Perón two days before had left the entire nation in mourning. Some of the players, expressing regret at the passing of their leader, did not want to play. But they did play, and they tied the East Germans 1–1, bringing their World Cup run to an end, just as it had ended for my old lady's Uruguay.

For everyone in my neighborhood, the World Cup was over, and life gradually returned to normal, despite the national state of mourning. School had been canceled, so we took advantage of the opportunity to play soccer in the streets. We didn't watch any more games on TV—at least until the day of the final. We watched that one, not because we cared about who would win, but to savor the duel between Cruyff and Beckenbauer.

PERFUMO SPEAKS

When I spoke with the captain of the 1974 Argentine team, "El Mariscal" (The Marshal) Roberto Perfumo, I found out the real reason why some of his teammates didn't want to play their final match against the East Germans. It wasn't because of any particular sense of respect for Perón, but rather because they simply wanted to go home.

"We were disgusted," the great Perfumo told me in Buenos Aires when I interviewed him for this book. "After what happened against Brazil and Holland, it just didn't make any sense to keep on playing. The team was a complete disaster. We were somewhere between unprepared and poorly prepared. We had replaced our coach at the last minute. We played just to see what would happen, to finish it. That's all. We all knew that we weren't going any further," he affirmed with a certain twinge of pain in his voice. Then he added one parting thought: "That's not why you play in the World Cup. And that's why what happened to us happened."

The interview took place in a sports bar in Recoleta. We spoke about other World Cups, about River, and also about television, since he is now working as a commentator on his own show for ESPN Deportes.

He also spoke about being the first player to be "repatriated" for that World Cup: in other words, he was recalled from his usual position of playing for Brazil's Cruzeiro.

When I asked him about the 1–1 draw with Italy—when he scored an own goal after they had taken a 1–0 lead on a goal by Houseman— Perfumo laughed and said, "I looked up at the scoreboard, and it said, 'Goals: Houseman and Perfumo,' as if we were winning 2–0! I wanted to die!"

Germany '74 was his World Cup farewell. And he could take with him a number of extraordinary memories and performances. "England '66 was my best World Cup," he recalled with pride. "It was my first, and—despite being so young and playing a tough position—things turned out pretty well for me. I got attention from a lot of people, and the press wrote some very complimentary things."

TRIVIA
After which World Cup did Roberto Perfumo retire from the national team?

Then they were eliminated during the qualifying series for Mexico '70, followed by the frustration of Germany '74. But he left through the front door. After that World Cup, he returned to the ranks of River, and led them to their first championship in eighteen years!

LATO'S THIRD PLACE MATCH

As I mentioned, the Brazilians lost 2–0 to Cruyff and Holland, finishing second in their group. As such, they would be playing in the third-place match against Lato and Poland, which would have been in the final themselves if it weren't for Gerd Müller.

Müller scored the only goal of their semifinal match, which put West Germany in the final. Plus, it was his thirteenth career World Cup goal, equaling the total of Just Fontaine...though the Frenchman scored all of his in one single World Cup!

Lato played that same role against the Brazilians. His lone goal gave Poland a 1–0 victory, and sole possession of third place in the world. It was Poland's best performance in their history.

They would equal the feat four years later, in Spain '82.

THE GRAND FINALE IN MUNICH

On July 7, 1974, the Olympic Stadium in Munich was filled with 75,000 people. West Germany was playing in their second World Cup final; for Holland it was their first.

It was, in a way, a repeat of the 1954 final in Bern. Once again it was the Germans facing the pretournament favorites—in this case, the Dutch—with the added benefit of the two brightest stars of the day appearing on the same stage: Cruyff and Beckenbauer.

It was also a matchup of the two best coaches of the day: Rinus Michel of Holland against Helmut Schoen, who had directed West Germany in three consecutive World Cup appearances.

Cruyff began to shine right from the start. Fifty-five seconds into the match—after no fewer than eighteen consecutive passes between Dutch players without a single German touch—Cruyff flew into the opposing penalty area and was brought down by Verti Vogts (the same Verti Vogts who would years later go on to become Germany's coach). Johan Neeskens converted the penalty, and Holland was on top 1–0.

It was the first penalty kick in a World Cup final.

But the Germans were not shaken. They took control of the action, and in the 25th minute another penalty was awarded . . . this time in their favor. Paul Breitner took it and tied the match.

The Germans continued to press and attack, and just before the first half came to a close, Müller appeared with a powerful and sweeping 180-degree shot that put West Germany ahead 2–1.

The goal proved to be historic. It was the fourteenth and final goal ever scored by "The Bomber" in World Cup competition, and it also broke the record of most goals ever scored by a single player, eclipsing the previous mark—thirteen—set by Just Fontaine.

TRIVIA

When was the first penalty kick in a World Cup final awarded?

It also turned out to be the goal that sealed the victory for the Germans, who—with a great deal of discipline and a champion's luck—managed to beat back the avalanche of orange that came at them in the second half. They were attacked from all sides. On two occasions, their great goalkeeper Sepp Maier made majestic saves off his line, and three other times Dutch rifle shots ricocheted off the posts.

The match ended 2–1, in favor of the hosts, and the history of Bern from 1954 had indeed repeated itself. Germany was crowned world champions, overthrowing the pretournament favorites. They would reach the final match again in 1982, '86, '90, and 2002, proving time and again that they deserve their status as titans of world soccer. What will happen in 2006?

Place your bets!

Argentina 1978: Mario Kempes's World Cup

Finally!

It was forty years in coming, but at long last it arrived. After much begging and pleading, FIFA granted Argentina the right to host a World Cup.

The entire nation dedicated itself to the necessary preparations, with the full support of the dictator General Jorge Rafael Videla, who took the same sort of approach Mussolini had in Italy '34: make the event into a propaganda machine for his regime.

The slogan was "Twenty-five Million Argentines Playing in the World Cup," and it was set to a jingle that still runs through our heads every once in a while. And they invested what seemed like all the money in the world—over $700 million—to renovate stadiums, airports, highways, trains, and hotels.

The European teams, however, were still concerned with security for the event, since the Montoneros—leftist guerrillas who were waging combat with the *milicos*—had been threatening to sabotage the event.

FIFA echoed those concerns, but Videla and his partisans guaranteed that nothing would happen.

And they kept their word: the regime cracked down with an iron fist, and to this day nobody is sure just how many people disappeared during that month of June, 1978. But the eleventh FIFA World Cup—which would bring what I call the World Cup's Modern Era to an end—went off without incident.

Argentina '78

SIXTEEN FOR THE LAST TIME

Another reason I call this the last of the Modern World Cups is on account of the growing pressure to increase the number of participating nations. But FIFA wouldn't do it just yet. Once again there were sixteen finalists, and they used the same format as they had four years earlier in Germany: four groups of four teams each, with the top two teams advancing out of each and forming two new groups of four. The winners of these secondary groups would again meet for the title of World Champions, this time in Buenos Aires.

The draw was held at the Teatro San Martín in Buenos Aires, and here is how the groups emerged:

> **Group A** (Buenos Aires and Mar de Plata): Argentina, Hungary, Italy, and France—the "Group of Death"
>
> **Group B** (Rosario and Córdoba): West Germany, Poland, Tunisia, Mexico
>
> **Group C** (Buenos Aires and Mar de Plata): Austria, Spain, Sweden, Brazil
>
> **Group D** (Mendoza and Córdoba): Peru, Scotland, Holland, Iran

As you can see, Spain, Hungary, France, and Peru had returned to the World Cup stage. The notable absentees were Uruguay, England, and Czechoslovakia.

WHO ARE THE NEWCOMERS?

The only selections with no World Cup experience were the Iranians (representing Asia) and the Tunisians (representing Africa).

Iran tied with Scotland, but lost to Holland and Peru. Tunisia had a better showing. They opened against *los tri*, and came through big with a 3–1 victory, which also doubled as the start of Mexico's debacle. After that match, Tunisia lost to Poland and ended the first round with a tie against West Germany.

The new faces appearing at this World Cup included a generation of very interesting players, but one needs only to mention five names: Zico, Platini, Rossi, Passarela, and Hugo Sánchez. Not all of them met with much success here, but they did make their marks and show signs of what they would offer up in future World Cups.

TRIVIA

Which World Cup saw the debuts of Zico and Platini?

The most outstanding of the bunch was Daniel Passarela, the captain and central defender of both Argentina and River.

And right up there with him was France's Michel Platini. He was only twenty years old, and yet he was playing with considerable skill. He had scored a goal against Argentina, and set up many of his teammates, but in the end it wasn't enough. France would fall in the first round.

The Brazilian Zico played three matches and scored one goal, a penalty shot against Peru. He also gave a little preview of the class he would display—and which Brazil would fail to capitalize on—four years later, in Spain.

The Italian Paolo Rossi also showed what he was capable of, and he went on to shine brilliantly in 1982. He celebrated his World Cup debut with a goal against France, and he followed that up with a second strike against Hungary in the second match. Italy went through to the second round, and Rossi scored the lone goal in a 1–0 victory over Austria. In the end, Italy finished fourth.

TRIVIA

Which was Paolo Rossi's first World Cup?

Mexico's *"niño de oro,"* Hugo Sánchez, didn't have the same sort of luck. He wasn't yet "Hugol." In fact, he never really shined on the World Cup stage. People everywhere would have to wait three more years for his arrival in Spain—as a striker, first for Atlético and then with Real Madrid—before being able to fully appreciate his class and his nose for the goal. In Argentina '78, everyone—including himself—was bursting with desire. But he was shut out, and *los tri* managed to score only two goals . . . while giving up twelve! Ouch!

With Teófilo "El Nene" Cubillas and my very good friend Tom Mulroy.

SPEAKING OF MEXICO . . .

There was no explanation. And there still isn't.

Mexico had returned to the World Cup after an eight-year absence that began after their appearance as hosts for the unforgettable 1970 tournament. You'll recall that they were eliminated by Haiti en route to Germany '74, but this time they qualified from the CONCACAF region with relative ease, playing on their home turf.

Their coach was José Antonio Roca, and, with a new roster full of young faces, they seemed in store for a good run in Argentina.

Among those selected to play were: Pilar Reyes, the goalkeeper for Monterrey's Tigres; Guillermo "El Wendy" Mendizábal from Cruz Azul; Victor Rangel from Toluca; the man with the most famous Afro in all of Mexico, Leonardo Cuellar of UNAM; and the two stars from national champions América: Toño de la Torre and the great "Capitán Furia," Alfredo Tena, who today is a coach himself.

TRIVIA

In which World Cup did Hugo Sánchez make his debut?

Of course, they also called up the country's newest soccer sensation, Hugo Sánchez, who was barely twenty years old.

They won all of their matches leading up to the World Cup, scoring twenty goals while conceding only five. That same year, the U-20 (i.e., under-twenty) team had an extraordinary run at FIFA's World Youth Cup in Tunisia. They reached the final before finally bowing out on penalties to the Soviet Union. But even with that loss, they had left an indelible imprint on the collective Mexican consciousness.

A new generation of players was emerging, and it foretold good things down the road for the national team.

Which perhaps is the reason why coach Roca decided to base his final roster on younger talent, sacrificing the veteran leadership that had gotten *los tri* through qualifying. Their average age was a mere twenty-two years, making Cuellar one of the "older" players at twenty-six.

Many considered it to be the best Mexican team of all time.

But so much youth coupled with so much optimism proved fatal for Roca and *los tri*. Their first

With Hugo Sánchez.

test was against the African qualifiers, Tunisia, on June 2nd, in the city of Rosario. As I mentioned above, the Tunisians ate them alive, even though Mexico started out winning 1–0 on a penalty by Arturo Vázquez Ayala of Pumas.

Their second match was in Córdoba, and it was against the defending world champions, West Germany—a trial by fire for the young selection if ever there was one. They gave up the first goal in the 14th minute, and then others followed in the 29th and the 37th. West Germany knocked home three more in the second half, handing Mexico their worst defeat in history, a 6–0 shutout! The last comparable Mexican defeat was a 6–3 loss to Argentina all the way back in the 1930 World Cup.

Apparently the Río de la Plata air was not to the liking of *los tri*.

Their final match was against a Poland team that still counted Lato among its players. A win would have taken away a bit of the sting—and oh, did they try! But it was not to be. They almost reached halftime with the scoreboard empty, but Poland scored in the 43rd minute. Mexico responded after the break, with Rangel tying the game in the 52nd minute.

But it was all downhill from there.

Poland found the back of the net twice more, and the match ended 3–1 in their favor. Mexico's final stat-sheet included a ratio of two goals for and twelve against—and one unfulfilled dream. They bowed out of the World Cup in last place.

"Ay mamacita linda, cómo duele!" was the collective cry of pain echoing throughout the house.

But the pain didn't end there. En route to Spain '82, Mexico would hit rock bottom.

EL FLACO'S PLAN

After Germany '74, in a moment of clarity, the Asociación Argentina de Fútbol (AFA), decided to get a conscientious head start on their own World Cup, four years down the road.

The first thing to do was name a new coach, someone who would take a firm hold of the reins and come up with a cohesive plan of hard work for the future, something that the Argentine selection never had before.

The responsibility fell to one César Luis Menotti, a tall, skinny (hence "El Flaco"), cigarette-smoking thirty-six-year-old with long hair and an artist's manner from Rosario. They called him "the soccer philosopher." He had previously been the coach of his hometown club,

Newell's, and in 1973 he led modest Huracán to the championship, along with the help of its three stars, Houseman, Babington, and Brindisi.

TRIVIA
Who was
Argentina's coach
in 1978?

As a player, Menotti was elegant if a bit ineffective. He played alongside Pelé during a brief stint with Santos of Brazil, and then with Juventus of Italy. His great skill was in his ability to study and analyze the game itself.

"El Flaco" dedicated himself to a methodical work ethic, one without improvisation. He called his approach one of "criteria and struggle." In four years, he put together a solid, homogeneous squad without any big-name individuals, one that—according to him—would find a balance "between putting on a show and fighting for a common goal." In this case, the goal was to win the World Cup.

Thanks to this new approach to work and strategy, Argentine soccer can be divided into two distinct periods: the time before Menotti, and the time after him. For the first time in Argentine soccer history, the interests of the national team took precedence over the interests of the clubs. As a result, in 1975, the two great capital-city teams—River and Boca—were reluctant to release players to the selection. So Menotti filled his ranks with young players from other clubs around the country, with a few veterans of the previous World Cup thrown in. They were: "El Pato" Ubaldo Fillol; Mario Kempes; Alberto Tarantini and his pupil at Huracán, René Houseman.

Among the newcomers were: Luis Galván; Osvaldo Ardíles; Américo Gallego; Leopoldo Luque; as well as the captain, Passarela. Under pressure from both the public and the press (let alone Almirante Lacoste, president of the World Cup Organizing Committee), Menotti was forced to call up the star player from River, Beto Alonso, but although he was on the roster, "El Flaco" never started him.

"DIEGO, YOU'VE GOT TO WAIT"

If it had been up to him, Diego Armando Maradona would have joined that list of players and made his World Cup debut there, in 1978, at the tender age of seventeen . . . the same age as Pelé when he arrived in Sweden.

In his autobiography, *Yo Soy El Diego* (I Am El Diego), Maradona confesses that—despite his friendship and respect for Menotti—he is still bitter about not being included on the roster for Argentina '78.

"I haven't forgiven Menotti for that, nor do I plan to," Diego writes. "I believe that I could have played. I was as ready as ever."

"El Flaco" cut him from the final twenty-two-man roster a month before the event, because, said Menotti, "he was very young." For Don Diego it was a bitter blow that changed his life.

"That day, which was the saddest day of my career, I swore that I would get back. It was the greatest disappointment of my life, one which forever marked me, defined me," he confesses. "I was determined to play in many World Cups."

Diego would have to wait four years to make his national team debut, and four more after that to conquer the world. Though, in 1979, some of the sting was removed with being crowned World Youth Champions in Japan.

THE RETURN OF NENE

After eight years of absence, Peru returned to the World Cup stage, again led by their superstar Teófilo "Nene" Cubillas, who had gained a considerable amount of experience during stints with the Swiss club Basel and the Portuguese club Oporto.

Other veterans were Héctor Chumpitaz and Hugo Sotíl, who had been there for Mexico '70, but the majority of the roster was made up of new faces, such as Juan Oblitas and Guillermo La Rosa.

Nene displayed his class once again. In their first match, against Scotland in Córdoba, he scored twice, including a sensational strike from outside the area—one of the most beautiful highlights of that or any Cup. Peru won 3–1.

In their second match, this time in Mendoza, they fought to a 0–0 tie with none other than the Dutch, though sans Cruyff. In the final encounter of the first round, they faced Iran, and Cubillas must have laced up his scoring shoes, because he had himself a hat trick. That gave him five goals in the first round alone, which—coupled with the five he tallied in Mexico '70—put him among the top five goalscorers in World Cup history.

They were on to the second round, but things there would change drastically.

MY FOURTH WORLD CUP

The confidence of a team with four solid years of preparation and the resulting enthusiasm of an entire nation were hit with a bucket of icy water on the second day of play, June 2, 1978.

Argentina opened against Hungary, which had returned to the tournament after Sweden '58. Every Argentine was consumed by expectation. Nobody went to work, nobody went to school.

Including me.

I was seventeen years old, and I'd just started college. The only thing that mattered to me in those days was the World Cup, starting with that first match against the Hungarians. Those who had either dough (*guita*, as they say) or connections got tickets to the game at the Estadio Monumental. Us poor folks had to make do by clustering in front of our little TV screens, or the big screens that broadcast the match via closed-circuit channels.

My wonderful mother surprised me with what they call an *abono*—a package of prepaid tickets—to watch every match via closed-circuit big-screen TV in Luna Park, the famous Buenos Aires scene of boxing matches and other grand events. I don't know how much she paid for them, but I know she must have really dug deep into her purse. She had recently divorced my father, and money was short, and I knew she was working overtime for my sake.

And there was only enough for one of us to go. She stayed home to watch the action on our little TV set—a sacrifice, to be sure, but then she didn't have the same vested interest as I did, since her beloved Uruguay hadn't qualified for that World Cup.

I was able to see and experience a World Cup; rather, I was able to see and experience my fourth World Cup . . . but this time it was on the big screen, and in living color.

CRUYFF'S PROTEST

More than a protest, it was a rebuke, a pointed denunciation of Argentina's military regime.

The news surprised not only Holland, but all of Europe. In Argentina, however, it wasn't widely reported. In fact, I'd go so far as to say that many of us didn't even know until we saw the Dutch arrive without their all-world star, Johan Cruyff.

That's how we finally found out—months before the event itself—that the great number 14, the leader of the "Clockwork Orange," had withdrawn from the national team in protest of General Videla's human-rights violations. In Argentina, the press censorship did not allow us to hear about the Dutch protest (to say nothing of what was happening), though we were well aware of the violations and the disappearances.

TRIVIA

Why did Johan Cruyff not play in Argentina '78?

Sad to say, Cruyff's was the only such voice, and the national state of euphoria at finally hosting a World Cup drowned out the truth, the denunciations, the protests, the international criticisms, and the outrage of the lone player who took that principled stance.

What a shame there were no others!

THE HOME OPENER

Finally, June 2 was upon us. Argentina looked good out of the gate, but it was Hungary that struck first, in the 10th minute, putting away a rebound off the keeper Fillol. A frigid silence fell over both the Estadio Monumental and Luna Park, where my friends and I were decked out in *albiceleste* jerseys.

"Son of a—!" was the only thing that you could hear across the darkened pitch.

Our hearts were lifted five minutes later, however, when an Argentine free kick ricocheted off the Hungarian goalkeeper, and the mustachioed Luque took advantage to score the tie goal.

From that point on, the action was fairly even, despite the fact that we missed out on scoring some goals. Hungary played their own very European style. They defended well, and launched the occasional, yet dangerous, counterattack.

Just when it seemed as if the match was headed for a tie, Luna Park lit up with joy at a goal by Daniel Bertoni in the 83rd minute.

Next up was France, four days later, on the same stage. Argentina took the lead on a penalty converted by Passarela just before the half—his first World Cup goal. Platini, who had himself quite a game, also notched his first World Cup goal that day, tying things up in the 61st minute. Two minutes later, he very nearly had his second, but the ball passed inches beyond the post.

TRIVIA

When was Michel Platini's first World Cup goal?

The French were playing inspired ball and had us pinned deep in our side of the field. But an Argentine counterattack was all it took to regain the lead, with Luque scoring his second goal of the tournament on a lovely gem of a shot from outside the area, one of the best goals of the Cup. We went on to a 2–1 victory, assuring ourselves of a spot in the second round. We did lose our final match, to Italy, by the score of 1–0, which relegated us to second place in the group, but we were on to Rosario.

Amid singing and exuberant celebrations, we all filed out of Luna Park and made our way to the Obelisco on the 9 de Julio avenue to celebrate in the frigid night with all of Buenos Aires.

RIVELINO BIDS FAREWELL

This was the third and final World Cup for the unforgettable Brazilian Roberto Rivelino. He didn't play much, nor did he score. In fact, he only cracked the starting lineup in the opener against Sweden. He came on as a second-half substitute against Poland in the second round, and in the third-place match against Italy. The latter appearance would be his farewell: June 24, 1978, is the exact date, there in Buenos Aires to both the Brazilian national team and to the World Cup. (Trivia alert!)

TRIVIA

What was Rivelino's final World Cup?

He left a legacy of splendid, often impossible left-footed goals that came off of free kicks and booming strikes from well outside the box. In Brazil, he continues to be revered as one of their ten greatest players of all time.

BRAZIL IN TRANSITION

Like the '74 Brazilian squad, the '78 team was a shadow of the glories that had been 1958 and 1970. They were still in a transitional phase, and the heirs to Didi, Pelé, Garrincha, Jairzinho, and Rivelino had yet to emerge.

Now the stars were Dirceu, the *seleção*'s top scorer with only three tallies, and a young Zico, who had yet to show the best of his abilities.

In the first round, they tied Sweden 1–1 and Spain 0–0 before coming away with a lucky 1–0 win over Austria. But in the second round they picked up speed. They defeated Peru 3–0, fought to a scoreless draw with Argentina, and downed Poland 3–1. And in the third-place match, they beat the mighty Italians 2–1.

In all, Brazil had knocked in ten goals in seven matches, which was a significant drop-off from previous performances.

Things would truly improve in Spain '82, when Zico came into his own, and Sócrates and Falcão burst onto the scene as well.

GOT TICKETS?

I got tickets to the second round! Amazing!

For the first time in my life, I was going to see a live World Cup match! And not one, but two! The only drawback was that neither ticket was to see Argentina—my luck did not run *that* far. For finishing second in their group, the Argentine team would be playing away from Buenos Aires, which is where my tickets were for. My good friend

Augusto Kartún had given them to me because he wouldn't be using them, as he and his family were going to Rosario to watch Argentina.

For this second round, two highly competitive groups of four teams were established:

Group A (Buenos Aires and Córdoba): West Germany, Italy, Holland, Austria

Group B (Mendoza and Rosario): Argentina, Poland, Brazil, Peru

My tickets were for Wednesday, June 14th, at the Monumental de River. The match was between Italy and West Germany. It was an unforgettable game, not only because I was alone in the cold and because it was my first, but also because nothing happened. Although on paper it promised to be one for the ages, in reality the match was a scoreless draw.

But I was happy. I saw two of my favorite goalkeepers—two of the best of in the world—Zoff and Maier. I was also able to see the new stars Paolo Rossi and Karl-Heinz Rummenigge. The second match was better: Holland versus Italy, a classic that took place the following Wednesday.

It was something else. I was lucky enough to see the veterans from the 1974 Netherlands team: Neeskens, Rep, Krol, Haan, and Rensenbrink. The game was highly entertaining and often quite emotional. One of the best of the entire Cup.

Italy took the lead early, on an own goal by the Dutch defender Brands, but he redeemed himself majestically with a second-half cracker of a goal from outside the area.

Italy employed their famous *"catenaccio"* defense in an attempt to slow down the "Clockwork Orange" attack, but the results were ineffectual. In the 77th minute, Arie Haan made history with the best goal of the entire year, a booming strike from over forty yards out that angled in past Dino Zoff. Holland went on to win 2–1, leaving them in first place with a ticket for the final match.

Obviously, *I* didn't have tickets to that one. Let alone money to buy them. So I returned to my trusty Luna Park to watch the match on the big screen.

A SCARE, KEMPES, AND A MIRACLE

Meanwhile, back in Rosario, things turned out well for Menotti and his boys, though not without a scare.

First you have to understand that, in the first round, Mario Kempes was shooting blanks. Not a single goal. But in the second round, "El Matador" was out of control. In fact, he ended up as the tournament's top scorer, with six goals in only five matches.

His coming-out party was against Poland, on the fourteenth of June. He scored twice in the victory, and all of Argentina was thrilled to see him running free and firing, shooting with accuracy.

Then came Brazil, but not much activity. Just an empty scoreboard for both teams.

The scare took place in their third match, on June 21, against Cubillas's Peruvian squad. On that same day, just a few hours before the match, Brazil had beat Poland 3–1, meaning that Argentina would have to defeat Peru by *four goals* if they wanted to creep ahead of Brazil on goal differential and advance to the final match.

Panic gripped the entire nation.

Conjectures and fears abounded. I was caught up in the discussion on the bus heading to Luna Park. "It's tough." "Almost impossible." "We'll have to see." "Maybe we can." "Maybe not." "Peru's tough." "But watch out. God is with us. I know it."

To make a long story short, the stars and planets were in alignment that day, and Argentina pulled a miracle out of their collective sleeve. They even scored two goals to spare! A 6–0 victory left shouts of joy echoing from Quiaca down to Tierra del Fuego.

Of course, that win can only be described as incredible. Many people couldn't believe their eyes. And because Peru's keeper, Ramón "Chupete" Quiroga, was a naturalized Peruvian who had been born in Argentina, rumors of a payoff were flying every which way.

Had a bribe been offered? Accepted?

Nothing was ever proven, and when you see footage of the game you feel the legitimacy of the Argentine goals. The *albiceleste* just ate up the field that day. And Kempes proved to be the one with the biggest appetite. Two of the six goals were his. Luque also added two of his own, and Tarantini and Houseman had one apiece.

Whether or not there was any truth to the rumor of Quiroga's collusion, Argentina was in the final match, their second such appearance in World Cup history.

(Peru, for their part, had an excellent first round, but for some inexplicable reason, they seemed to fall apart in the second. They lost all three of their matches without so much as a single goal to their credit.)

THE GRAND FINALE IN THE MONUMENTAL

I t was also the second final match for the Dutch, although they had only had to wait four years since their last one. Once again, they were facing the hosts on their own turf.

Argentina's first appearance in the Grand Final was forty-eight years earlier in the Centenario in Montevideo, when they were downed 2–1 by Uruguay. And once again they were facing the best team in the tournament.

It was a special Sunday, June 25th, in the cold Río Plata winter. But the Estadio Monumental in the Nuñez neighborhood of Buenos Aires was boiling over with Carnival's atmosphere. Reams of tickertape and paper streamers floated through the air and fell to the ground like so much snow. Over 77,000 delirious voices were chanting in unison.

Emulating Mussolini during his own final, Videla and the rest of the Junta Militar were also seated in their luxury boxes, taking advantage of the visibility and bursting with pride in their team, though perhaps not quite as much as "Il Duce" had.

A few blocks from there, in the stands at Luna Park, the big screen seemed even bigger than usual that day. The Argentine jersey, bluer than ever. The manes of our players, longer than usual. My gang and I could not believe our luck: we were about to see our country play in a World Cup final.

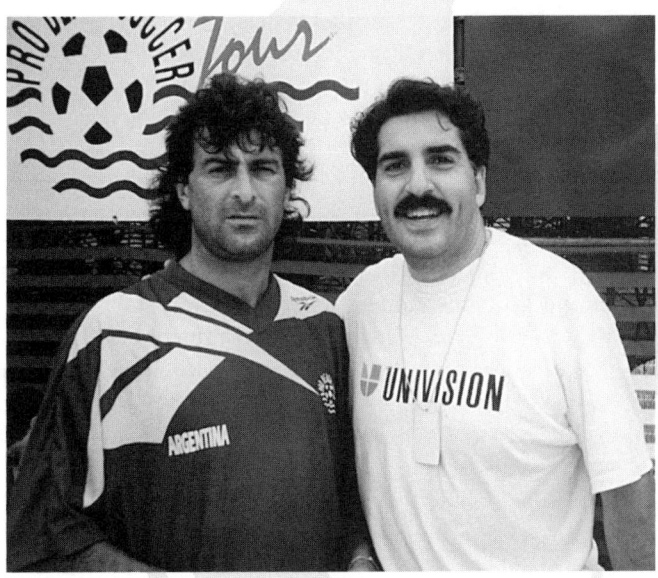

With Mario Kempes.

We felt as if we were right there on the field with them.

The start of the game was delayed because the Argentines were protesting a cast on the right hand of the Dutch player Rene van der Kerkhof. It took ten minutes to solve the problem. Finally the match could begin. An eruption of joy. More tickertape. It was hard to gauge the action for the first few minutes. Then, bit by bit, Holland began to settle into their rhythm, and soon a powerful header by Neeskens just grazed past the post. Then came a booming strike by Nicholas Rep, which Fillol saved marvelously. Shaken, the crowd there at Luna Park looked at one another wordlessly.

This seemed to serve as a wake-up call for our boys. They began to elevate their game, and take proper hold of the reins. The Dutch, perhaps a bit deafened by the thundering crowd, began to lose control and play hard.

In the 30th minute Argentina looks inspired. Kempes is alert, and elusive. In the 37th minute he receives a pass from Luque and dribbles between a number of Dutch legs toward the goal. He shoots. He scores.

¡GOOOL! shouted everyone in Luna Park. It might well have been heard all the way back in Amsterdam. Everyone leapt from their seats, wild with applause, embraces, tears. The replay of the goal only heightened the excitement.

On the field, the team fell back and began to work the clock. The Dutch players reacted, but dully so. They looked at one another, confused. They played lethargically. And that's how they went into the half: with the giant electronic scoreboard reading "Argentina 1, Holanda 0" and shining under the afternoon sun.

But the second half would be another story altogether.

More coordinated, rested, and clearly anxious, the Dutch players came out looking hard for the tie. The avalanche of orange was not about to sit back and wait. They showed why they had made it to the final, and why they were one of the world's best teams. The dribbled, they passed, they rotated, they blocked, they pressed, they ran up and down, they probed and penetrated the Argentine defense from all angles.

But Fillol was playing inspired soccer in front of his own goal. Neither he nor any of his defenders ever lost their cool. They maintained their order and discipline, content to play the counterattacking game.

With ten minutes left in the match—and, naturally, with every Argentine fan feeling that the World Cup was theirs—the dam could hold no more, and the wave of orange poured through.

Goal to Holland.

Dirk Nanninga had come on as a substitute for Rep, who was exhausted from his effort, and with one touch of the head, he tied the match with nine minutes left to play.

I don't know if I was scared.

All I remember is an icy feeling that penetrated all of us there in front of the big screen, already on our feet with worried looks in our eyes. Praying.

Fortunately for us, the stars in the night sky were not aligned with Holland. Their attacks continued, and with only one minute to go—and everyone was getting ready for overtime—Robert "Bobbie" Rensenbrink hit the post hard, which took the wind right out of our sails. I shut my eyes and turned away. I just couldn't watch anymore. I went through all the saints from my childhood, begging them for mercy and compassion.

I never found out whether they heard me, or if maybe Saint Menotti was just given some divine instructions. But the fact is that Kempes, Luque, Bertoni, Gallego, Tarantini, Ardíles, and Passarela came out on fire in the overtime period, determined to take the match back. We began to play our great, orderly offensive game. The Dutch players seemed to be tiring, seemed to be letting their guard down a bit. We, however, were in peak physical form. As the end of the first overtime period wound down, "El Matador" Kempes rose up again with another strike.

Goal.

GOAL!

¡GOOOL! we all cried at the tops of our lungs and from the bottoms of our hearts. It was a cry laced with tears of elation and topped with delirium.

We jumped for joy, bouncing off one another, embracing and kissing and dancing right there in the stands. The big Luna Park screen exploded with fireworks, and the whole place shook. It was a veritable Argentine earthquake, and the seismic waves were felt as far away as Holland, all the way across the globe.

And there was more.

My saints and all the soccer gods must have been feeling generous that day. Their invisible rays descended from Mount Olympus to light up the long-haired Argentine players and impel them toward yet another goal. With just a minute left in overtime—and the crown all but on our heads—Daniel Bertoni rose up to seal the victory with another great goal. The crowd went wild. Incredible. Was it really happening?

I couldn't stand it any longer.

It was as if I were watching everything in slow motion, in silence, to the nervous rhythm of my beating heart. The Argentines were world champions! A few minutes later, the giant screen showed a picture of Daniel Passarela lifting the FIFA World Cup.

It was the happiest day of my soccer life.

(One more fact . . . Kempes was the first player in World Cup history to both play on the triumphant side *and* finish as the tournament's top goalscorer. He had six.)

TRIVIA

Who was the World Cup's first top goalscorer to also bring home the FIFA trophy?

A SAD EPILOGUE

The euphoria of victory was clouded by the sad political reality of our country. The military remained in power for another six years, leaving over three thousand disappearances and dragging the country into a senseless war with England over the Falkland Islands.

Without our knowing it, the joyous cries pouring out of the Monumental that afternoon drowned out the anguished cries of political prisoners being tortured in the Escuela de Mecánica de la Armada, just a few blocks from the stadium.

Five:
The Contemporary Cups (1982–2002)

The Contemporary Cups:
Spain '82 to South Korea/Japan '02

First came Jules, and then came João. The first sowed the seed, the second harvested the fruit. But he also cleaned it, polished it, packaged it, marketed it, sold it, and transformed it into a commercial and athletic phenomenon unprecedented in world history.

With João Havelange, the president of FIFA since 1974, the World Cup of Soccer entered a new age, as it went from being simply an important and popular sporting event to being an international socio-economic phenomenon. FIFA had more members than the United Nations, and Don João wielded more influence than the Pope himself.

After eleven installments over fifty-two years, the number of participating nations jumped from sixteen to twenty-four. And then up to thirty-two. And with more teams participating, more people wanted to see the games on television. That was when broadcast rights began to be bid on, resulting in a dance of millions and millions of dollars.

Immediately, the most prominent multinational corporations on earth began to fight over commercial control of the event. Companies like Adidas, Coca-Cola, McDonald's, Fuji, Anheuser-Busch, and MasterCard (among others) outbid their competitors, becoming exclusive World Cup sponsors. As a result, FIFA's coffers were overflowing, making it the wealthiest international athletic organization on earth.

And it all went back to the promise Don João made when he took over the reins from Jules Rimet: "I've come here to sell a product, and that product is soccer."

Along the way, Havelange set the World Cup in a country virtually

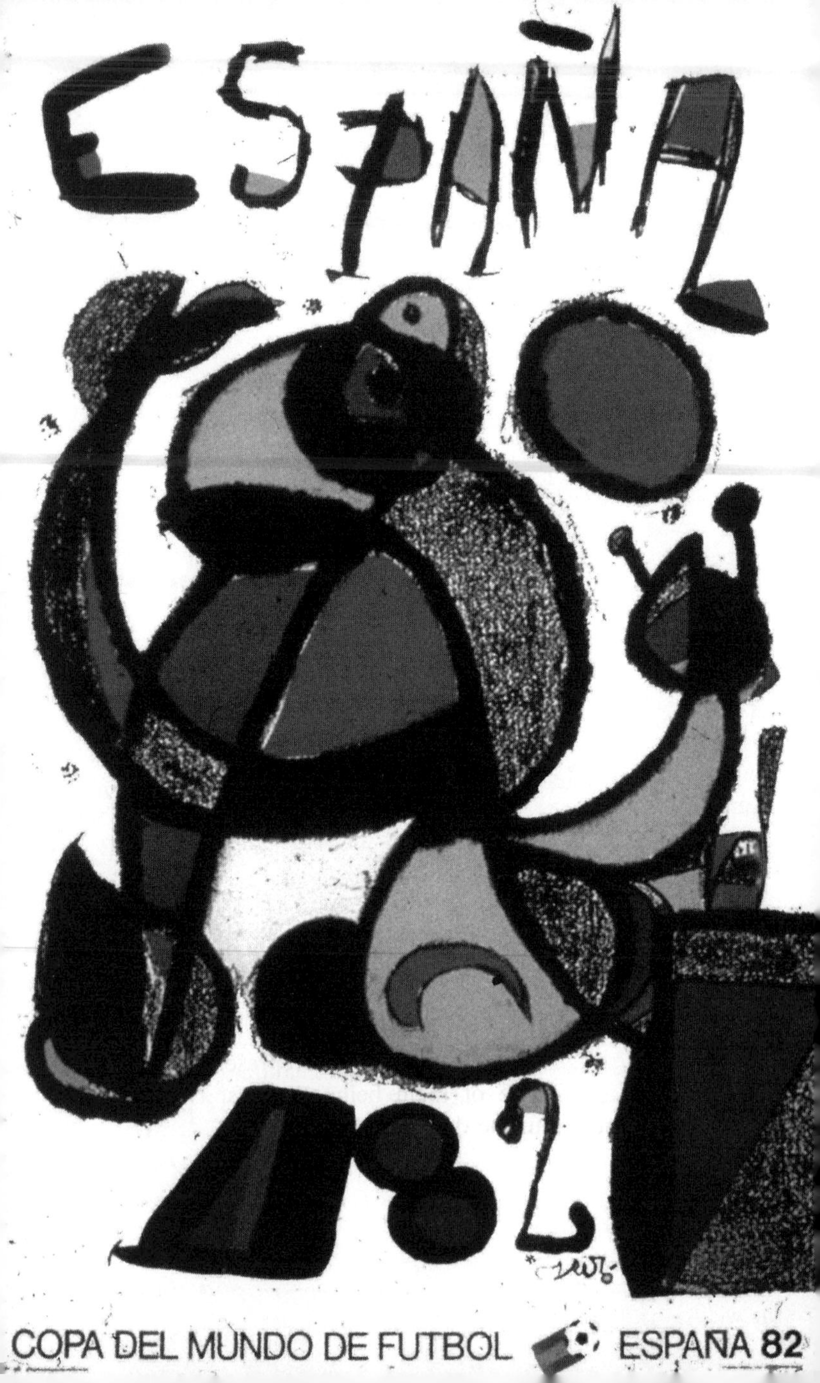
ESPAÑA
82
COPA DEL MUNDO DE FUTBOL
ESPAÑA 82

without soccer (the United States, the largest consumer market on earth) and convinced two longtime rivals, Japan and South Korea, to collaborate on an Asian World Cup.

He also managed to expand the FIFA brand to embrace various age brackets, as well as women. And so were born the Women's World Cup, as well as the Under-23, Under-20, Under-17, and Under-15 World Cups.

When he retired from FIFA in 1998, after twenty-four years at the helm, Don João guaranteed the continuity of his work and vision by naming his friend and right-hand man, Switzerland's Joseph "Sepp" Blatter, as his successor.

Under the direction of its new president, FIFA has negotiated new international television rights, signed with new exclusive sponsors, and, in 2010 the World Cup will be held on the African continent, in South Africa for the first time.

Now let's take a look at the fabulous Contemporary Cups.

Spain 1982: The Cup that Brazil Lost

The cradle of the Fiesta Brava was as prepared as ever for a new *fiesta*, one as valiant and colorful as the running of the bulls. Only this occasion was the twelfth FIFA World Cup of Soccer: Spain '82. It would have to be, after all, because there were more invitees than ever. Twenty-four to be exact.

As I mentioned, Havelange's FIFA had added eight more teams to the original sixteen, and they were allocated in the following way: one for CONCACAF, one for Africa, one for Asia and Oceania, and four for Europe. South America was the big loser in the reassessment, getting stuck with the same old three slots it had before. All they got was the right to play off against one of the European teams (in this case, Bolivia lost to Hungary).

In other words, at Spain '82, Europe was represented by no fewer than fourteen teams, one of them being the host country. South America had three (plus the defending champions, Argentina), while North and Central America/Caribbean, Africa, Asia, and Oceania had two apiece.

The stage was set, ready for the opening kick, on the thirteenth of June there at the Nou Camp in Barcelona. Across the rest of the Iberian peninsula, the tapas bars, the flamenco dancers, the guitars, and the wineskins were all ready for the *fiesta*.

THE 24 CLUB

There were twenty-four teams broken down into six groups of four, and the matches were played in thirteen Spanish cities:

Group A (Vigo and La Coruña): Italy, Poland, Peru, Cameroon
Group B (Gijón and Oviedo): West Germany, Algeria, Chile, Austria
Group C (Barcelona, Elche, and Alicante): Argentina, Belgium, Hungary, El Salvador
Group D (Bilbao and Valladolid): England, France, Czechoslovakia, Kuwait
Group E (Valencia and Zaragoza): Spain, Honduras, Yugoslavia, Northern Ireland
Group F (Sevilla and Málaga): Brazil, U.S.S.R., Scotland, New Zealand

Madrid and Barcelona were the locales for the second round, which consisted of four groups of three teams each. The winners of each of these groups would then play off in a semifinal series, from which the two finalists would emerge.

"TANGO" AND "NARANJITO"

One was an Adidas ball, while the other was the mascot. Both traditions had been carried into Spain '82. "Tango" was the same basic ball that was used in Argentina '78, though with certain improvements, such as a higher plastic-to-leather ratio. And "Naranjito" was the official mascot, which—as the name would indicate—was a little doll shaped like an orange. And it must have been quite a macho mascot, because a lot of people thought the name should have been "Naranjita."

TRIVIA
What was the name of the official mascot of Spain '82

I have to admit that I never understood the whole orange thing. I never saw it as a symbol of Spain. Of all the iconic images of that beautiful land—the matador, the bull, the flamenco dancer, the gypsies, El Quijote, the priests, anything really—the orange was the *last* thing to come to mind.

DEBUTS AND RETURNS

More teams playing meant more new faces.
Africa sent two new teams, Algeria and Cameroon. Asia and

TRIVIA
What team did Carlos Alberto Parreira coach in Spain '82?

There were also two newcomers: Kuwait and New Zealand. The Kuwaitis had the novel idea of bringing in Carlos Alberto Parreira as their coach—the very Parreira who made a champion out of Brazil in '94 and who is returning as coach for Germany '06.

Europe didn't have any newcomers, but there were four teams making their first appearance since Mexico '70: England, Czechoslovakia, the U.S.S.R., and Belgium. Holland's "Clockwork Orange" squad was no more, making them the great absentee of 1982.

South America saw the resurgence of Chile, which was making its first appearance since '74, though that continent failed to provide a credible Uruguay, which was still in a state of soccer crisis, now missing their second consecutive World Cup.

Finally, the CONCACAF region sent the two infamous rivals from 1970, Honduras and El Salvador. Both sides had won their spots in a pre–World Cup competition in Tegucigalpa, which saw the surprising elimination of Mexico.

THE OLD MAN AND THE KID

Two somewhat odd records were set in Spain '82. On the one hand, it featured the oldest player ever to compete in a World Cup: the famous Italian keeper Dino Zoff, who was forty years young.

On the other end of the spectrum was the youngest player ever to compete, younger even than Pelé was in 1958. I'm talking about the Scot Norman Whiteside, who was seventeen years and forty-two days old at the start of the World Cup, whereas "O Rei" was much closer to eighteen when he set the mark.

TRIVIA
Who was the oldest player to compete in Spain '82?

Years later, Zoff's record would be broken by the Cameroon player Roger Mila at U.S.A. '94, who was forty-two when he took the field. Coincidentally, Whiteside's mark was also broken by a player from Cameroon, Samuel Eto'o (of Barcelona fame), in France '98. He was a mere sixteen years and several months when he debuted.

THE APPEARANCE OF "EL MÁGICO"

His goals are still the stuff of legend in El Salvador and Cádiz. His moves were unforgettable. His nocturnal adventures, extreme. Jorge Alberto "El Mágico" González was the greatest undisciplined player of all time. But what a player!

He was the twenty-one-year-old star of FAS in San Salvador when he stepped forward in Tegucigalpa to help his nation qualify for the '82 Cup. And although his team's performance in Spain provided nothing to for the record books, his personal display was enough to get him a contract with Cádiz, which was then still in the upper echelons of Spain's league.

TRIVIA
In which World Cup did "El Mágico" González play?

El Salvador made its debut against Hungary in record-setting fashion—and may all Salvadorans forgive me for mentioning it here! It was the worst defeat in World Cup history, a 10–1 pounding.

It hurts even to say it!

"El Mágico" could only do so much that afternoon of June 15th in Elche. His team's lone goal came from Baltazar Ramírez, which was also the only goal El Salvador ever scored in World Cup competition.

After the tournament, "El Mágico" was bought by Cádiz. There he found a number of years of success, but also of controversy, due largely to his bohemian attitudes and his thirst for nightlife. But he is remembered, and most certainly missed. With him, Cádiz enjoyed some of their best years.

A RETURN TO THE "JOGO BONITO"

Brazil finally got back on track with a new generation of superstar players. Thanks to players like Sócrates, Falcão, Eder, and Zico, Brazil had returned to its flamboyant and spectacular style of soccer, the famous *"jogo bonito,"* or "beautiful game," that was always in such high demand by the Brazilian public. (They expected much.)

This new *"Scratch"* was coached by Tele Santana, and they opened their campaign on June 14th in Seville against the Soviets. They won 2–1 on the strength of two long-distance strikes, one by Sócrates and the other by Eder.

TRIVIA
In which World Cup did Sócrates and Falcão make their debuts?

In the next match, they fell behind early to Scotland but quickly remedied that with goals by Zico, Oscar, Eder, and Falcão. They finished as 4–1 victors and were through to the second round with the best soccer of the tournament. In their third match, they swiftly dispatched New Zealand 4–0 on a pair of goals by Zico and one apiece by Falcão and Serginho.

THE HONDURAN DEBUT

The 1980s was the golden age of Honduran soccer, thanks to a generation of exceptional players. Participating in Spain '82 was a fit-

ting tribute to the talent of men like Gilberto Yearwood, Roberto "Macho" Figueroa, Porfirio Betancourt, Julio César Arzú, Héctor "Pecho de Águila" Zelaya, Tony "La Aguja" Laing, Prudencio "Tecate" Norales, and two great friends of mine, the team's captain Ramón "Primitivo" Maradiaga and "El Kaiser," Jaime Villegas.

Under the watchful eye of coach José de la Paz Herrera—better known as "El Chelato Uclés"—the Hondurans took full advantage of the extra World Cup slot allocated to CONCACAF, as well as the fact that they hosted the 1981 pre–World Cup qualifiers, to punch their tickets for Spain. They finished first in the region, passing Mexico en route.

They drew an opening match in Valencia against the hosts themselves. It was June 16th, one day after El Salvador was so soundly beaten, and many people feared the same result for the Hondurans.

The Honduran squad took an early lead—in the 7th minute, in fact—off a goal by Zelaya. They held their advantage on the scoreboard (much to the Spaniards' dismay) all the way until the 65th minute, when their hosts scored the goal. A Honduran defender had committed a foul outside the area, and the Argentine referee awarded a penalty, and the match concluded in a 1–1 tie. Honduras had made quite an impression, with a style of soccer that was at once organized and effective—but also joyous.

For their second appearance, they traveled to Zaragoza to face Northern Ireland, with similar results. Another 1–1 tie (goal by Laing), and they were still alive at the World Cup.

Their third match was against Yugoslavia, who were coming off a

The Honduras team.

Para Fernando Flore[s] buen amigo de Honduras y gran ser humano afectuosamente

Julio 8, 2001

loss to Spain and a tie with Northern Ireland. If Honduras could win, they would be through to the second round. A third draw might also suffice, but that would depend on other, external results. They played again in Zaragoza, on June 24th, and the match was a great one. One might say that it had it all.

With three minutes left in the match, the "penalty ghost" reared its head yet again, in the form of a dubious move by Jaime Villegas against Yugoslavia's Vladimir Petrovic. The Chilean referee, Gastón Castro, blew his whistle. The Honduran players mounted a heated protest, with the result that their Gilberto Yearwood was sent off. Petrovic himself converted the penalty, giving Yugoslavia the win, 1–0.

Throughout the years, I've been able to relive what happened that distant day in Zaragoza through chats and interviews with various members of that famous Honduran team. Jaime Villegas, for example, has always said: "Fernando, I swear to you that I didn't touch him. I swear it." And he says it with such conviction that I can't help but believe him. Especially when the match film corroborates him.

TRIVIA
Which country eliminated Honduras in Spain '82?

"It was a black day for Honduras. So close, and yet so far away!" recalls "El Kaiser" Villegas. "Those are the hardest parts of the game to come to terms with. When you least expect it, in sweeps the referee to ruin everything."

ARGENTINA DEFENDS HER TITLE

I almost didn't even know that the '82 World Cup would be taking place in Spain. By then I was living with my mother in the United States, and the hard life of an immigrant didn't permit me the luxuries of television—or being a soccer fan. She was working for a travel agency in New York, ferrying travelers to Washington and Florida.

I was barely even able to see a single game, out of all the ones broadcast by Univision Canal 41 in New York . . . which, in 1982, was still called SIN, and wasn't actually in New York but in rather Patterson, New Jersey. Tony Tirado was the commentator, and every time someone scored he would repeat his call in English for the benefit of all the gringos in the audience tuning in.

The thing is, I didn't see Argentina defend its title. And I regret that fact to this day, but there's nothing to be done. Other priorities took precedence. I lived those emotions a few years later, in 1986, when Maradona brought us a second World Cup title. That one I *was* able to enjoy.

With Jaime Villegas in San Pedro Sula, Honduras.

Speaking of Don Diego, in 1982 he finally realized his dream of playing in the World Cup. He had appeared in—and won—the World Youth Cup in Japan in 1979, but Spain marked his first appearance with the full national team.

His debut was against Belgium, and their famous keeper Jean-Marie Pfaff. There was nothing much to report. The match took place in Barcelona on June 13, and we lost 1–0. Was it an unlucky date?

TRIVIA
What was Maradona's first World Cup match?

The second match was against Hungary, and it was there that the genius of the great number 10 came to the surface. In it, he scored both his first World Cup goal (off the post) as well as his second (a left-footed cracker), and we won 4–1.

TRIVIA
What was Maradona's first World Cup goal?

I'd heard about Maradona's skills and abilities from some Argentine tourists, and it made me quite curious to see him for myself before the Cup came to a close. It took a few days for me to get my schedule sorted out so I could situate myself in front of a television. But it was a good time to do it: Argentina versus Brazil in the second round. We'll deal with that one later.

SHADES OF THE FALKLANDS

If I wasn't following the World Cup too closely, I was following the war.

Ever since April 2nd of that same year—the day Argentina invaded the Falkland Islands—I followed the news via radio and the papers. That was when I discovered that we in the United States knew more about the conflict than they did in Argentina, since the military dictatorship was "sanitizing" the information and spinning the news to make it appear as if they were winning.

And since the national team was off in Spain, it was easier than ever to distract the public. Two days before their World Cup debut, on June 11th, the British navy sank the Argentine battleship *General Belgrano*, and three hundred Argentine sailors lost their lives. But the Buenos Aires headlines were focused on the national team's debut against Belgium.

On the 14th—just a day after falling to the Belgians—we lost the war and surrendered in Puerto Argentino. But the papers there were more interested in the upcoming game against Hungary, scheduled for four days later.

It was one of the darkest periods of our history, yet soccer ruled the editorial pages and calmed a nation's pain.

"ADIÓS," NENE

Spain '82 was the farewell World Cup for the sensational Peruvian star Nene Cubillas. And it was bittersweet.

The Peruvian team was out in the first round, without showing any of the brilliance that had defined their performances in 1970 and '78. And Nene was shut out, held without a goal.

Their first match was in La Coruña, against Cameroon, and it ended in a scoreless draw. Their second was a 1–1 draw with Italy, but Peru didn't score for themselves.

Their final first-round match was against a Polish team that still featured the legendary Grzegorz Lato, as well as a new young star with similar talents by the name of Boniek. The Poles dropped five big goals on Peru, whose lone goal came off the foot of La Rosa, and only near the end of the match.

It was an unfortunate end to Cubillas's magnificent World Cup career. Fortunately, his compatriots don't remember him for the failure in Spain; rather, they focus on the virtuosity of his play, his spectacular goals, and the unforgettable moments he left behind.

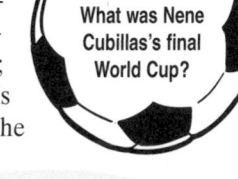

TRIVIA

What was Nene Cubillas's final World Cup?

"ADIÓS," DON ELÍAS

Chile had returned to the World Cup after an eight-year hiatus, but they bowed out without any fanfare, and wouldn't be back for another sixteen years, until France '98.

In 1982, the duo known as "Za-Sa" did not yet exist. Iván "Bam Bam" Zamorano was fifteen years old, and Marcelo Salas was merely eight; in other words, Chile didn't yet have the benefit of players of that caliber.

Their main figures—players like Elías Figueroa (36) and Carlos "El Chino" Caszely (32)—were in the twilight of their careers, and the younger generation—like Patricio "El Pato" Yañez, Juan Carlos Letelier, and Eduardo "El Bonva" Bonvallet—were all but imperceptible presences in Spain. They bowed out just as Uruguay did in Germany '74: a team filled with old glory and few promises.

After Pinochet bid the team farewell at La Moneda (where several players refused to have their pictures taken with him), la roja headed for Spain full of hope and optimism. Under the direction of coach Luis "Locutín" Santibáñez, they had qualified with relative ease, vanquishing Ecuador and Paraguay, neither of which scored upon them.

But it all went downhill from there.

They lost all three matches in a group that looked to be one of the easier ones, even with West Germany in there. They started off with a 1–0 defeat at the hands of Austria in Oviedo, then fell 4–1 to the Germans, before fighting hard but losing to first-timers Algeria 3–2.

It was the end of an era for Chile, and the swan song for their greatest player, Elías Figueroa. In 1998, when "Bam Bam," Salas, Estay, and Rojas were ready, Chile returned to form, but that was a few years off.

FIRST-ROUND SURPRISES

The first surprise was that, in their first match, unheralded Algeria defeated West Germany and its stars, Hummenigge, Breitner, Briegel, Littbarski, and their newcomer, goalkeeper Harald "Tony" Shumacher.

The second was that Group A ended in a three-way tie between the Germans, the Austrians, and the Algerians. It is rumored (though I don't believe it) that the Germans reached an agreement with the Austrians to let them win 1–0, thus keeping the poor Algerians out on goal differential. That was just talk.

Another big surprise was that Italy was able to advance without winning a single match. They played Poland to a scoreless draw and tied both Peru and Cameroon 1–1 each. They finished second in the group, tied with Cameroon at three points apiece but ahead on that tricky goal differential.

As you'll see, Italy was able to recover their form and get a good, fresh start in the second round.

THE SHEIKH COMMANDS

Carlos Alberto Parreira's Kuwaiti team nearly toppled the Czechs in their debut. Instead, they found themselves with a 1–1 draw. But in their second match, against France, they proved the embarrassment of the tournament. But not because of their play; rather, it was because of Parreira's boss, the Shiekh Fahid Al-Ahmad Al-Sabah, the president of the Kuwaiti Football Federation.

They played in the Estadio José Zorrilla in Valladolid, and France was up 3–1 in the second half. In an inexplicable turn of events, the entire Kuwaiti defense stopped dead in their tracks, thinking that the referee had blown his whistle, while the French strikers continued to play and scored their fourth goal. Immediately, the Kuwaiti team protested, and tried to explain to the Soviet referee what had happened—that they had heard a whistle coming from the stands—but their pleas fell on deaf ears, and the goal was validated.

Up in his box, the sheikh ordered his team to abandon the match and leave the field. Can you believe it?

Parreira stepped onto the field—as did some FIFA officials, journalists, and the sheikh himself—and together they surrounded the referee. Nobody knows what was said, but suddenly he changed his opinion of the call and overturned the goal. The Kuwaitis returned to the field, and the French, bewildered, but unruffled—simply said, *"C'est la vie."* The match was restarted, and before all was said and done, France had scored their fourth goal—for the second time that day. Winners, 4–1.

After the World Cup had ended, both the sheikh and the Soviet referee were expelled from FIFA.

And that's that.

"LA SEGUNDA RONDA"

Round 2 featured twelve teams: the top two finishers in each of the six groups. The idea the organizers had was to form four new groups of three teams each, with the four winners advancing to the semifinals. Matches would be played only in Barcelona and Madrid. And here is how it all broke down:

> **Group A** (Estadio Nou Camp, Barcelona): Poland, Belgium, U.S.S.R.
> **Group B** (El Santiago Bernabeu, Madrid): West Germany, England, Spain
> **Group C** (Estadio Sarria, Barcelona): Italy, Argentina, Brazil (ouch!)
> **Group D** (Estadio Vicente Calderón, Madrid): Austria, France, Northern Ireland

MORE SURPRISES!

The first was that Spain fell flat; the second is that Italy let loose; and the third is that Brazil bowed out.

The famous Spanish *furia* did not materialize when it was needed, and the result was elimination. Many sarcastic journalists across the country wondered aloud whether the team was really all that "furious" after all.

Their first match of the second round was in Madrid's Bernabeu,

against West Germany. The first half ended 0–0, but with the start of the second, the Germans began running circles around the Spaniards. They scored twice in the first thirty minutes. Spain finally got on the board in the 81st minute, but it was too late, and they lost 2–1.

Their second opponent was England. *¡Ay!*

Spain needed a win to advance to the semifinals. And I have to say that they did show a bit more of the *furia* than they did in the first round, but it wasn't enough. They played inspired but scoreless soccer, and the match ended 0–0. Spain had been bounced from their own World Cup, and they left the field under a rain of catcalls, hurled beverages, and spit from their dissatisfied fans.

But Brazil's fate was sadder still.

They displayed the best soccer of the tournament, scored on every team they faced, and yet it wasn't enough to overcome Italy's Paolo Rossi.

ITALY AWAKENS

Nobody can explain the drastic change that Italy underwent between the first and second rounds.

They had advanced by the skin of their teeth, without having won a single game, and with only two goals in their favor. But on June 29th, when they stepped onto the field at Barcelona's Estadio Nou Camp, their luck changed.

Maybe it was the outstanding defense that they used on the Argentines, or the tight coverage that Claudio Gentile used to handcuff Maradona. But whatever the reason, Argentina was unable to penetrate the Italian area, and Don Diego was shut down. Italy won 2–1, their first victory of the tournament.

In his autobiography, Maradona tells how every time he received the ball, "Gentile would give me a little hack in the calves." Years later they would meet again in Italy, and Gentile admitted that he played "to prevent him from playing."

After that defeat, "Brazil got us good," said Don Diego.

A RED CARD FOR MARADONA!

It was the only match from Spain '82 that I found in New York. I wanted to see Diego Armando Maradona in his first-ever World Cup, and it was the best on-paper match, for it was the Argentina versus Brazil classic, played at Barcelona's Estadio Sarria on July 2, 1982. It was also the third straight time the two nations faced off in a World Cup match.

But it would have been better to skip it!

The match was evenly played and had its exciting stretches, but as time wore on, it became apparent that Brazil was more fit than we were. They tried to cut Diego down in his tracks with so many hard fouls that finally he lashed out himself and kicked Batista in the groin.

"The kick I threw at Batista's nuts was supposed to be for Falcão," Maradona writes. Either way, he was ejected for it, and Argentina was left to play a man down.

Zico, Serginho, and Junior went on to score a goal apiece, and it wasn't until the 89th minute that Ramón Díaz got one of his own to salvage some of Argentina's honor.

"I came out of that tournament in pretty bad shape," Maradona reflects in his biography. "Everyone on earth—including myself—thought that it was going to be my World Cup. I had the most to lose. Nobody had as much at stake as me, and nobody wanted things to turn out for the best more than I did."

After the Cup ended, Don Diego returned to Spain to play for Barcelona. It was the most expensive transfer in the history of La Liga up until that time. They paid Boca Juniors "8 *palos verdes*" as they say in Argentina: $8 million.

ROSSI 3, BRAZIL 2

Italy's fourth match of the Cup was against Brazil, and Paolo Rossi had yet to score a goal. But his drought would end that day, the fifth of July, at Barcelona's Nou Camp.

Both teams had beaten Argentina, and so the winner of this matchup would go on to the semifinals. And it was something of a grudge match, since Brazil had beaten the Italians 2–1 in the third-place match four years earlier in Argentina.

Rossi got to work early that day. He had his first goal in the 5th minute. But the Brazilians were not shaken. They settled into their own rhythm, dancing a samba around the Italians, who had dropped back in defense, trying to preserve their lead. Six minutes later, Sócrates tied the match.

Brazil continued to press and very nearly got their second, but old Zoff was solid that afternoon. In the 25th minute, Italy mounted a counterattack that resulted in another goal by Rossi.

Rossi 2, Brazil 1. And that's how it went into the half.

After the break, Brazil bombarded Italy's defensive wall in search of the tie. They had increased both the speed and the precision of their

play, and it seemed as if the equalizer would come at any time. It took eighteen minutes, but it came. A deep strike from Falcão—some dubbed it the goal of the tournament—leveled things at 2–2.

Without lowering their guard, they pressed their advantage, already convinced that the Italians were sitting ducks. But, what do you think happened? Rossi capped off another counterattack, resulting in his third goal of the day.

Rossi 3, Brazil 2. *Ciao!*

And that's the way it was. Nobody could believe what had happened—neither Rossi's hat trick nor the elimination of the best team in the field, and the best team Brazil had fielded in twelve years.

But that wasn't the only trick up Rossi's sleeve.

ROSSI 2, LATO ZERO

Rossi continued his loose, inspired play on the Spanish turf.

In the first semifinal against Poland, the famous Italian with the number 20 jersey scored twice more to put his side in the final match in Madrid.

It proved to be Lato's farewell match; he was playing the last card in the deck of his career, which had started back with Mexico's Atlante. However, his legacy would remain, and Poland still has yet to produce another goalscorer of similar caliber or class to that of their famous bald striker.

And Rossi?

He was still sharp, and still had a few rounds left in the clip for the final.

A SEMIFINAL FOR THE AGES

With the elimination of Brazil, the best team left seemed to be France. Their performance was due to the strength of their midfield.

That was where three of the great figures in French soccer developed into a band of brothers. They were Michel Platini, who was the current star of Juventus and playing in his second World Cup, coupled with two newcomers: Jean Tigana, a dark-haired youngster with class and intelligence, and the marvelous Alain Giresse, France's little giant, the five-foot-four-inch bundle of dynamite.

They lost their first match of the tournament 3–1 against England in Bilbao, but they recovered quickly against Kuwait and Czechoslovakia.

TRIVIA

Who were France's "Three Musketeers" in Spain '82?

In the second round, they downed Austria 1–0 and pounded Northern Ireland 4–1, two of those four goals coming from Giresse.

Which is how they reached the semifinals against the ever-dangerous West Germans in Seville, on July 8. Regular time ended with the score tied at 1–1, the goals coming by way of Littbarski and Platini. So they went to overtime, which was nothing new to the Germans, who had a bit of experience with these marathon matches.

France dominated the extra period, and in only nine minutes they had added two goals to their one, thanks to Trésor and Giresse. France was on its way to the final match, and West Germany was once again cut down in the semis, as had happened against the Italians in Mexico '70.

But hold on a second!

Who is that player coming onto the field?

It's no less than Karl-Heinz Rummenigge. The stands come alive. Being injured, he hadn't been in the starting lineup, but the German coach, Jupp Derwall, was desperate. He came on as a substitute for Briegel, who had already given his all.

What happened next is the stuff that movies are made of. The kind of thing that takes place once every hundred years.

Moments after play had restarted, Rummenigge had himself a goal. West Germany was back in the game, and the French were shaken. Minutes after that, Fischer scored one off a half volley, tying the match at three apiece. It was going to penalty shots, for the first time in World Cup history.

BITTER PENALTIES

All of France felt like dying! In West Germany, they couldn't believe it. And in Seville, people were chewing on their nails while photographers gathered at the end of the field, where the penalties would be taking place.

Even after the first five shots, the two sides were still tied 4–4. The German keeper Schumacher and his French counterpart, Ettori, had saved one penalty each.

So they were down to the final stretch. Tension was at the breaking point. Whoever blinked first would lose.

The Frenchman, Bossis, stepped to the spot first. He shot, and Schumacher turned it away at the post. Now it was all up to the foot of Hrubesch. If he scored, the Germans were through to the final. And he did! West Germany 5, France 4.

It was certainly the most dramatic match of Spain '82, and ultimately one of the most dramatic of all time.

France slunk into the third-place match against Poland, and lost there as well, 3–2.

SCHUMACHER'S KNOCKOUT BLOW SHAMEFUL!

In the semifinal match, the Frenchman Battiston had been running full speed for a ball bouncing into the German penalty area. Schumacher came off his line hard and there was a furious collision. The ball bounced harmlessly away. Schumacher returned to his post, while Battiston lay on the turf, his fists clenched.

Up until then, it had simply seemed like a hard play in an intense match. But Battiston did not move. His teammates were concerned and gathered around him to see if they could help, but the poor man was unresponsive. He was completely unconscious. And Schumacher stood in the mouth of his goal, calmly watching the scene as if nothing had happened.

Soon, however, the replays began to flash across the screen, and the world began to see how Schumacher—*fuácata!*—had intentionally hit the Frenchman in the jaw, laying him out on the ground.

Battiston was taken off the field on a stretcher with a cerebral contusion and three broken teeth. Schumacher was unmoved. He didn't so much as go over to see how his victim was doing. Nor did the referee call him on it. I understand that to this day, Schumacher continues to offer his apologies, though Battiston has yet to accept them. Twenty-four long years later.

THE FINAL IN MADRID

Madrid, Estadio Santiago Bernabeu. Sunday, July 11, 1982. Italy versus West Germany. Both squads, twice champions before, were about to face off in the twelfth World Cup final.

That final also featured the tournament's top two goalscorers playing face-to-face: Rossi and Rummenigge, with five apiece.

Both sides had experience in settings such as this. It was the fourth appearance for each: Italy had been there in '34, '38, and '70, the Germans in '54, '66, and '74.

In other words, everyone was expecting one for the ages.

In the event, it wasn't quite like Sweden '58 or Mexico '70, but the match did have its moments, especially when you consider that both teams were built around staunch defenses. The first half ended 0–0, and the Italians had failed to convert a penalty.

As I mentioned, Rossi had been playing sharp, inspired soccer during Italy's run. The second half was barely under way before he opened the scoring with a tight shot from inside Schumacher's six-yard box.

Ten minutes later, Tardelli fired a powerful shot from the edge of the area for Italy's second. The Germans were crumbling, but Italy was not yet satisfied and continued to press their advantage, taking complete control of the match. Their third goal came with only nine minutes left to play. It was Tardelli again who broke swiftly from his midfield post and reached the edge of the German area, where he crossed to Altobelli, who took Schumacher inside and beat him by the near post.

Italy 3, West Germany 0.

Two minutes later, the Germans countered with a strike from Breitner. (Trivia alert! The same Breitner who converted the penalty in the '74 final.) But that would be all.

The Italians were world champions, and Paolo Rossi was the tournament's top scorer, with seven. It was only the second time—after Kempes in '78—that the man with the golden boot played for the team that won the golden trophy.

With the victory, Italy joined Brazil as the only three-time world champion. And those two nations would see each other in the final twelve years later, at U.S.A. '94.

TRIVIA

Who was the top goalscorer from Spain '82?

Mexico 1986: Maradona's World Cup

It had been slated for Colombia, but in the end it went again to Mexico, which became the first country to host twice.

Because of economic problems that included a mounting foreign debt, Colombia withdrew its bid in 1983. Immediately, both Mexico and the United States announced their candidacies. FIFA carefully weighed the experience and athletic infrastructure of both nations, and eventually decided on Mexico. (The close relationship between Don Guillermo Cañedo and Havelange certainly didn't hurt.)

So the World Cup was returning to one of its most memorable stages. Sixteen years had passed since Pelé & Co. had wowed the world with their soccer skills, but the images lived on in the minds of people who watched the games unfold across the globe.

But who would ever have imagined that another South American was about to steal the show on the very same stage?

EARTHQUAKE!

Mexico II brought back memories of another World Cup: Chile '62. Once again, an earthquake struck a host nation in the year leading up to the event. It struck in September of 1985, partially destroying several neighborhoods of Mexico City, along with some outlying areas. More than 10,000 people lost their lives, though the true total was never revealed. The Mexican government did not want to alarm either FIFA or the world more than was necessary.

Fortunately, the primary site—the Azteca—was undamaged, and Mexico persevered through their period of mourning and rebuilding, toward their second hosting of a World Cup.

SUN AND TELEVISION

As was the case in 1970, television determined the match times. And now there was more reason for it than ever, with so many more people tuning in, and so much more sponsorship money.

In order for the Europeans to be able to enjoy the spectacle, many games were scheduled to kick off at noon, under Mexico's brilliant summer sun. Mexico City's altitude still gave some people cause for concern, but the 1970 World Cup had proven that it was nothing the players couldn't overcome.

Perhaps they even performed better!

NEW FACES, OLD ACQUAINTANCES

The number of participating countries remained the same as it was in Spain '82: twenty-four teams. The difference was that South America had one more representative this time, for a total of four in all: Brazil, Argentina, Uruguay, and Paraguay. Uruguay—my mother's ancestral team—was making their first appearance since 1958, and *los charrúas* were back for the first time since '74.

CONCACAF was represented by Mexico (as host) and Canada, which was making its World Cup debut.

Africa sent two teams, Algeria and Morocco, and Asia did as well: Iraq and South Korea, which was back after a twenty-two-year hiatus.

The glaring absences included Austria, Czechoslovakia, Sweden,

Yugoslavia, and Holland. The Dutch seemed to have lost their soccer muse, and had not appeared since 1978. They were replaced by another newcomer that, like the "Clockwork Orange" of old, played with a new and revolutionary style. I'm talking, of course, about Denmark.

DENMARK

The six groups of four teams were spread across nine Mexican cities. Here's the breakdown:

> **Group A** (Mexico City and Puebla): Italy, Bulgaria, Argentina, South Korea
>
> **Group B** (Mexico City and Toluca): Mexico, Belgium, Paraguay, Iraq
>
> **Group C** (León and Irapuato): France, Canada, U.S.S.R., Hungary
>
> **Group D** (Guadalajara and Monterrey): Brazil, Spain, Algeria, Northern Ireland
>
> **Group E** (Querétaro and Guadalajara): West Germany, Uruguay, Denmark, Scotland
>
> **Group F** (Monterrey and Guadalajara): Poland, Morocco, Portugal, England

The top two teams in each group would move on to the second round, along with the four best third-place finishers—a new feature of this World Cup.

RETURN OF "LOS GUARANÍES"

On June 4th of that year, Paraguay opened at "La Bombonera" in Toluca, where they beat the Iraquis 1–0. (It was their fourth trip to the World Cup stage, and their first since Sweden '58, where they got bombed hard themselves, 7–3, by France.)

The winning goal was scored by Julio César Romero—the famous "Romerito"—who was one of the best Paraguayan players of all time, and who also spent time with the New York Cosmos, Brazil's Fluminense, and Mexico's Puebla. In their second match, against Mexico, he scored again, and Paraguay came away with a 1–1 tie.

Their next matchup was with a Belgian team featuring

TRIVIA
What South American nation played in Mexico '86 after a twenty-eight-year absence?

Jean-Marie Pfaff and Jan Ceulemans, and it ended at two goals apiece. The *guaraníes* goals came from the best Paraguayan player of the day, Roberto Cabañas, who also played for the Cosmos, as well as Cali's América, France's Lyon, and Argentina's Boca.

Paraguay finished runners-up in the group, and were through to the second round, where they ran into England and its new star, Gary Lineker, who scored a pair of goals. The match ended 3–0, in favor of England, and Paraguay headed home until France '98.

TRIVIA

Which nation did the goalkeeper Jean-Marie Pfaff play for?

THE RETURN OF "LOS TRI"

After not advancing very far in their own World Cup in 1970 (and after the failure in '78 and the absences in '74 and '82), the Mexicans were ready to redeem themselves internationally, and bring a bit of joy to their people after the terrible earthquake the previous year.

Their preparations were fresh, intelligent, and organized around the strengths of a new generation of athletes—like the keeper Pablo Larios from Cruz Azul; Fernando "El Sheriff" Quirarte from Chivas; Javier "El Vasco" Aguirre from Atlante; Francisco "El Abuelo" Cruz from Monterrey; Manuel Negrete and Luis Flores from Pumas; Carlos de los Cobos from América; Tomás Boy from Tigres; and, of course, the great Hugo Sánchez, who was in those days flourishing in Spain.

There was also a twenty-two-year-old kid with a great personality and an excellent future who went on to become one of the top strikers in Mexican history: my good friend and the famous number 27, Carlos Hermosillo. Back then, he was scoring goals for América, where he'd made his professional debut at the tender age of nineteen.

Unfortunately for him (and possibly for Mexico), Carlos did not see any action during that World Cup, leaving us all to wonder what might have been, especially on the day on which *los tri* were eliminated.

The team started off on the right

With Mexican player Carlos Hermosillo.

foot. They opened on June 3rd in the Azteca against Belgium, who had defeated them in 1970 on that same field. But this time they were victors, 2–1, with goals coming from Quirarte and Hugo, the latter getting himself the first of his World Cup career.

Their second match was a 1–1 draw with Paraguay, the goals coming from Romerito and Luis Flores of Pumas fame. In their final first-round match, *los tri* had to fight much harder than they had expected in order to eke out a 1–0 victory over Iraq. The goal was Quirarte's, his second of the tournament, and it was enough to give Mexico first place in their group. They were on their way to the quarterfinals for the second time in their history, and the first since 1970.

BORA'S FIRST

Mexico '86 was the first of five World Cups on the résumé of the famous and colorful—and ubiquitous—Serbian, Bora Milutinovic.

On this particular occasion, he was coach of the Mexican team, after having success in that country as both a player and a coach.

In 1990, he would take Costa Rica to their first World Cup tournament, and in 1994 he led the United States into their first second-round appearance. After that, he was at the reins of Nigeria in 1998 and China in 2002.

It will be a difficult record to break.

TRIVIA
What was the first team Bora Milutinovic coached in a World Cup?

MATTHAEUS'S SECOND

Someone else making history with his string of World Cup appearances was Lothar Matthaeus. He also participated in five, equaling the record originally set by my friend "La Tota" Carbajal.

Mexico '86 was technically Matthaeus's first appearance as an incumbent, since he had played a few minutes of West Germany's match with Chile four years earlier in Spain. Now, though, he was twenty-four years old and rounding into form as the star of the team, shining alongside veterans like Schumacher, Rummenigge, Briegel, and Littbarski.

The next World Cup would be his true breakout party, but at Mexico '86 he certainly sowed the seeds. The Germans ended up second in their group, and although he had yet to score, he would soon make his mark. In the second round, at UNAM's Estadio Olímpico, he

scored in the 90th minute to give West Germany the slimmest of victories over a tough Moroccan team.

With that goal Matthaeus became Germany's savior—the one they looked to to lead them through to the finals.

THE '86 "SCRATCH"

It looked a lot like the Brazilian squad of '82. Same coach (Tele Santana), and same style of play, flashy and flowing. And they were met with the same bad luck.

Sócrates, Junior, Falcão, and Zico were on the roster, but only Sócrates and Junior were true veterans. The '86 squad also featured some players who would go down in the annals of World Cup lore. There was the dangerous right-winger Branco, famous for his excursions up the sideline and his powerful free kicks; the midfielder and playmaker Alemão; and the center forward Careca, who had missed Spain '82 due to injury but would go on to score five times in Mexico. After the World Cup, he moved to Italy (Naples), where he continued to flourish alongside Maradona.

TRIVIA
Which World Cup saw the debuts of Brazil's Alemão, Branco, and Careca?

The first round was a walk in the park for the Brazilians. They won it with ease, and they played all three of their matches in Guadalajara's Jalisco, which was "their house" from Mexico '70. The locals treated them like their own: hometown favorites.

First up was Spain. A goal by Sócrates gave them a 1–0 win. Next came Algeria, and they won again by the same score, this time off the foot of Careca. (Trivia alert: it was his first World Cup goal!)

Those two wins alone were enough to guarantee them a spot in the second round. Even so, they dispatched Northern Ireland 3–0 in their final first-round match, a pair of goals from Careca and one by Josimar. They were on to the semifinals with a full head of steam.

But that's where their luck abandoned them.

"EL PRÍNCIPE" DEBUTS

Another big-name debut at Mexico '86 is someone I've been fortunate enough to spend some unforgettable time with—someone for whom I have a great deal of love, respect, and admiration. He won a championship with River, and is known the world over as "El Príncipe" of Uruguayan soccer, the heir to the throne that is the glories of 1930 and 1950. My good friend Enzo Francescoli.

With Enzo at the helm, Uruguay was able to return to the big event after the twelve-year absence following Germany '74, when the last great generation of Uruguayan players bowed out.

Uruguay's first match in Querétaro's "La Corregidora," was against West Germany, actually, and it wasn't too bad, emerging with a 1–1 draw. But the second installment, in Neza, would go down as one of the darkest moments in the history of Uruguayan soccer. One that not even Francescoli could do anything about.

It hurts so much to even say it that I'll just whisper it here: (they lost to Denmark, 6–1. *¡Ay!*)

The only positive thing to come out of that match was Uruguay's lone goal, scored by "El Príncipe" himself, his first on the World Cup stage.

But that's it.

They didn't score against Scotland; but, on the other hand, the Scots didn't score against them, either. After a 0–0 tie, Uruguay had miraculously qualified for the next round as the best of the third-place teams in group play. There they met their next-door neighbors, Argentina, who were riding to glory on the shoulders of Maradona.

TRIVIA

What was Francescoli's first World Cup?

They lost 1–0 and headed home, eliminated, exhausted, and with their collective tail between their legs.

Eventually Enzo recovered from the failure, at least personally. At the conclusion of the World Cup, he moved to France, where he won a

"President" Fernando Fiore with "Prince" Enzo Francescoli and "King" Pelé. A very special photo!

championship with Marseille. After that, he played in Italy, before ending up in Argentina, where he won another championship with River.

His second opportunity in the World Cup would come in Italy '90.

MY MOTHER BREAKS WITH "LA CELESTE"

As you might expect, Uruguayans were not very happy (shall we say) with the performance of their squad in Mexico that year. And my dear mamá was no exception.

So much so, in fact, that the beating they took at the hands of the Danes was, for her, the last straw. After all those years of being the Number One Fan of the Uruguayan National Team, she finally threw in the towel after that one awful match against the Danes.

"How far have we fallen?" she asked, heartbroken, after watching the game on TV. "I'm not wasting any more of my time on those frauds," were her parting words.

And that's how it was. The old lady had retired from watching World Cup matches—and from worrying about Uruguay's fate in them.

MY FIFTH WORLD CUP (AND IT WASN'T ALL BAD!)

As I mentioned, Uruguay versus Denmark was the only match from Mexico '86 that my mother watched at home. We were living in New Jersey, and we watched on the same channel we always did, SIN 41, before it became Univision.

The commentator was the same one from the '82 Cup: Tony Tirado from Peru. Only now he was accompanied by one of my compatriots, the late Norberto Longo. I never would have guessed that a

mere two years later I would be working with them both on television.

But those are life's unexpected twists! I'll tell you later about how we met. In any case, I watched the rest of that summer's World Cup matches on the TV at the Go Tours office where I was working. I saw nearly all of them there, with the

With my friends in the famous basement in Queens.

exception of Argentina's games, which I watched with a group of fellow compatriots—among them "El Ñato" Nongelli, whose Queens, New York, basement served as our gathering place.

Whenever I wanted to go see a match, I either called in sick or said I had a doctor's appointment. And since my boss was a total gringo, he didn't know that the World Cup even existed. Thank God! Anyone else would have noticed a conspicuous coincidence between the days I was sick and the days on which Argentina played.

Besides Ñato and me, the usual suspects included his cousin "El Colorado," "El Pichi," "El Tano" Vicente, and "El Doctor" Carlitos Carugatti. We all drank either maté, wine, or beer. We would order pizzas, or, if it was a weekend game, Ñato would fire up the grill. It was a smallish place with a low ceiling, and I remember that it was dangerous to celebrate goals with too much abandon. On the day we beat Uruguay 1–0, the goal by Pasculli was very late in arriving. When it finally did, I leapt with so much joy that I slammed my head into the ceiling.

My friends still remember that goal . . . but more for what happened to me! They were some unforgettable evenings.

DON DIEGO STRIKES BACK

Up until then, Diego Armando Maradona had not had a good World Cup experience.

With the notable exception of the 1979 World Youth Cup in Japan—which he won with Argentina—the event had left him quite dissatisfied. Let's not forget that Menotti had left him off the roster in '78, and that he was sent off in '82, before Argentina was eliminated as a whole.

According to his biography, when he returned to Buenos Aires, he declared that he was going to "wipe from my mind" the experience of that World Cup, and "start thinking about '86."

And that's exactly what he did. Right from the opening whistle of their first match against the South Koreans there in the Estadio Olímpico, it was obvious that Diego was back. He was in fine form, agile and flashy. Argentina won 3–1, with two of the goals coming from his friend and fellow striker Jorge Valdano. Maradona had set him up for both.

Playing against Italy in Puebla, he scored the winning goal: an impossible strike from the endline—no angle at all—that took the keeper, Giovanni Galli, and the rest of the world completely by surprise. It was the only score in a 1–0 victory, and it assured Argentina of a spot in the second round. After that, they downed Bulgaria 2–0 and Uruguay

1–0 on the strength of more Maradona goals. But we still hadn't seen anything yet.

The best was yet to come.

"EL BUITRE" DEBUTS

Their failings at their own World Cup in '82 had left the Spaniards with heavy hearts. Now, however, the *"Furia Roja"* had arrived in Mexico with waves of optimism: they had a new generation of players, some of whom were really quite good—exceptional, even. Among them was the best Spanish player to come down the pike in a long time: their new goalkeeper, Andoni Zubizarreta, one of the best to ever stand between the posts.

Also new to the Spanish squad was a marvelous midfielder and star of Real Madrid named José Miguel González Martín del Campo, better known as Michel; and perhaps the best striker to ever come out of Spain, a twenty-three-year-old kid who also starred for Real Madrid: Emilio "El Buitre" Butragueño.

TRIVIA

When did "El Buitre" Butragueño make his World Cup debut?

His God-given role, there in Mexico—though he probably didn't realize it—was to exact revenge for the defeat that Uruguay suffered at the hands of Denmark. (At least, that's how I saw it.)

That day, the eighteenth of June, in Querétaro's "La Corregidora," "El Buitre" took it upon himself to stop the "Danish Train" with not one, not two, not three, but four goals. Four! It was the best performance ever given by a Spaniard in the World Cup.

The match ended 5–1 in their favor, and for the first time in their history, Spain was through to the quarterfinals. Before that, their best result was all the way back in 1950, when they finished fourth in the world.

In Mexico, Spain started off with a 1–0 loss to Brazil. But they quickly recovered and defeated Northern Ireland in their second match by a 2–1 margin, the first goal of which was struck by Butragueño—the first of his World Cup career.

After that came the destruction of Denmark, and then yet another heartbreak. I'll explain more.

PLATINI SAYS "AU REVOIR"

With him, we said goodbye to Tigana, Giresse, Battiston, Rocheteau, Bossis, and Amoros—that whole family of fabulous players that brought so much glory to *les bleus* during the 1980s. They truly were the heirs of Fontaine and Kopa, as well as the forefathers of Zidane, Trezeguet, and Henry.

They played their last World Cup matches there at Mexico '86, and they did so with the utmost in class, if not with what they deserved and were perhaps denied: a spot in the finals. It had slipped through their fingers in Spain '82, and it would in Mexico '86 as well.

Their first round had been relatively simple, without much noise. They started off in León, where they downed the rookie Canadians 1–0. After that, they drew with the Soviets 1–1 in Irapuato. Their unveiling of sorts occurred in their third match, where they faced Hungary, eliminating them 3–1.

In the second round, *les bleus* steamrolled two world champions, until the third stopped them dead in their tracks. It was then that they gave their *"au revoir."*

France would return twelve years later, as hosts.

But what's also certain is that they left behind some unforgettable memories of a creative and effective style of play. And their brightest star, the thirty-one-year-old Michel Platini, joined the ranks of the greatest players of all time.

THE ROUND OF GOALS AND PENALTIES

Historically, the second round of a World Cup offers equal doses of games for the ages and heart attacks.

But Mexico '86 broke the mold.

The historic moments were provided by Mexico and Maradona. The former advanced to the quarters on a great goal by Negrete, while the latter did the same thing, though not with one but two.

The attacks totaled four, and all of them involved overtime. Three even went to penalties. Nothing like that had ever taken place before. The matches were between Belgium and the Soviets (overtime), Belgium and Spain (penalties), Mexico and West Germany (penalties), and, the worst of all (or, rather, the best, the most intense) was between Brazil and France (penalties).

The clash between the Belgians and the Soviets was a real battle of goals. What a game! It lasted 120 minutes and ended 4–3 in favor of the Belgians, who were through to the quarterfinals for the first time in their history.

There they ran into "El Buitre's" Spain, and history repeated itself.

MANOLO'S BICYCLE

Before Maradona's famous "hand of God" goal against England, the Azteca was the scene of another sensational goal.

It occurred on June 15th, during the game between Mexico and Belgium, in the 35th minute of the match. "El Vasco" Aguirre centered to Manolo Negrete, who was waiting for the ball at the edge of the eighteen-yard box. It came in a bit high, and the only way to reach it would be to go up and get it. Which is what Negrete did: he leaped into the air— but not for a header. He was going for the bicycle kick.

TRIVIA
Who had the assist on Manuel Negrete's famous bicycle-kick goal at Mexico '86?

LONG LIVE THE BIKE!

You must have seen the video somewhere along the line. The ball came off Manolo's boot like a rocket, then slammed into the Bulgarian goalpost—and into the back of the net. Borislav Mihaylov had no chance.

Classic!

Besides being the best goal of his career—and the best by any Mexican in a World Cup—it was also one of the greatest of all time, along with Maradona's. In fact, both goals are immortalized on a pair of commemorative plaques that hang outside the entrance of the Azteca.

When Manolo visited us at the *República Deportiva* in 1999, he recalled modestly how, for him, it was a normal thing to shoot in such a manner. "I always took shots like that when Pumas would practice," he said. "We all would whenever we played *fútbol-tenis* amongst ourselves."

That afternoon at the Azteca—when he saw the ball coming in just a bit high—he reacted the same way he did a thousand times before in training: he threw himself back, cocked his right leg, and met the ball in midair.

The only difference was that he was doing it in a World Cup match. And it was a goal. Mexico went on to win 2–0.

The second goal was scored by his teammate from Pumas, Raúl Servín. It came in the 61st minute and wasn't as spectacular as the first, but it still counted and it had the effect of securing Mexico's place in the quarterfinals.

BRAZIL IS OUT

For some, it was the best match of Mexico '86. For others, it was one of the worst of all time.

For everyone else, it was a supremely intense match, with each team seizing the advantage from time to time, a match featuring grand entrances, beautiful goals, and spectacular saves. A tie might have done more justice, but one of these two teams would have to be eliminated.

It took place in Guadalajara's Jalisco, on the twenty-first of June, 1986. Two of the flashiest teams on earth, France and Brazil, were squaring off in the quarterfinals. Brazil was coming off a 4–0 thrashing of Poland; France had downed world champions Italy 2–0.

Two great scorers would be going head-to-head: Platini and Careca. Their duel was evenly played, and each scored in the first half. But just when it seemed as if the contest was destined for overtime, something inexplicable happened: Zico entered the match for Müller, and was immediately assigned to take a penalty kick in the closing minutes.

Cold, and maybe a bit nervous, he failed.

Incredible!

So the match did end in a 1–1 tie, and went into overtime. In the thirty additional minutes, the balance could have easily shifted in either team's favor. Both pressed hard for a winner, and both came up with big saves to preserve the tie.

TRIVIA

Who failed to convert a penalty at the end of the Brazil versus France match in 1986?

And that's how it went. The scoreboard remained unchanged, and it was left up to penalties. It was the second consecutive time that France had to decide a World Cup match in such a way, an echo of their game against the Germans in Spain '82.

In the penalty round, both Platini and Sócrates met with the same misfortune as Zico and failed to convert their attempts. But then there was Julio César, and it was all over. He failed as well, and France was in the semifinals.

Nobody could believe it, least of all the millions of Brazilians watching back home on TV. For the second consecutive World Cup, the *"Scratch"* had played beautiful soccer but still found themselves denied, just outside the gates of the final.

With Brazil gone, the stage was set for the Maradona Show on the following day.

"ADIÓS," MEXICO

June 21, 1986, would go down in history as the Day of the Penalties. After France and Brazil came Mexico and West Germany. The game took place on the field of the Universitario de Monterrey that same day. For ninety minutes, the Mexicans played well enough to win,

but some German luck (and a pair of huge saves by Schumacher) held them off. Time ended with the scoreboard blank, and the match went into overtime. It was the second match of the day—and the third of the tournament—to post a World Cup record.

The scoreboard was still clean after thirty additional minutes, and thus headed for penalties. Again: twice in one day and three times in one World Cup. Again: records.

Here is where Schumacher entered the picture and proved to be the bane of all of Mexico. The German goalkeeper managed to save four penalties that day! One, two, three, four—something as historic as this was stupefying.

TRIVIA
How was Mexico eliminated from their own World Cup in 1986?

Negrete kept the home team from being shut out, being the only one to convert his try.

Mexico had been eliminated, but they weren't without reasons to feel proud. It was their best World Cup performance ever, and they did it on their home soil. And they had proven to be capable hosts, as Mexico '86 was already a commercial and popular success.

Will the curse be lifted in Germany '06?

We shall see!

MARADONA'S TWO LEFTS

One was with the hand, the other with the foot. But both were big lefts. I'm talking about the most sensational performance by a single player in a World Cup match, one that instantly went down in history and that is still recalled with affection and a touch of nostalgia. Especially by us Argentines.

The setting was, fittingly enough, the Azteca, which was filled to capacity that twenty-second of June. Over a hundred thousand souls were there to see the quarterfinal match between England and Argentina, rivals in both soccer and politics. People were still talking about Rattín's ejection in 1966, and about the stupid Falklands War of 1982.

The first half was completely one-sided, with Argentina pressing and England defending. Maradona was ranging far and wide across the pitch, searching for a chink to exploit in the British defense, but their back line was closed up tight as could be.

But all that changed five minutes into the second half.

A bad clearance by the English defense left a dangerous ball bouncing back toward their own goal, where Maradona was waiting. The goalkeeper, Peter Shilton, came off his line to punch the ball away, but Maradona got there first, just barely touching the ball with his head—and with the help of his left hand—into the back of the net. Goal! All of England protested, but the call stood.

Argentina 1, England 0.

In a basement in Queens, a few thousand miles from the Azteca, my friends and I laughed and debated the goal's validity. We didn't celebrate much. "Was it legit?" we asked one another. The video replays seemed to show Maradona raising his left hand as he went up for the header, but it still seemed inconclusive. Today, of course, after reviewing a wealth of visual evidence—and after El Diego himself has confessed that the goal was scored with the help of "the hand of God"—there is no more doubt.

That afternoon, we weren't quite sure. But what did it matter . . . we were winning!

The "hand of God" was completely forgotten a mere four minutes later, with the advent of Maradona's second goal. I won't even try to describe it, because I'm sure you've all seen it a thousand times or more over the past twenty years. Suffice it to say that he broke free in his own half of the field, went on a sixty-yard run over ten seconds of game time, took on no fewer than five English defenders along the way . . . and all the while Tirado's voice was pouring from the television set, shouting (as he had been all World Cup long): *"Diego! Dieguito! Diegote!"*

I'll offer up one last fact: according to the writings of Jorge Valdano, Diego later told him that during the course of that sixty-yard run, he had been looking to pass to him the entire time but couldn't "find the space" to do so.

Thank God! History might have been written differently.

The legendary soccer commentator from Mexican television, Don Ángel Fernández, jokingly told me once that when Maradona scored his famous goal, Queen Elizabeth took off running through the halls of Buckingham Palace, shouting, "Who is that man? Is he one of my subjects?"

TRIVIA
Which World Cup goal became known as "the hand of God"?

She wished!

It was the greatest World Cup goal of all time, the most famous, the most ostentatious, and it set the tone for the rest of Argentina's championship run. Back in Queens, my friends and I dashed out of the basement to celebrate as God would have willed it: with a little soccer scrimmage at a park in Flushing.

Oh . . . I almost forgot. England scored once toward the end of the match, in the 81st minute. It was courtesy of Gary Lineker, who went on to finish as the tournament's top scorer, with six goals to his name.

Congratulations!

SPAIN IS OUT, TOO

That afternoon, the festival of ties and penalty shots that defined Mexico '86 continued.

Now it was Belgium and Spain's turn. The *furia* was coming off the 5–1 beating they gave to Denmark, and the Red Devils had left the Soviets in their own wake.

This match, too, took place on the twenty-second of June, this time at Puebla's Estadio Cuauhtemoc, and Spain did everything in their power to win. But it just wasn't their day. The game was tied 1–1 after ninety minutes and so went into overtime, where Spain continued to fight on, trying to take advantage of their superior physical fitness, as the Belgians were exhausted from their battle with the Soviets.

But the Spanish goal never materialized. The thirty minutes of overtime ended with the score still knotted at one apiece, and—for the third time in a twenty-four-hour span—a World Cup match would be decided from the penalty spot.

Belgium's strikes proved the more true, and their lease on life continued, though they would be facing El Diego in the semifinals.

THE SECOND AZTECA FINAL

Sixteen years had passed since the last such event, but the *fiesta* was still the same.

And the guest of honor was once again the best player of the Cup, and the best player in the world at the time. In 1970, over a hundred thousand spectators filled the stands to watch the show Pelé put on. This time, 114,580 were on hand to see Maradona.

West Germany, led by the great Franz Beckenbauer, had struggled—following a rather up-and-down path, as was their custom—to reach this point. In the first round, they had drawn with Uruguay, defeated Scotland, and fallen to Denmark. Then they cruised past Morocco before finally outlasting Mexico in penalty kicks. But they'd saved their best for the semis, where they put a solid ninety minutes together and ousted France 2–0.

Argentina, led by Carlos Salvador Bilardo, rolled in like a freight train. And Diego Armando Maradona was its engine. After eliminating England with his two goals, he repeated the feat in the semis by dropping another pair on Belgium.

Back at Ñato's house a special menu had been put together, and the guest list expanded. The basement was packed with people—all Argentines, all anxious, both over the play on the field and the steaks out on the grill.

The match started off tight. Matthaeus was all over Maradona, reminiscent of Beckenbauer marking Charlton back in the '66 final. Neither of the two sides was able to fully settle into their game plan. But Argentina was the first to find their form. Slowly they began to control both the ball and the match, but still they struggled to breach the wall of the German defense. It took twenty-three minutes, but they did break through, thanks to a set play. It might have been the only way.

Matthaeus fouled José Cuciufo along the right sideline. Jorge Burruchaga lofted the free kick into the six-yard box. Schumacher went up to punch it clear, but he never quite arrived. Instead, it was the Argentine center, José Brown, who rose up to meet the ball, heading it straight and true, deep into the back of the German net.

Goal! *¡Goool de Argentina!*

Back in the basement in Queens, we stopped eating and reservedly jumped for joy...careful not to bang our heads on the ceiling. Argentina 1, West Germany 0.

¡Vamos Argentina, carajo!

Even after conceding the first goal of the match, the Germans inexplicably continued to hang back and defend. This opened things up for Maradona and his teammates, who continued to press their advantage, trying to thread their way through their opponents' back line. But they couldn't seem to break through again. And that's how the first half came to a close. It wasn't the best half of play—for Maradona, or anybody else, really—but we were ahead.

The second half was better.

In front of the Azteca Stadium in Mexico.

Argentina came out in strike mode, and the Germans were still defending. In the 10th minute, Maradona initiated a play at midfield that ended at the feet of Jorge Valdano, who broke free up the left-hand side. He reached the German area, and when Schumacher came out to contest him, Valdano displayed a deft and subtly elegant touch, playing the ball to the right—and into the back of the German net.

¡Goooool! everyone yelled, whether at the Azteca, in Queens, or back home in Argentina.

That was it! At 2–0, we were already feeling like world champions. But . . . watch out . . . this was West Germany, after all. They don't go away easily.

Indeed, they weren't done yet. They took advantage of the subsequent letdown in the Argentine attack and began to create some dangerous opportunities near Nery Pumpido's goal. Until that point, our keeper hadn't had much to do that day.

In the 75th minute, West Germany had themselves a corner kick on the left-hand side. It was taken by Völler, flicked on by Brehme, and Rummenigge got enough of his foot to the ball to send it into the net. Goal West Germany.

All eating in the basement in Queens came to a halt.

Five minutes later came a similar play: Brehme took a corner kick from the left side, Berthold headed it toward the goal, and Völler headed it home to tie the match at two goals apiece.

TRIVIA

Who scored the winning goal for Argentina in Mexico '86?

Our hunger was completely gone. Nobody said a word. The only sounds in the room were the voices of Tirado and Longo coming from the television.

There was still nearly ten minutes to play, and if we didn't get ourselves together, the Germans were going to do it again. Thank God we had Maradona on the field that day. Barely a minute after the second German goal, he gathered the ball near the center circle. He saw Burruchaga open, and lofted a fine long pass his way. "El Burru" broke quickly away from Briegel, heading toward Schumacher's penalty area with the ball close at his feet. When the German keeper came out to close down the angle, Burruchaga clipped it past him, just inside the far post.

¡Gooool! ¡GOOOOL carajo!

Now the championship was ours for sure!

The tickertape (à la '78) did not fall, but the Azteca crowd celebrated with flags, horns, and thunderous applause. Back in Ñato's basement, we took another helping of blood sausage and opened another bottle of wine.

Argentina 3, West Germany 2.

We were two-time world champions! Maradona received the FIFA World Cup from Mexican president Miguel de la Madrid, kissed it, and held it aloft proudly for everyone to see. He was on top of the world, and this was his coronation as the new King of Soccer, the best player on the planet.

I wasn't even hungry. All I wanted to do was go play soccer. So we left the Queens basement and ran out to celebrate with a pickup match in Flushing park.

Italy 1990:
Schillaci's World Cup—(Whose?)

Everything was going well. Until we got to Italy.

The general consensus is that this was the worst World Cup. In '90 the biggest stars failed to live up to their billing, and the tournament's top goalscorer was a relative stranger. There were a pair of emotional encounters, but nothing to compare with the history of this grand event. And, unfortunately, the record-setting number of ties and games decided by penalty kicks reached all the way to the final.

It was all quite unexpected.

We're talking about Italy, after all: the world soccer power, cradle of some of history's greatest players, and the home of the most expensive and competitive league in Europe.

But the fact of the matter is that—with a few exceptions—the fourteenth FIFA World Cup of Soccer, Italy '90, left much to be desired.

ITALIAN ENTHUSIASM

The fault was not with the organizers, nor with the Italians in general. The entire nation was ready to put on a spectacular show in marvelous cities with majestic stadiums. They had all the resources and enthusiasm they could need.

This was the first World Cup to feature night games, which was done (as you'll no doubt guess) for television purposes. Games were

scheduled according for times that would draw the greatest worldwide viewing audience. Not too late, not too early. Remember that by 1990, the World Cup was already an ultracommercial event, and the broadcast rights fetched many millions of dollars.

Everywhere you went you were reminded of the event by the ubiquitous posters and souvenir stands. And speaking of souvenirs, the official mascot for Italy '90 was a strange-looking doll, not unlike a robot, formed out of blocks similar to a Rubik's Cube, though in the colors of the Italian flag (green, red, and white), with no feet, and a ball for a head. It's name was Ciao.

PLEASANT SURPRISES

Despite everything to the contrary, Italy '90 held a few pleasant surprises.

Colombia was back after an absence of twenty-eight years, while Costa Rica, and Ireland made their World Cup debuts, bringing fresh blood and fresh faces, as well as an energy and desire to impress. It flew in the face of the staunch defensive mind-set of most other participants, and all three were able to advance into the second round. Ireland got as far as the quarterfinals.

Egypt was another big surprise. They returned to the world stage after a fifty-six-year absence, and not even the Dutch could defeat them. Only England was able to break down their defense and emerge with a slim victory.

The Americans also made a good impression. They had qualified for the first time since 1950, and despite the fact that they were unable to win a first-round game, they did show promise and progress as a soccer nation.

Of all the smaller nations that participated in Italy '90, the best performance was turned in by Cameroon. With a joyful style of play, they defied all expectations and advanced to the quarterfinals, where they played one of the best matches of the entire summer.

THE REPRIMANDS: MEXICO AND CHILE

One was because of a player; the other was because of the directors. In Chile's case, the goalkeeper Roberto Rojas put on such a show on the field that he ended up costing his country the chance to play in that year's World Cup, the next one as well, and several other international competitions.

Here's what happened: in September of 1989, Chile was playing their final qualifying match against Brazil, away, at the Maracanã. Both teams were tied in the South American standings, and only the winner would go on to the finals. The first half closed 1–0 in favor of Brazil. Near the start of the second half, someone in the stands lit a flare and threw it in the direction of Rojas. It landed very close to the Chilean keeper—but did it hit him? Rojas fell to the ground, writhing in pain, and there seemed to be blood on his face. It did seem serious. His teammates did not wait for a stretcher to arrive, carrying him into the dressing room themselves. The Chilean captain pulled his remaining players from the field, and the match was suspended.

FIFA, CONMEBOL, the Federación Chilena de Fútbol, the Confederação Brasileira de Futebol, and the rest of the soccer world began their investigations of the incident. After examining video footage and interviewing other players, they concluded that Rojas had suffered a self-inflicted wound to his eyebrow. FIFA suspended him, his captain, the team doctor, and the head trainer for life, and they banned the Chilean team at large from competing in the 1994 World Cup.

For several months, Rojas steadfastly denied having caused his own injury. But soon his conscience began to hang heavy on him. He admitted his ploy in May of 1990.

THE CASE OF FALSE IDENTITIES

Mexico's deal was far more complicated.

They called it *El Caso de Los Cachirules*, which in Mexico means "The Case of the False Identities."

It involved one of the Mexican Soccer Federation's "coaches" who falsified birth certificates for some of the players in order to shave a few years off their age. The practice had been going on for many years before it was uncovered by an investigative journalist. Though the discovery was largely thanks to the idiocy of the Federación itself: several official publications listed the names of players who had also participated in the 1988 Pan-American games, but with different dates of birth.

And so the inquiries began. The press took it and ran, and eventually the folly reached FIFA, which did its own investigation that resulted in a two-year ban from international competitions. The punishment included being banned from the 1990 World Cup.

Basically what had happened was that the federation would send older players to some Mexican town where he would meet with a patently

TRIVIA
Why did FIFA ban Mexico before Italy '90?

corrupt local official who would issue them a new, counterfeit birth certificate. With two less years to his name, the player was ready to go.

Of course, the practice wasn't limited to Mexico. The problem is that they were caught with their hands in the cookie jar.

THE TWENTY-FOUR CLUB

Italy '90 was the third World Cup to feature twenty-four teams.

And the format would remain the same: six groups of four teams each, with the top two in each group advancing to the elimination round, along with the four best third-place finishers. Here is the draw:

Group A (Rome and Florence): Italy, Austria, Czechoslovakia, U.S.A.

Group B (Milan, Naples, Bari): Argentina, Cameroon, Romania, U.S.S.R.

Group C (Turin, Bologna): Brazil, Sweden, Costa Rica, Scotland

Group D (Milan, Bologna): West Germany, Yugoslavia, Colombia, United Arab Emirates

Group E (Verona, Udine): Belgium, Uruguay, Spain, South Korea

Group F (Cagliari, Palermo): England, Holland, Ireland, Egypt

THE GREAT ABSENCE

France. After three consecutive wonderful performances in the World Cup, the French would not be traveling to Italy.

The generation of Platini had given way to a new one that didn't quite measure up. And, sad to say, Platini himself had something to do with the failure. He started off the qualifying stages as France's coach, but things were going so bad for *les bleus* that a change was quickly made. Henri Michel was called in, but it was already too late. They weren't able to dig themselves out of the hole, and France was left out of the finals for the first time in many years.

THE RETURN OF COLOMBIA

Speaking of new generations, what about Colombia?

It was their greatest of all time. An incomparable constellation of stars: elegant players and exceptional talents that defined a new era of Colombian soccer and elevated them to a higher international level. So much so, in fact, that they would be dark-horse favorites to with it all in U.S.A. '94.

The names are now familiar: José René Higuita, the late Andrés Escobar, Bernardo Redín, Luis "El Chonto" Herrera, Leonel Alvarez, Luis Carlos Perea, Freddy Rincón, and the brightest star of them all, the sensational Carlos Valderrama, "El Pibe" of Colombian soccer.

The magic behind this great team—the man who found and formed most of those players—was the dentist Francisco "Pacho" Maturana, the man who modernized Colombian soccer. A year before the World Cup, he had won the Copa Libertadores with his team, Medellín's Atlético Nacional. After he made his national-team debut against Israel, his ticket to Italy was guaranteed.

TRIVIA
Who was Colombia's coach for Italy '90?

This was Colombia's second World Cup appearance, after their unforgettable performance in 1962.

They opened against the United Arab Emirates in Bologna's Estadio Renato Dall'ara on the ninth of June. (Germany '06 will also kick off on the ninth of June.) They played as was to be expected: with joy and effectiveness, striking and defending well. They won 2–0, with the goals coming from Redín and "El Pibe."

TRIVIA
Which World Cup saw the debut of "El Pibe"?

Colombia's second match was against Yugoslavia. For their efforts they deserved at least a tie. They dominated almost the entire match, and all but scored on a number of occasions. But the Yugoslavians managed to keep them under wraps, and capitalized on their opportunity to score. Colombia lost 1–0.

The third match was decisive. They had to win in order to stay alive, or else hope that a draw would leave them among the top third-place finishers. And they were staring directly at one of the finalists from the last World Cup: West Germany, led by Lothar Mattaeus and coached by the venerable Franz Beckenbauer.

The two teams were still stuck on 0–0 in the 89th minute, when Pierre Littbarski finally got the Germans on the board. ¡Qué pena! Colombia would be going home.

But wait . . .

One minute later, "El Pibe" threaded a pass through several German defenders to Freddy Rincón. He entered the area and beat the

TRIVIA
Who was the coach of West Germany during Italia '90?

keeper, Bodo Illgner, sneaking it right between his legs. Goal! The match ended in a draw, and Freddy & Co. were through to the second round.

I think they're still celebrating in the streets of Colombia!

RETURN OF THE U.S.A.

Mexico's ban ended up helping the United States.

It was the triumphant return of one of the World Cup's original teams...though you might not have thought of them like that. But remember, the U.S. played in '30, '34, and '50, where they defeated the English 1–0. After that, they dropped off the map.

> **TRIVIA**
> Name the two Latino stars of the U.S. team at Italy '90?

But the American team that made its way to Italy in 1990 represented the most successful generation in the history of U.S. soccer, and they'd proven themselves to be one of the top ten teams in the world. Their roster included names like Tony Meola, Alexi Lalas, John Harkes, John Doyle, Paul Caligiuri, Eric Wynalda, and two young men with roots in the Río Plata region and who are both members of the National Soccer Hall of Fame: Marcelo Balboa and Tab Ramos.

Both Marcelo and Tab had paid their dues in the States, in the APSL, and both had been standout members of their college teams, the former with UC San Diego, the latter with North Carolina.

But their debut in Italy '90 was one to forget. They faced Czechoslovakia in Florence on June 9th, and were completely dismantled by a score of 5–1. Caligiuri had the only goal for *los gringuitos*.

Despite the rough start, Team U.S.A. was not afraid to step back out on the field for their second match—against the Italians, no less—in Rome's Olympic Stadium. Italy struck early, in the 11th minute of play. And we all know what happens when Italy strikes first: they drop back and apply the *"catenaccio"* defense. This time was no different. Our boys sought to find the equalizer, but it proved an impossible task. They lost 1–0 and were left without hope of advancing.

Their third and final game was against Austria, who had also been eliminated heading into the match. They lost again, 2–1, but even so, the experience had galvanized a group of young players filled with class, energy, and promise.

Many would be back in 1994, where they would write an important page in the history of U.S. soccer.

DEBUT OF "LOS TICOS"

First there was Mexico. Then came Costa Rica also known as *los ticos.* The colorful Serbian coach Bora Milutinovic was back in the World Cup, though with a brand-new team. Like Colombia and the United States, Costa Rica was entering an age of great players.

Their most memorable figures were the goalkeeper Gabelo Conejo, Roger Flores, Germán Chavarría, Oscar Ramírez, and the striker Juan Arnoldo Cayasso, as well as one who would later go on to success in Mexico, Hernán Medford. They also featured the player who will be coaching *"el tricolor tico"* in Germany '06 (his second consecutive such appearance): Alexandre Guimaraes.

Los ticos shared Group C with the mighty Brazilians and two European sides: Scotland and Sweden. On paper, it was a very difficult group. Everyone hoped that Bora's squad would have a strong run, but what happened was beyond even that.

Unlike almost every other first-time team, *los ticos* started off with a win. They faced Scotland on June 11th, and a Cayasso goal at the start of the second half was enough to give them a 1–0 victory.

A Costa Rican *fiesta. ¡Pura vida!* as they say.

Their second match was against Brazil. And contrary to what many expected, *los ticos* were not intimidated. On the contrary, they had their feet well under them that day, and frustrated the Brazilians for much of the match, handcuffing them until Müller finally got them on the board. It would prove to be the only goal of the day, as the *ticos'* attack was shut out. Brazil won 1–0, but the international press had taken notice of the Central Americans' abilities.

TRIVIA

What was the second team Bora Milutinovic took to a World Cup?

June 20th of that World Cup summer would be a historic day for Costa Rican soccer. Bora's selection was facing Sweden and needed a win in order to advance to the second round, as Colombia had done the previous day in Milan.

Near the end of the first half, they were on the short side of a 1–0 score. Enter Medford, and everything changed. Flores found the equalizer in the 75th minute, and with only two minutes remaining, Medford had himself the winner.

If there was any doubt before, now there was a true *fiesta* going on throughout Costa Rica. *Los ticos* had given their country the most glorious moment in their soccer history.

They were in the second round. Incredible!

But what the World Cup giveth, the World Cup also taketh away. The joy would last but three days. On June 23rd, in Bari, they faced off

against the mighty Czechs, who had earlier bombarded the United States. The Costa Rican dream was over. Ronald Gonzáles scored for *los ticos*, but the Czechs had four of their own, for a 4–1 victory.

Bora and his team returned home, sad yet satisfied. Upon their arrival, they were given a hero's welcome. And very well deserved, I should say.

TRIVIA
Who eliminated Costa Rica from their first-ever World Cup?

KLINSMANN'S DEBUTS

In Germany '06 he will make his debut as coach. In Italy '90 he made his debut as a player.

I'm referring, of course, to the great German striker Jurgen Klinsmann, star of Stuttgart and Bayern Munich in Germany, Inter Milan and Sampdoria in Italy, Monaco in France, and Tottenham in England, where he finally retired in 1998, at the age of thirty-four, the veteran of three World Cups.

When Italy '90 got under way, Klinsmann was playing for Inter Milan, and his first two World Cup matches that summer were played on Inter's home turf: Giuseppe Meazza field. Maybe that's why he started off on fire. In his—and West Germany's—first match, against Yugoslavia, he scored his first World Cup goal en route to a 4–1 win.

In the second match, against the United Arab Emirates, he struck again, and the Germans had a 5–1 victory. It was their most auspicious offensive start in years, and it was thanks in no small part to Klinsmann.

TRIVIA
In which World Cup did Jürgen Klinsmann make his debut?

Their third match was (as I mentioned) against Colombia, whom they tied 1–1. And they continued to play well as they opened their second-round play. Klinsmann scored again to help down Holland 2–1, and their march toward the final continued.

I had the great pleasure to get to know this amiable German in a soccer setting. We had both been invited to bid farewell to a common friend, Carlos Hermosillo, at the Estadio Azul in Mexico in 2001. Klinsmann played on a team of international stars, while I played on one composed of journalists and television commentators.

Both teams shared the same locker room, and so we were able to meet. He graciously signed a ball that I always keep with me for World Cup autographs, and when he was preparing to head out onto the field, he realized that he had forgotten his shin guards. Since I had already played in the press match, I offered him mine to use, and he accepted.

What an honor!

Jurgen Klinsmann played in Carlos Hermosillo's farewell match wearing my shin guards!

And he scored one from midfield!

When the match ended, he thanked me effusively, which I didn't quite understand. It was just a pair of shin guards. Who wouldn't have loaned them out, especially to a player of his caliber? I was certainly touched!

In fact, Klinsmann never forgot my generosity. I saw him again in 2005 during the Confederations Cup, and he greeted me warmly, with memories of that locker-room meeting back at the Estadio Azul.

OTHER FIRST-TIMERS

There were several other young players of considerable worth who made their debuts at Italy '90, but none of them left quite the impression that Klinsmann did.

TRIVIA
What do Maldini, Baggio, Gullit, van Basten, and Hagi all have in common?

They include the Dutchmen Ruud Gullit, Marco van Basten, Ronaldo Koeman, and Frank Rijkard (who today is the coach of Real Madrid); the Italians Franco Baresi, Paolo Maldini, and Roberto Baggio; the Uruguayans Ruben Paz and Ruben Sosa; and Romania's Gheorghe Hagi.

THE BRAZILIANS OF 1990

They were good, but nothing like the 1970 squad.

Once again, the three-time world champions were renovating their lineup after the retirements of Sócrates, Zico, and Falcão.

Holdovers from the '86 *seleção* included Alemão, Careca, and Müller. And of the new players that came to Italy that summer, five of them would eventually help lead Brazil to their fourth World Cup title. They were the goalkeeper Claudio André Taffarel, the dangerous left winger Branco, the great containment midfielder Dunga, and two young strikers who didn't see much action that summer: Romario, who only appeared in one match, and Bebeto, who didn't appear at all. The coach was Sebastián Lazaroni.

TRIVIA
What was Romario's first World Cup?

There were no real slipups in the first round, but neither did they blow anybody away. They beat Sweden 2–1 before struggling mightily to down Costa Rica 1–0. In their last match, they managed only a 1–0 win over the lowly Scots.

They advanced to the second round, where they faced the Argentines, who this time were led by the great Caniggia. And you all know what happened there.

SCHILLACI SAVES LA PATRIA

Schilla-*who*? Where'd he come from?

It seems strange, but nobody had heard of him. He wasn't even supposed to be a starter. But as surprising as it may seem, he came out of nowhere to lead Italy into the semifinals.

His name was Salvatore Schillaci, affectionately known as Toto. He was twenty-six years old and a native of Palermo. He played six seasons with Messina in the Italian second division before being traded to the powerful Juventus one year before the Cup. There, he helped the team to an Italian league title, as well as a UEFA Cup title. For his efforts, he was given a last-minute spot on the *azzurri* roster.

Toto was on the bench when Italy kicked off their first match against Austria. But as time passed and the scoreboard remained blank, Coach Azeglio Vicini decided to use him as a second-half substitute. Four minutes after stepping onto the field, Toto scored the winner.

He didn't start the next match either, the one against the United States, but again he was brought in as a second-half sub, and his play helped Italy to another 1–0 win.

For the final first-round match, against the Czechs, the coach relented and placed him in the starting lineup. Schillaci did not disappoint. He opened the scoring in the 9th minute: his second goal of the Cup. By that point, all of Italy was talking about Toto. Everyone wanted to know more about the sensational kid from Palermo who spoke the language of goals. Italy went on to win 2–0, and was through to the second round.

There they faced Uruguay, and Toto's starting job was assured. The first half ended without a goal for either team, but Schillaci came out firing in the second half, and soon he had Italy on the board. They went on to yet another 2–0 win, and Totomania was sweeping the peninsula.

They faced Ireland in the quarterfinals, and all the world's eyes were on Schillaci. The stands were alive with Italians crying: *"To-to! To-to! To-to!"*

And who do you think had the decisive goal?

Why, Toto, of course. It seems like a Hollywood script, right? It was his fourth goal in five matches.

TRIVIA

Who was the top goalscorer from Italy '90?

Italy was through to the semifinals, where they would face Argentina in a bout that was billed as "Schillaci vs. Maradona."

MARADONA AND THE TWO-TIME CHAMPIONS

Speaking of Maradona, he was back for his third World Cup, and filled with fortune and fame.

At the time, he was enjoying a successful career with the Italian club Naples, and the people there loved him. He helped them to the Italian league title for the first time in their history in 1984, and to a European title in 1989.

He was joined on the Argentine team by several old friends from their championship run in 1986, such as Nery Pumpido, Oscar Ruggeri, Sergio Batista, Jorge Burruchaga, Ricardo Giusti, and Julio Olarticoechea. The coach was once again Carlos "El Narigón" Bilardo.

First-timers on the Argentine squad included Abel Balbo, José Basualdo, and two others who would go on to make some unexpected history: Claudio Caniggia and Sergio Goycochea. The former would knock Brazil out of the competition: the latter would set a record for penalties saved.

When the World Cup began, they were considered favorites along with Italy, West Germany, England, Holland, and, of course, Brazil. Nevertheless, they all failed to live up to expectations, and though Argentina did manage to reach the final, it was almost as if they did so simply with the luck of a defending champion. Throughout their run, they struggled to score, and their style of play was a shadow of the inspired show they put on during Mexico '86.

TRIVIA

Who scored the goal against Argentina in the opening match of Italy '90?

A hint of things to come was revealed in their opening match, on June 8th, in Milan. There Argentina faced Cameroon, and fell 1–0 on a goal by Omam Biyik, who would later go on to play for Club América.

And so began the long and winding road to the championship final. With difficulties at every step.

For their second match, they traveled to Maradona's club's stadium in Naples, where they defeated the Russians 2–0, but it came at the cost of their starting goalkeeper. In a collision with a teammate, Nery Pumpido broke his leg and was knocked out of the rest of the World Cup. He was replaced by his backup, Sergio Goycochea, who soon became the most prominent player on that team.

Next they faced Romania in that same stadium, and they drew

1–1. They weren't even in second place in their group. Short on glory, they shuffled into the second round as one of the third-place qualifiers.

That's where things got really interesting. Keep reading, and you'll see what I mean.

MY FIRST WORLD CUP ON TELEVISION

Not watching it on television, but working in television.

If you're keeping count, Italy '90 was the eighth World Cup of my life, but the first one that found me working in front of a TV camera. That's why it will always occupy a special place in my heart, despite the generally poor quality of play and Argentina's distressing performance.

When that summer's World Cup began, I had been working in television for about two years. My most recent appointment was as host of a Canal 41–Nueva York news program, along with a lovely Cuban woman named Marcia Julián, called *5:30 En Punto*. The legendary anchor Gustavo Godoy had given me the opportunity.

I had made my television debut with Telemundo in 1988 as a reporter for *Día a Día* and *Deportes Telemundo*. That's how I met Tony Tirado and Norberto Longo, who had left Univision by then. The lead Telemundo commentator for Italy '90 was the new voice of Spanish-language soccer, my friend Andres Cantor, who was accompanied by Longo, freshly returned to Univision. (You know how this business can be!)

On account of the World Cup, our New York program did not come on at its regularly scheduled time. It was pushed back to a night-time slot that we called *5:30 En Punto en el Mundial*. That's where we reviewed the day's games and offered our analysis. It was the first time that I was ever able to see every single World Cup game, and to comment on all the plays, players, and goals. I loved it. I had found a new vocation, something that has led me to where I am today.

Now that I was on television, I had to maintain some measure of "objectivity" and control my emotions every time Argentina was on the field. It wasn't easy. Their match against Italy was so nerve-racking that I was sweating bullets.

But in the end I was able to. I learned how to distance myself from what was happening down on the pitch.

MILLA VS. HIGUITA

All of Colombia's first-round joy went up in smoke with a single mistake by René Higuita.

Everyone was used to seeing him come off of his line—and even his area—to play for a spell like an extra sweeper, and it had garnered him a lot of attention over the years. One day, though, such excursions were bound to cost the team a goal. But what nobody ever imagined was that the day would be June 23, 1990.

The Colombian squad, still riding the emotional wave of their arrival in the second round, was facing the "Green Lions" of Cameroon, who were themselves ecstatic. The stage was the San Paolo in Naples. It was evenly played, with the Colombians perhaps getting the better of the play. There was no score after ninety minutes, and the match was the first of the second round to go into overtime.

There the Africans began to gain some advantage, especially the star of their roster. His name was Roger Milla, a thirty-eight-year-old veteran (and the oldest player of the tournament) who had been convinced to come out of retirement for one more run. And it proved to be the right move, because in this match he would be the hero.

He opened the scoring in the 106th minute, and three minutes later he found himself facing Higuita, who had come well off his line to make a play on the ball. The Colombian keeper tried to put a move on Milla, just as he had a thousand times before in his career. But this time his opponent dispossessed him of the ball and summarily deposited it in the back of his unguarded net.

Colombians both on the field and off—both in the stands and in front of their televisions—simply couldn't believe it. How could Higuita have risked all that in a game of such magnitude?

Redín responded nearly at the end of overtime, but the damage had already been done. Cameroon was advancing to the quarterfinals, and Colombia was on their way home with a horrible taste in their mouth.

TRIVIA
What African team eliminated Colombia in Italy '90?

CANIGGIA DISPATCHES BRAZIL

I really should say "Caniggia and Goycochea," because they each did their part to dispatch Brazil in Italy '90.

They met in Turin on June 24th. "El Goyco" smothered everything that Careca and Müller threw at him, though they helped by sending a few shots wide and putting two others off the post. It marked the fourth time that the two South American powerhouses went toe to toe in a World Cup.

And as was to be expected, Maradona helped define the match.

He gathered the ball at the center circle and drove toward the

Brazilian area. When he arrived, and just before being tackled, he crossed to Caniggia, who was roaming alone along the left flank. Taffarel came out to cut down his angle, but Caniggia played it past him for the goal.

It was the 80th minute. Brazil could no nothing more. Argentina wins, 1–0. It was the first time Argentina ever beat Brazil in a World Cup.

But for Brazilians, it was the fifth straight World Cup with the disappointment of not reaching the final.

THE ROUND OF TIES

Of the first eight second-round matches played in Italy '90, four were tied after ninety minutes and had to be decided in overtime.

The first, as we've seen, was between Colombia and Cameroon. Next it was Ireland and Romania, who ended 0–0 and went to penalties before Romania finally prevailed.

TRIVIA

What World Cup broke the record for the most second-round matches to end in ties after ninety minutes?

The following day, Spain and Yugoslavia were tied at 1–1 until the latter squad scored in overtime for the win. That same day, England and Belgium played ninety minutes of scoreless soccer before the Brits finally knocked in the winner, again in overtime.

A World Cup record was set, as additional matches in the quarters and semifinals were unable to be decided in regulation.

The only teams (besides Argentina) that were able to get their results in the time allowed were Italy, which downed Uruguay 2–0, and West Germany, which beat Holland 2–1.

What was happening to soccer?

MORE PENALTIES

Things went from bad to worse.

In the quarterfinals, the winners got their results by the slimmest of margins. Those who didn't were forced to play overtime. The only memorable thing about this particular stretch of Italy '90 was the excellent play of the Argentine goalkeeper Goycochea (and the match for the ages that took place between England and Cameroon).

After eliminating Brazil, Argentina faced Yugoslavia in the quarters. The game was in Florence, on June 30th. In the first half, one of the Yugoslavian players was sent off, but we were not able to take advantage of the numerical advantage. The match ended nil to nil, and headed for overtime.

In the penalty round, "El Goyco" became a national hero after he saved not one but two shots. Incredible! And it was even more vital, because before his second save, Maradona, who had been playing hurt and was less than a hundred percent, failed to convert on his attempt.

Thanks to our goalkeeper, we won the match and advanced to the semifinals.

That same day, Italy beat Ireland with a single goal. And who do you think it came from? Why, Toto, of course! The only name on the statsheet.

The following day, July 1st, in Milan, the Germans defeated the Czechs by a similarly slim margin. And—you might not believe this— the lone goal came on a penalty kick taken by Klinsmann.

*Booo*ring!

The final encounter of those insufferable quarterfinals saved a bit of face for that World Cup. Finally! In fact, after the vibrant emotions stirred up by Costa Rica and Colombia, this was the best match of the summer.

All thanks to Cameroon.

They were up against the best English team since the side that won it all back in 1966. Gary Lineker and David Platt led the way, each of them playing in his second and final World Cup. The scoreboard lit up in the 25th minute with a goal by Platt. Cameroon tied things up on a penalty in the 61st, and four minutes later they took the lead with another lovely strike. When they were on the verge of victory—in the 83rd minute, to be exact—Gary Lineker was brought down in the box, and the Mexican official Edgardo Codesal, blew his whistle. Lineker took the penalty himself, and converted to even the score at two goals apiece. Full time came to an end and now overtime was upon them.

And what do you think happened?

Exactly! Another penalty. Codesal had blown his whistle yet again.

Lineker's take was true once again, and England had themselves a 3–2 win, thus ending the dreams of the first African team to reach a World Cup semifinal.

HURRAY FOR PENALTIES!

By this point, there was nothing else to do but simply enjoy the drama of the penalty shot. It was the only emotion to be gotten from Italy '90.

And the semifinals were no exception.

The first was between Italy and Argentina, on July 3rd, on Maradona's home turf in Naples. It was the second consecutive World Cup in which these two countries met (in Mexico '86, their first-round match ended in a 1–1 draw). It was also a hand-to-hand matchup between Maradona and Schillaci.

The Neapolitans were of divided heart. Who to support? The headlines in the local papers asked Diego's forgiveness, but they had to support Toto and the mother country in this case.

The match was evenly played and somewhat uninspired. The first notable event was when Schillaci opened the scoring in the 17th minute. Then, the Italians dropped back into their defensive mode, as per their norm. They held off the Argentine attack as long as they could, but in the 67th minute Caniggia put home a header with his back to the goal. It was especially significant in that it was the first goal conceded by the Italian keeper Walter Zenga to that point, a record of 517 scoreless minutes spanning five games.

TRIVIA

How many scoreless minutes did Walter Zenga maintain in Italy '90?

Full time ended that way, 1–1, and overtime did as well. Bring on the penalties!

Goycochea was once again the hero, and in doing so he set a World Cup record by stopping his third penalty of the tournament. It came at the expense of poor Roberto Donadoni, who for many years was blamed for the Italians' exit. One more time, luck was with us.

With the loss, Italy found themselves in the same place as Spain did back in 1982: on the outside, looking in on their own World Cup final. But in the consolation match, they beat England 2–1, with one of the goals coming by way of Schillaci. It was his sixth of the summer, enough to give him the Golden Boot award as the tournament's top scorer.

In the other semifinal, which took place in Turin, West Germany faced England in another historic rematch. It was the fourth time the two sides had faced off at a crucial stage of the World Cup; they had met after the '66 final (England), the 1970 quarterfinals (West Germany), and the second round of Spain '82 (tie).

The match was an emotional one, even if the score-board remained blank for the first hour. That's when Andreas Brehme opened the scoring for the Germans. The English pressed hard for the tie, and found it twenty minutes later—in other words, with only ten minutes to play—thanks to Lineker. After that, they went into overtime, and then (of course) to

TRIVIA

Who won the Golden Boot award at Italy '90?

penalties. The Germans rose to the occasion, and left England along the wayside.

Beckenbauer and his boys were through to their second consecutive final.

ROME'S SECOND GRAND FINALE

Please, just don't let there be another shoot-out!

That was the prayer heard round the world the day of the final, July 8th. It was a rematch four years in the making: Argentina and West Germany.

Fifty-six years had passed since the last final in Rome, back in Italy '34, which was the first one to be tied after ninety minutes of play and decided in overtime. Everyone hoped that history would not repeat itself, and that the Argentines and the Germans would have themselves an active and lively match, putting a positive cap on the prorogations and penalties that had come to define Italy '90.

They came close. There was no overtime, but there were penalties, one of which—unfortunately—defined the entire match.

And who do you think the official that day was?

Edgardo Codesal! Who else could it have been? The man attracted penalties like a magnet.

I wasn't working at the station that day, because it was a Sunday. I decided to watch the game at home, alone, because I didn't

want to burden anyone with my anxiety. The night before, I had a pre–thirtieth birthday party with some friends of mine. Mamá made me a delicious cake, which she purposefully decorated with the Argentine flag. Early the next morning, I ushered out the last few remaining guests, and—without sleeping or cleaning the house—I readied myself for the Grand Finale on television.

Argentina would be without four of their players, who were suspended for their accumulation of yellow cards. This completely altered Bilardo's strategy, and the Germans used the situa-

TRIVIA
Who was the first player ever to be sent off in a World Cup final?

Celebrating my 30th birthday in New Jersey.

tion to their advantage. In fact, they veritably dominated the match, and were often on the verge of goals.

We countered their attack as best we could, sometimes more urgently than was needed. Pedro Monzón entered the game in the second half, and he made history: he became the first player ever to be sent off in a World Cup final. Before the end of the match—during which the referee seemed like the defining man on the pitch—Gustavo Dezotti was also red-carded for rough play, and Maradona was shown the yellow for protesting the call.

But the match will always be remembered for a penalty.

Codesal blew his whistle with five minutes to play. Not only was it controversial, it would determine the outcome for the first time in finals history. Rudi Völler was brought down in the box by José Serrizuela in what seemed like a clean tackle. The protests issued, but to no avail.

Ironically, Goycochea—who had become a national hero for his penalty-saving abilities—could not stop the most important one of all. The most important of his life, perhaps. Brehme struck. "El Goyco" dove, but could not reach it.

That was the end of the match, and of the World Cup. West Germany was a three-time champion.

That's all she wrote.

The promise of a great World Cup faded into memory and time. Germany would reach another final, while Argentina has to content itself to this day with memories of glory from 1978 and '86.

I finally went to bed and tried to sleep, but I couldn't. I was too worked up, too full of anger and frustration. Some birthday present! It was hours before I fell asleep. I replayed the match a thousand times over in my head before finally I surrendered.

That night I dreamed about penalty after penalty flying into the net behind me.

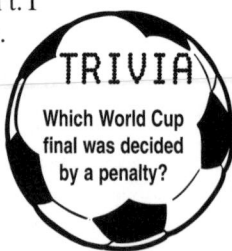

TRIVIA

Which World Cup final was decided by a penalty?

United States 1994:
The World Cup of Baggio and Romario

In his eagerness to spread soccer throughout every corner of the planet, João Havelange and FIFA managed to do the impossible: bring the World Cup to the United States of America, the home of baseball, the NBA, and football.

This was the land of soccer moms and kids running around after a ball in a suburban park. Not macho and passionate *fútbol*, played in stadiums filled with thousands of frantic fans.

Nevertheless, they were able to market "the product" effectively —in fact, contrary to the prevailing fears, U.S.A. '94 set an all-time record for attendance, its total of 3.5 million surpassing the previous standard set during Italy '90. It was an all-around huge success. There were great games, classic goals, and two bright stars who fought right up until the final match for the title of Most Valuable Player.

The Fifteenth FIFA World Cup of Soccer was taking place right here in the U.S.A. My adopted home!

Welcome!

ONE HOT CUP

And I'm talking about real heat, not the warmth of love and friendship. I'm talking about temperatures.

The fifty-two matches were played under a blazing sun, high humidity, and suffocating heat. Think about what it means to play ninety minutes of soccer in the noonday summer heat of Dallas, Orlando, New York, or Boston. Unbearable. And all of it on television, as we've said. The games had to start early enough so that the European viewers wouldn't be up too late. But nobody died, and they all played hard. Some harder than others. U.S.A. '94 gave us emotional matches and unforgettable performances by several international stars.

It also offered the drama of Maradona, the tragedy of Andrés Escobar, games in a domed stadium, a forty-two-year-old "old man," a historic

TRIVIA
What was the name of the official mascot for U.S.A. '94?

elbow, a Bulgarian surprise, and a new official mascot, a pup named "Striker."

Oh yes, and a new ball, the Adidas Questra, which was the latest in high-technology plastic.

TWENTY-FOUR FOR THE LAST TIME

U.S.A. '94 was the last World Cup to feature twenty-four teams. The heights the event had reached—coupled with the ensuing commercial demands—meant more people and more teams. It was decided that eight more would be added for 1998.

The "24 Club" was again divided into six groups of four teams each. And just as with Mexico '86 and Italy '90, the top two in each group would advance, along with the four best third-place teams.

Also, this World Cup was the first to award three points for a first-round win. It was a change specifically engineered by FIFA to discourage the ties and ensuing penalty shoot-outs that had so plagued Italy '90.

This is how the draw looked:

> **Group A** (Detroit, Los Angeles, San Francisco): U.S.A., Switzerland, Colombia, Romania
>
> **Group B** (Detroit, San Francisco): Cameroon, Sweden, Brazil, Russia
>
> **Group C** (Chicago, Dallas, Boston): Germany, Bolivia, Spain, South Korea
>
> **Group D** (Chicago, Dallas, Boston): Argentina, Greece, Nigeria, Bulgaria
>
> **Group E** (New York, Washington, Orlando): Italy, Ireland, Norway, Mexico
>
> **Group F** (New York, Washington, Orlando): Belgium, Morocco, Holland, Saudi Arabia

France and England were glaring absences. The French lost in the last minute of their last qualifying match against Bulgaria. The English, despite coming off their strong showing in Italy '90, finished third in their group behind Holland and were left home, as well.

On the other hand, the draw included a pair of newcomers: Nigeria, representing Africa, and Saudi Arabia, representing Asia.

In the case of Bolivia, it wasn't a debut per se, but for a full generation of Bolivians, it was as good as one.

BOLIVIA AND ITS DEVIL

A devil of flesh and blood, and indomitable on the field. Bolivia qualified for their third World Cup (after previous appearances in 1930 and '50) by playing the best soccer of their history. And they were led by an intelligent and gifted midfielder, Marco Antonio Etcheverry, better known as "El Diablo." He's one of the few South American players to have won championships in four different countries: in his native Bolivia with Bolvar, in Chile with Colo-Colo, in Ecuador with Emelec, and in the United States with DC United. His career also included stints with Spain's Albacete (they never let him play) and Cali's América. In Bolivia's green jersey, he reached the finals of the 1993 Copa América; and his greatest accomplishment: a trip to U.S.A. '94.

His U.S.A. '94 debut was nothing if not dramatic. He was fresh off an injury that had kept him on the sidelines for months, and in his first game back he was red-carded.

TRIVIA
What was Marco Antonio Etcheverry's first World Cup?

It happened in the first game of the World Cup, in which Bolivia faced defending champions Germany at Chicago's Soldier Field. "El Diablo" entered the match in the 79th minute, and was sent off in the 82nd. I don't think he even touched the ball!

Bolivia lost 1–0 on a goal by my friend Jürgen Klinsmann, but the quality of their performance was worthy of a tie.

In Miami with "The Devil" Marco Antonio Etcheverry and "The Angel" Gianluca Sergei Fiore.

Their second match was against South Korea, and they did little with it in a 0–0 tie. In their last match they fell to Spain 3–1, and with that they were packing their bags. They returned home, still with the desire to see "El Diablo" shine in front of the eyes of the world. That would come later, on that same North American soil, when Etcheverry joined Major League Soccer's DC United and went on to win three championships with them.

BORA AND THE "GRINGUITOS"

Once again, Bora was back in a World Cup. The soccer mercenary had helped his third team reach the finals. They paid him to field a competitive team, but Bora surpassed expectations by leading them into the second round. And showing promise, too! Only Bora could have pulled off such a feat.

> **TRIVIA**
> What was Bora Milutinovic's third team as a World Cup coach?

The marvelous Americans used their home-field advantage and fan support to enter the round of sixteen. And they did so with strong play from strong players, including two Latino stars making their second World Cup appearances: Tab Ramos and Marcelo Balboa.

Team U.S.A. was basically the same as the team from Italy '90, but much more prepared. Bora's influence was evident in their play: disciplined, excellent physical form, solid defense, and dangerous counterattacks.

The other holdovers from the previous World Cup included goalkeeper Tony Meola, defenders Thomas Dooly and Alexi Lalas, midfielder John Harkes, and strikers Paul Caligiuri and Eric Wynalda. They teamed with several players with bright futures, like Ernie Stewart, Coby Jones, and Joe-Max Moore, not to mention one of the most talented U.S. players of all time, Claudio Reyna, who was kept from the field this time around with a thigh injury.

And the roster included another Latino, the Uruguayan veteran whose experience proved invaluable to the team's efforts. I'm referring, of course, to my dear friend Fernando Clavijo, who is currently the coach of the Colorado Rapids and a member of the Hall of Fame.

These boys started off the competition by making history. Not because of their play, but because of the stadium itself.

> **TRIVIA**
> What was the first World Cup that Ernie Stewart, Coby Jones, and Joe-Max Moore played in?

THE OPENER IN THE SILVERDOME

It was the Silverdome in Pontiac, Michigan, just outside of Detroit. And it was the first domed stadium with natural grass ever used in a World Cup.

It was an experiment by FIFA that sought to take advantage of technology developed by University of Michigan scientists. The turf was seeded and grown outdoors and brought into the dome in two hundred giant hexagonal patches that were brought under the dome and put together to form the playing surface. After each match, they were removed for watering and sunlight.

Ingenious, right?

After the World Cup, they threw out the natural grass, and the Silverdome returned to its old artificial turf on which the NFL's Detroit Lions play their games.

That's where Team U.S.A. made their debut against Switzerland on June 18th. The Swiss opened the scoring in the 39th minute, but five minutes later—just before the break—Eric Wynalda scored on a booming free kick. When Eric visited us on *República Deportiva* five years later, he told us that it was, without a doubt, the greatest goal of his career. Both for the timing of it as well as the emotion.

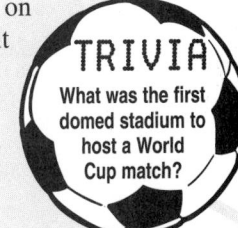

TRIVIA
What was the first domed stadium to host a World Cup match?

The match ended at one goal apiece.

In their second game, Bora's boys made even more history. This time against Colombia.

COLOMBIA—AMONG THE FAVORITES

Everyone believed in them, starting with Pelé himself, who, prior to U.S.A. '94, said that Colombia was one of his picks to win it all.

And he had good reasons, too.

"Pacho" Maturana's roster was composed of the same stars that had appeared in Italy '90. Many were finding success in foreign leagues, and they had qualified in first place in their South American group, ahead of Argentina.

And not only that, they handed the Argentines the worst defeat in their history: a 5–0 thrashing that Argentines still haven't forgotten ... or forgiven!

"El Pibe" Valderrama and his teammates Leonel Alvarez, Andrés Escobar, "El Chonto" Herrera, Luis Perea, and Freddy Rincón united with promising newcomers like "El Chicho" Serna, Iván Valenciano, the great keeper Oscar Córdoba, and the swift and sensational striker Faustino "El Tino" Asprilla.

Expectations for the team were running high. The press was focusing on them, especially on Valderrama's hair. But when the day of their opener came, they were exposed.

It was in the Rose Bowl in Pasadena. Their opponents, Romania, only went on the attack three times, but all three ventures resulted in goals. It was an ugly 3–1 defeat to start things off with. But there was no reason to give up hope. There were still two matches left, and they could still advance with wins in those.

Enter Bora and Team U.S.A.

A DEADLY GOAL

In retrospect, the match between Colombia and the United States was a horrible black mark on the history of Colombian soccer.

That day, the twenty-second of June, they lost the match. And a few days later, one of their most charismatic and beloved players would lose his life.

This is the tragedy of Andrés Escobar, the Colombian defender who scored an own goal in the loss to the U.S., and was later gunned down outside a Medellín restaurant by a fanatic. His death dramatized the reality of Colombian soccer in those days, when threats and other external pressures affected the team on the field of play.

TRIVIA
What Colombian player was murdered after scoring an own goal in a match with the United States?

It all began in the 35th minute. Escobar tried to clear a cross in front of the Colombian goal, but instead he deflected it into his own goal, past the helpless keeper Córdoba. Later, at the start of the second half, Ernie Stewart scored a second U.S. goal, effectively breaking Colombia's spirit, until the final minute of play, when Adolfo "El Tren" Valencia got one back.

The magic was gone, and it marked the end of the great Colombian team of the 1990s. They never fully recovered, and Escobar never imagined the cruel fate that lay in store for him back home.

DIEGO'S EPHEDRINE

Maradona's drama is nothing when compared with that of Escobar. But since it happened first, it felt, at the time, like a tragedy to us Argentines. And it marked the end of Maradona's career, both in the World Cup and with the national team in general. The sad end of a career without parallel.

We had struggled to qualify, needing a play-off against Australia to reach the finals, and in our debut, in Boston (actually in nearby Foxboro Stadium), on June 21st, we showed our hunger. Maradona was showing his brilliant old form, and for a brief moment we all fell under the spell again. He had got himself in fine shape so that he would be able to play one more World Cup for his daughters. As he put it, so that "Dalma and Gianinna could see their papá concentrating, training, and playing."

He was accompanied by a few other veterans from 1990 (Goycochea, Sensini, Guggeri, Caniggia, Basualdo, and Balbo) as well as by a new generation of stars, like Diego "El Cholo" Simeone, Ariel Ortega, José Chamot, Fernando Redondo, and a sterling young striker who played his club soccer in Italy and was about to come into his prime, Gabriel "Batigol" Batistuta.

"We had a hell of a team," writes Maradona in his autobiography.

We started off with a 4–0 dismantling of Greece, including three goals from Batistuta (what a debut!) and one cracker of a goal from Maradona. If we could keep up that kind of play, we could find ourselves in the championship, we all were thinking. In the second match (June 25th, also in Boston), we defeated Nigeria 2–1 guaranteeing ourselves a spot in the second round.

I was fortunate enough to be present that day: the second time in my life when I was at a World Cup match, and the first time I got to see my country play.

At the time, I was working for Deportes Univision in Miami, and during the World Cup I was hosting a *Primer Impacto* segment that summarized the games of the day. That's when I started collecting soccer jerseys. Every day I would wear a different team's colors when I presented my segment from the "satellite room."

TRIVIA
How many goals did Gabriel Batistuta score in his World Cup debut?

On the weekends, I was given permission to see a few games on my own time. One of these was the Nigeria match, which turned out to be Maradona's last one. It was barely over—the team was still celebrating joyfully—when an official doctor came up to Mardona and led him away for a drug test.

We all know what happened next.

TRIVIA
What banned substance did Maradona test positive for in U.S.A. '94?

He tested positive for the banned substance ephedrine. Everyone was shocked to hear the news. "How could Diego do that to the team?" we all were asking ourselves. He had fooled us all.

Maradona has tried to explain the results on more than one occasion, insisting that he never intentionally

tried "to gain an advantage. It was a mistake." In his autobiography he gives details and blames the team doctor for unintentionally giving him a medication that contained the banned substance. That's all. We may never know how "innocent" the doctor's prescription was, or how much "better" Maradona felt after taking it.

"The truth—the only truth—from the 1994 World Cup," he writes, "is that [team physician] Daniel Cerrini was in the wrong, and I was blamed for it. That is the only truth."

But the fact is that he was expelled from further participation in that World Cup, and FIFA suspended him for a period of eighteen months.

Argentina's third match was against Bulgaria, and we lost 2–0. We started off the second round against Romania, and the boys played one of the best matches of the entire summer, despite the psychological burden of having lost Maradona. I'll never forget it. It was July 3rd, at the Rose Bowl in Pasadena, and I was there in the stands, praying.

Unfortunately, the Romanians had the better of us that day, and broke our hearts by a score of 3–2. Adiós, U.S.A.

I returned to Miami to give my daily summary, but I just wasn't all there. I hope nobody noticed.

MEJÍA BARÓN'S "TRI"

Mexico was back in the World Cup after the embarrassing false identity scandal, which had gotten them banned by FIFA from Italy '90.

But getting there wasn't easy.

Things had changed in the CONCACAF region, and qualifying was no longer a sure thing. In fact, it took Mexico right up until their final match—when they beat Canada 2–1 in Toronto—before their tickets to U.S.A. '94 were punched.

The qualifying campaign began with high hopes, under the direction of a new coach, César Luis Menotti, who had changed the face of Argentine soccer and led them to the World Cup title in 1978.

Nevertheless, things didn't quite go as planned. Amid poor results and political bickering, Menotti resigned his position and was replaced by Dr. Miguel Mejía Barón, the former coach of Pumas and, before being moved up, of Monterrey.

U.S.A. '94 brought out the best in a new generation of players. The previous group had lost their World Cup opportunity in the wake of the FIFA ban, including Jorge "El Brody"

TRIVIA
Who did Dr. Miguel Mejía Barón replace as coach of Mexico during the qualifying series for U.S.A. '94?

Campos, Claudio "El Emperador" Suárez, "El Nacho" Ambríz, Marcelino Bernal, Joaquín del Olmo, Benjamín Galindo, Misael Espinosa, García "El Beto" Aspe, Luis "El Zague" Roberto Alves, Luis Garcia, and Hugo Sánchez.

And my good friend and colleague at *República Deportiva* Félix Fernández was the backup goalkeeper with that team.

Many considered it the best squad in Mexican soccer history, and in U.S.A. '94, they proved why. They came out on top of a group that included Italy, Ireland, and Norway, and that was despite the fact that they lost their opening game.

That took place in Washington, D.C., on the nineteenth of June. It was an intense match, and unlucky for *los tri*. It seemed as if Mexico would score at any moment, but their goal never came. What did come was one by Norway, in the 88th minute, and the Norwegians would win by that margin.

But such an inauspicious beginning did not affect Mejía Barón's boys. In their second match—against Ireland, in Orlando— Mexico put on a clinic, and came away with a 2–1 win, both their goals coming from Luis García.

In the final match of the first round, *los tri* found themselves locked in a back-and-forth struggle with Italy. They fell behind early on, but thanks to a great goal by Marcelino Bernal from outside the area, they pulled level and advanced.

TRIVIA
What Mexican player scored twice in one game in U.S.A. '94?

For the second time in history, Mexico was in the second round of a World Cup. And there they ran into the team that would become the biggest surprise of the tournament: Bulgaria.

THE CURSE OF THE PENALTIES, PART II

The first one was in the '86 Cup, against West Germany. Now it was Bulgaria's turn.

It was July 5th, and it was a match that Mexicans will never forget.

The game took place in New York (actually, at Giants Stadium in New Jersey, across the Hudson River). Bulgaria broke first with a goal from Stoitchkov in the 6th minute. Shortly thereafter, García Aspe converted a penalty for the equalizer. The score remained at 1–1 for a long while, until something completely unexpected happened: for the first time in World Cup history a goalpost was broken and a replacement had to be brought in.

The match restarted after an eight-minute delay, and Mexico was on the attack. But the Bulgarian defense was superb, and they kept the score even until the end of ninety minutes of play. They went into overtime, but nothing changed. Mexico attacking, Bulgaria defending. After 120 minutes, it was up to penalties to separate the two sides.

¡Ayayay!

Why did Mejía Barón not bring in Hugo Sánchez as a substitute? That was the question on many people's minds. He should have been made available to take a penalty shot, right? Apparently not. He never entered the match, and we will never know why. (Some have speculated that Hugo himself did not want to play, for fear of missing a penalty shot. But I doubt that.)

You already know what happened. Once again, Mexico demonstrated an abysmal incompetence from the penalty spot, unable to find the back of the net like everybody else in the world.

First García Aspe failed his penalty, then Bernal, and then Jorge Rodríguez. Three missed penalties in a row. Incredible! Suárez was the only one to succeed his try. Bulgaria's Letchkov struck the last one true, and Mexico was bounced from the World Cup. And that's all she wrote.

Let's hope they can reverse the curse in Germany '06!

BRAZIL IN SEARCH OF THE "TETRA"

The *"tetracampeão,"* that is, the first nation to win a fourth World Cup title.

Carlos Alberto Parreira had left the Middle East and had taken up once more the reins of his own native country's team. Remember, he had been at the helm of Kuwait in '86 and United Arab Emirates in

In Miami with the 1994 Brazilian team.

TRIVIA

Who was Parreira's assistant during U.S.A. '94?

'82. And to guarantee the success of the *"Scratch,"* he brought in Mario "O Lobo" Zagallo as his assistant.

And the formula seemed to work. At least it brought good luck. Brazil returned to the final after a twenty-four-year drought that included the misfortunes in Mexico '86, Spain '82, and, to a certain extent, Italy '90.

The star of the team was Romario, who was coming into the prime of his career, and proving to be an excellent coupling with Bebeto. They were joined by three veterans from the 1990 squad, Dunga, Branco, and Taffarel, who were all in great form as well.

Right from the start it was patently obvious that Brazil was coming with everything. On June 20th, they beat the Russians 2–0 at Stanford Stadium (in Palo Alto, just north of San Francisco). Romario had one of the goals—the first of his World Cup career.

From that point on, the Brazilians were unstoppable. Four days later on that same field they downed Cameroon 3–0 on goals by Romario as well as Bebeto and Marcio Santos. Next they tied Sweden 1–1 in the Pontiac Silverdome (on the outskirts of Detroit). It was Romario again, now with three goals in three matches.

To start off the second round, they stared down the hosts on the very day of their nation's birth: July 4th.

What a present!

TWO RECORDS IN ONE DAY

And speaking of Cameroon, the "Green Lions," who had wowed so many people in Italy '90, seemed to have lost some of their roar at U.S.A. '94.

The only thing they really brought to the table this time around was Roger Milla's age record. He was now forty-two years old, and the oldest ever to play in a World Cup. His team drew their first match with Sweden, lost their second to Brazil, and was slowly dismantled by the Russians in their third and final match.

TRIVIA

What is the name of the oldest player ever to appear in a World Cup match?

They lost 6–1, the most lopsided defeat of U.S.A. '94. Milla had Cameroon's lone mark upon the scoreboard.

TRIVIA

What player set the record for most World Cup goals in a single match?

In that same match, which took place on June 28th in Palo Alto, another World Cup record was set: Oleg Salenko scored five of Russia's six goals! Another historical first.

Spec-*tac*-u-lar!

He ended tied with Bulgaria's Stoitchkov for the Golden Boot, with six goals.

BAGGIO: THE OTHER STAR

What Romario did for Brazil, Baggio did for Italy. It was thanks to his goals that Italy was able to reach the final.

When U.S.A. '94 came around, Baggio was also coming into his athletic prime. He had won the Italian league and the European championships with his club, Juventus. He had also been picked as FIFA World Footballer of the Year in 1993.

The difference between him and Romario was that Baggio did not have himself a single goal in the entire first round. He didn't get on track until the second round, not unlike his compatriot Rossi had done in Spain '82.

Italy started off with a 1–0 defeat at the hands of Ireland, at Giants Stadium. After that, they beat Norway 1–0 and drew with Mexico 1–1.

In the second round, they faced Nigeria, which was something of a surprise, having advanced for their first time ever. On July 5th, in Boston, the Nigerians struck first and maintained their advantage all the way until the 88th minute of play, when the genius of Baggio finally emerged to force overtime.

There, Nigeria committed a foul inside the area, and Baggio stepped up to convert the penalty. They went on to win 2–1, alive, though barely.

In the quarterfinals, they faced Spain on that same field, and once again Baggio emerged as a last-minute hero. It was an amazing match, one rife with emotion. The score was deadlocked at 1–1 until the 87th minute, when the great Baggio broke the deadlock and sent Spain home empty-handed, yet again.

The semifinal was against another surprising selection: the incredible Bulgarians, who had eliminated the Germans. Hristo Stoitchkov was their man at the helm. In another great match, Italy came out on top 2–1. And who do you think had both goals? In a five-minute span, no less?

Why, Roberto Baggio, of course.

By then all of Italy was enamored with their new national hero, the boy from Vicenza, the calm and spiritual twenty-seven-year-old Buddhist. Thanks to his blissful oneness with the ball, Italy was through to the final for the fifth time in their history.

And just wait to see what happens to our hero there ...

THE ELBOW HEARD ROUND THE WORLD

That's the only way to describe it.

Around the world, because everyone saw it happen. Live, via satellite.

The United States had made history for reaching the second round for the first time in their World Cup history, and it was there that they faced the mighty Brazilians, on Independence Day, at the Rose Bowl in Pasadena. Millions of fans and other spectators were tuning in to watch the match on television.

Did David stand any chance against Goliath?

The match is memorable not for the result (Brazil struggled to a 1–0 win on a goal by Bebeto) but rather for the brutal elbow that the Brazilian defender Leonardo threw at our beloved Tabaré Ramos of Team U.S.A. The knockout was even worse than the one that Schumacher dealt to Battiston in Spain '82. He hit Ramos on the right temple, leaving him stretched out on the turf with a cerebral contusion and a fractured skull.

TRIVIA

Which player knocked out Tab Ramos with an elbow in U.S.A. '94?

He almost killed him!

Ramos eventually recovered, but he was off the field for six full months, while he received and accepted Leonardo's heartfelt apologies. The Brazilian was red-carded and expelled from the remainder of the World Cup.

After the famous elbow incident, Brazil continued to hammer away at their opponents, though this time with goals. In what was really one of the best matches of the entire World Cup, they outgunned Holland 3–2 in Dallas, with the goals coming from Romario, Bebeto, and Branco. In the semifinal, they got past Sweden 1–0 on a goal by Romario in the 80th minute. It was his fifth of the tournament.

Brazil was on their way to their fifth World Cup final, and they were in search of their fourth World Cup title.

THE FINAL MATCH IN THE ROSE BOWL

The great stage on which so many college football and NFL games are played was now decked out in all her festive gear for a different sort of football: the World Cup final.

The opponents, Italy and Brazil, were both three-time world champions. Both were making appearance number five in the World Cup final.

TRIVIA

Where was the final match of U.S.A. '94 played?

Under a brilliant sun and a welcoming atmosphere, a great match was awaited. It was a rematch of Mexico '70, and both teams expected their respective stars—Romario and Baggio—to shine the brightest.

Well . . . in terms of the match, neither of them could do a thing.

Nothing! It was the most boring final in history, and it ended in a goalless draw.

Once again I had flown in from Miami to see the match. But I wasn't lucky enough to get tickets. And since press passes were few and far between, I was left without a way into the Rose Bowl. In my desperation to see the match, I paid a chauffeur I met outside the stadium ten dollars to let me sit in the back of his limo and watch it on the car's tiny TV.

Luckily I didn't miss much. If it had gone down as one for the ages, I would have slit my wrists.

Overtime was boring, as well. The scoreboard remained unchanged, 0–0, and for the first time in World Cup history, the champion would be crowned only after a penalty shoot-out.

TRIVIA
Which World Cup final was decided on penalty kicks?

What a pain! Or better yet: what an embarrassment! What would the gringos think? This wasn't the introduction to soccer that they needed to see. Havelange probably wanted to die.

Even in the penalty round, the ball didn't want to seem to go in the net. Baresi booted Italy's first chance, while Pagliuca saved Marcio Santos's try for Brazil. Still 0–0. After that, Albertini, Romario, Evani, and Branco were able to convert, and the contest stood at two goals apiece. Taffarel was equal to the shot by Mássaro, but Dunga converted his: 3–2 to Brazil.

Here is where the "Golden Bambino" took his turn. Surely Superbaggio would strike true, yes?

No! He missed it!

He put his shot over the crossbar—just barely over the crossbar—and into the blue Pasadena sky. And that is how Brazil won their fourth World Cup title: with little glory and more than a touch of pain.

Which is perhaps why the celebration there on the field was marked by as many tears as hugs.

TRIVIA
Who missed the pivotal penalty shot in the final match of U.S.A. '94?

Minutes later, Captain Dunga received the FIFA World Cup trophy from U.S. vice president Al Gore. I think the chauffeur should have given me my ten bucks back, don't you?

France 1998: The World Cup of Zidane, Zuker, and Ronaldo

Once again, France was the site of a grand festival. The first time was exactly sixty years ago, in 1938, when they hosted the last of what I call the Prehistoric Cups, just before the outbreak of the Second World War.

Now it was the end of the twentieth century, and the French—the creators of the Cup—were following Italy and Mexico into the realm of the two-time hosts.

This was the biggest World Cup of all, with the most people participating. The number of participating nations had grown to thirty-two, which gave many new people a reason to see a World Cup match for the first time. The only drawback was that there were no first-round surprises. All the big fish ate up the guppies, with the exceptions of

FRANCE 98

COUPE DU MONDE

© 1994 ISL TM

Croatia and Spain. Newcomer Croatia was the surprise third-place finisher, while Spain made a disappointing first-round exit.

Another novelty of France '98 was the introduction of the "golden goal," which was basically a "next goal wins" rule for overtime periods. This was also the World Cup of red cards, with 22 in all, and of yellow cards, as well, with 250 being shown. The reason for that increase could be the intensity with which the games were played. FIFA had eliminated the possibility of third-place finishers in group play advancing to the second round, limiting that privilege to only the top two teams in each. As such, teams played harder so as to avoid being left out.

So without further adieu, let's take a look at what happened in the sixteenth FIFA World Cup of Soccer—France '98, featuring the rooster "Footix" as its official mascot.

THIRTY-TWO TEAMS, EIGHT GROUPS

The increased number of teams allowed FIFA to give a spot to every one of its Confederations, and four more to Europe, whose membership had increased after the breakup of Yugoslavia.

Representing South America were the defending champions, Brazil, along with Argentina, Chile, and Colombia. CONCACAF sent

Mexico, the United States, and a newcomer: the "Reggae Boyz" from Jamaica.

TRIVIA
Which was the first World Cup to feature the inclusion of thirty-two teams?

Africa was, for the first time, sending five nations: Morocco, Tunisia, Cameroon, Nigeria, and another rookie, South Africa. Asian representatives were Iran, Saudi Arabia, South Korea, and first-timers Japan.

The Europeans included a new country, Croatia, which had been formed by the fragmentation of the former Yugoslavia. Before the Cup, nobody would have predicted just how well they would play, or that one of their players—Davor Suker—would emerge as the winner of the Golden Boot.

The draw was arranged as such, with venues all across France:

Group A: Brazil, Scotland, Morocco, Norway
Group B: Italy, Chile, Cameroon, Austria
Group C: France, South Africa, Saudi Arabia, Denmark
Group D: Paraguay, Bulgaria, Spain, Nigeria
Group E: South Korea, Mexico, Holland, Belgium
Group F: Yugoslavia, Iran, Germany, U.S.A.
Group G: Romania, Colombia, England, Tunisia
Group H: Jamaica, Croatia, Argentina, Japan

THE "SA-ZA" DUO

As you'll recall, Chile hadn't been to the dance in several years. Their last appearance had been Spain '82. After that, they suffered the wrath of FIFA and missed three World Cups in a row.

Now *la roja* was back with new desire and new figures who had found success across the globe. Two of them formed the team's offensive core: Marcelo "El Matador" Salas, and Iván "Bam Bam" Zamorano. Combining their two last name, Chileans came up with the joint moniker "Sa-Za" for this most potent goalscoring duo in Chilean history, and one that called to mind the "Ro-Ro" combo of Ronaldo and Romario in Brazil.

TRIVIA
To whom does the nickname "Sa-Za" refer?

"Sa-Za" was supported by a balanced squad of youngsters and veterans under the direction of Nelson Acosta, and they had gone through the South American qualifying series without many difficulties. The most outstanding of the supporting cast included Nelson Tapia, Francisco Rojas, Clarence Acuña, Nelson Parraguéz, and my great friend and star of Mexico's Toluca and Atlante clubs, Fabián Estay.

They got off to a good start in Bordeaux on the eleventh of June. Thanks to two goals from "El Matador," they were leading Italy 2–1 until the 85th minute, when the referee awarded the Italians a penalty. Roberto Baggio stepped up and fired home, and the match ended 2–2.

Their second game was in St. Etienne against Austria. Salas struck first, but once again Chile fell victim to a late goal, and another match ended in a draw. They closed out the first round with their third in three matches, but the 1–1 draw with Cameroon was enough to get them into the second round.

There, as had happened in their own World Cup in '62, they saw a familiar face: Brazil. ¡Uy!

Here there would be no ties.

In the first half, the three-time champions mounted three main attacks, and came away with three goals. One half of their "Ro-Ro" duo, Ronaldo, outperformed "Sa-Za" and scored twice. Chile was crushed underfoot, managing only one goal by Salas in a 4–1 defeat, and was heading home.

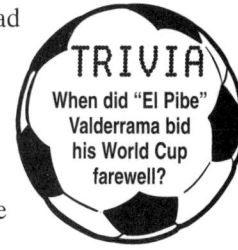

TRIVIA

Who eliminated Chile in France '98?

Despite three ties and a loss, Chile had made a good impression in France. After the World Cup, Marcelo Salas continued to see success in Argentina and Italy, as did Zamorano, who had a World Cup goal as a souvenir.

TRIVIA

How many goals did Iván Zamorano score in France '98?

But in the 2002 Sydney Olympics, he removed what thorns he had in him, and emerged as the games' top scorer. After that, he moved to Mexico, where he found further success with América, leading them to their first title in I don't know how long.

COLOMBIA: THE END OF AN ERA

That's exactly what it was. Colombia's great generation of the 1990s came to an end in France '98. It was playing in its final World Cup: after that, Colombia just hasn't been the same, failing to return to the grand stage in 2002 and now in 2006, as well. Even so, they left behind a great legacy of some unforgettable players.

Maturana was no longer with the team. He had been replaced as coach by his friend and assistant from U.S.A. '94, Hernán Darío "El Bolillo" Gómez, who would also go on to lead Ecuador to their first World Cup in 2002.

"El Pibe" Valderrama was still the star of the team, playing in his final World Cup alongside the

TRIVIA

When did "El Pibe" Valderrama bid his World Cup farewell?

likes of Leonel Alvarez, "El Tren" Valencia, Luis Perea, and Freddy Rincón. But the team was not the same; a shadow of its former self.

In their first match, they fell 1–0 to the Romanians in Lyon. After that, they defeated Tunisia with that same—well, opposite—score. The goal came off the foot of Preciado, but it would prove to be Colombia's only goal in that World Cup.

In the final Group G match, in Lens (in the north of France), England danced around them and bounced them from the competition

with a resounding 2–0 defeat. The second of the Brits' two goals came from a young David Beckham, his first in World Cup play.

Colombia was closing a great chapter in their nation's soccer history. But at the time of this writing, a new generation is forming and preparing to make themselves felt in the 2010 qualifying series.

Let's hope they find their way.

TRIVIA
Which nation eliminated Colombia from France '98?

"EL CHILA" MAKES HIS DEBUT

Paraguay arrived in France with its best team in many years.

They were doing without the likes of Cabañas and "Romarito," but they did have new stars who had cut their teeth in European, Brazilian, and Argentine leagues. Stars like Celso Ayala from River, Francisco Arce from Gremio, Carlos Gamarra from Benfica, Miguel Ángel Benitez from Espanyol, Roberto Acuña from Zaragoza, and Arístides Rojas from Independiente.

The most decorated of them all—and definitely the most colorful, famous, loud, and polemical—was their goalkeeper, at the time one of the best in the world at his position. I'm talking about José Luis Chilavert ("El Chila"), as famous for his work in front of the net as he was for his penalties and free kicks.

Above: *All smiles, Hernán "El Bolillo" Gomez.* Right: *Goalkeeper and goalscorer: José Luis Chilavert. A Paraguayan hero.*

After Argentina and world champions Brazil, Paraguay was the best selection in South America. They finished second in qualifying, right on the heels of the Argentines.

In France, they were assigned to Group D, along with Bulgaria, Spain, and Nigeria. On paper, it was one of the toughest. In the first two matches, "El Chila" was a hero between the pipes, but got little support from his offense as both games ended 0–0. For Spain, the draw meant their elimination, since they had already lost to Nigeria in their first match 3–2.

Paraguay then found their touch and defeated those same Nigerians 3–1 in Toulouse and advanced to the second round, just as they had in their previous appearance in Mexico '86.

And speaking of Nigeria . . . care to guess who was coaching the team? That's right: Bora Milutinovic. He had taken his fourth consecutive different team to the World Cup, establishing a new record in the process.

In the second round, Paraguay faced the hosts, and made history in the process. It was the first World Cup match to be decided by the golden-goal rule. Unfortunately, it wasn't scored by one of their own, but rather by Laurent Blanc, and with a mere seven minutes to go before penalties.

TRIVIA
Who was the goalkeeper for Paraguay in France '98?

AN AMERICAN DISASTER

The Age of Bora was over for the United States, who now seemed almost orphan-like in their play.

The team finished dead last at France '98, and Steve Sampson—the coach who had replaced Bora, and who had done a relatively good job in the qualifying rounds—paid the price. He was fired upon the team's return home.

TRIVIA
What was the first nation to win a golden-goal match in a World Cup?

Nobody could really say what had happened to the gringos. They had quality players and a long and solid period of preparation. Bad luck? Perhaps.

In their first match, they lost 2–0 to the "ancient" Germans, though the final score does not reflect their effort nor their quality of play on the field. In their second match, the same thing happened. In Lyon they faced Iraq—a keenly anticipated match owing to the political implications—and once again they played hard but lost 2–1. Brian McBride had the lone goal for the United States.

TRIVIA
Who was the U.S. coach for France '98?

They were officially eliminated, but they still had to play one more match, against Yugoslavia. Once again, it was a tale of missed opportunities. They had a number of openings, but failed to capitalize on them, perhaps stricken by some sort of amateur nervousness. They lost their third straight match, and had only one goal to their credit.

And that's how the team of Wynalda, Dooley, Coby, McBride, Moore, Stewart, and Reyna left France: with their tail between their legs, having given the worst performance in their World Cup history. Many people have criticized Sampson for not playing either of his veterans, Balboa or Ramos, more. They were on the roster but saw the field for only a few minutes each.

TRIVIA
How many matches did the United States win in France '98?

In South Korea/Japan, the United States got the chance to restore a bit of their lost luster. And let me tell you, they took full advantage! They had definitely learned from the lessons of France. But we'll talk more about that later.

ANOTHER CUP IN FRONT OF THE CAMERAS

France '98 was my third World Cup working in television. It was also the first time I had the opportunity to do the Univision broadcast, which is an honor I also had in 2002, and will have again in 2006.

That year, the channel "borrowed" me from Fuera de Serie and plopped me down in a sweltering Miami studio to welcome the viewers before every one of the sixty-four World Cup matches that summer. And to add a bit of trivia: it was the same studio that, one year later, would be converted into the home studio of *República Deportiva*!

I was joined in there by Jesse Losada, an ever-serious and circumspect man, as well as by a new Univision persona, a likable little guy who I'm sure you all remember best for his famous cry of *"Sa-té-li-té, sa-té-li-té."* I am speaking, of course, of Pepe Locuáz.

I fell, I suppose, somewhere between those two styles. I would enjoy going over the events of each game, but at the same time I would direct the "serious questions" to Jesse and the "humorous anecdotes" to Pepe. I honestly had a lot of fun there, though I admit I was dying to be over in Paris, broadcasting with Andrés Cantor and Norberto Longo, whom I introduced before every match.

After turning it over to them, we would remain in the studio and watch the match on the big-screen TV, and if we had a guest on the show that day, they would often stay and watch with us, suffering or celebrating, as the case might be.

I remember that the day Colombia was eliminated, our guest was the singer and composer Carlos Vives. How he suffered! If he didn't break down into tears, I think it was because of pride. But he was still able to return to his home country, happy and kind, just after the match was over.

I don't know how he did it! I'm still lamenting Argentina's exit from that same World Cup.

SPEAKING OF ARGENTINA . . .

My team had put together another formidable roster. They qualified as the first-place team out of South America, and all of the players were starring for European clubs.

Among them were the keeper Carlos Roa (Mallorca), Roberto Ayala (Napoli), José Chamot (Lazio), Roberto Sensini and Hernán Crespo (Parma), Claudio "El Piojo" López and Ariel "El Burrito" Ortega (Valencia), Diego "El Cholo" Simeone and Javier Zanetti (Inter Milan), Juan "La Brujita" Sebastián Verón (Sampdoria), and the man everybody loved, the great Gabriel "Batigol" Batistuta of Fiorentina.

After the embarrassment of Maradona and the sad elimination by Romania in '94, this was the time for redemption. The *albiceleste* boys arrived in France as favorites, thanks in no small part to their coach and former captain of the '78 and '82 squads, Daniel Passarela.

And, contrary to what had happened to us in so many other draws, we found ourselves in a favorable group. Group H, that is, with three teams with no World Cup experience: Japan, Jamaica, and Croatia.

But even so, we struggled to beat Japan and Croatia (the world had yet to learn just how good these guys were) by one goal to nil each. Jamaica, however, we put in their place, with a convincing 5–0 result. "Orteguita" had one and Batistuta had himself a hat trick, just as he did in U.S.A. '94 against Greece.

Undefeated and unscored upon, we were through to the second round filled with joy and optimism. At least, that's how I felt, watching there in the studio. The only problem was that we would have to face England next, and every time we play them in a World Cup, you just never know what's going to happen. For our opponents, it was a chance at revenge for the infamous "hand of God" game back in Mexico '86. For us, it was another chance to put them in their place, and regain some respect after the whole Falklands debacle.

TRIVIA

Who was on the receiving end of Batistuta's hat trick in France '98?

The match took place in St. Etienne, and it lived up to expectations. It was an amazing game, the best to that point, and one of the best of the entire summer.

The first half was simply spectacular. Batistuta opened the scoring in the 6th minute off a penalty, and four minutes later Alan Shearer had the equalizer. In the 16th minute of play, the new star of the English squad—Michael Owen, only nineteen years old at the time—pulled a Maradona and had himself one of the best goals of the Cup, after a long run that started at midfield and gutted our defense. But just before the break, Zanetti had a bomb of his own, and the match was even yet again.

It was the best first half of World Cup play in many, many years.

In the second half, emotions continued to surge. David Beckham was sent off for kicking Simeone, and the referee annulled a goal by Sol Campbell that could have been our undoing. But the match remained deadlocked at two goals apiece, and we were headed for overtime, and—please don't say it!—to penalties.

Thank heavens our keeper, Roa, had gained some inspiration from Goycochea's performance in Italy '90. He smothered two of the five English tries, and knocked them out of the World Cup. Yesss! It was a 6–5 win and we moved on.

But our destiny was by no means assured.

In fact, in another incredible match filled with drama and emotions, Holland took it all away from us. They got out to an early 1–0 lead on a goal by Patrick Kluivert, but five minutes later we evened up thanks to "El Piojo" López. The second half was the stuff of heart attacks. An Argentine goal seemed to be ever on the verge, but it never arrived. And just when it seemed that we were headed for more overtime, *boom!* Dennis Bergkamp nailed us with the second Dutch goal. The game—and the Argentine dream—were over.

I don't know how I did it, but I managed to compose myself and put on a good face even under the circumstances. I think that being in shock might have helped. I went on the air with the same smile as ever, though inside I felt as if I were dying. All I wanted to do was cry.

Once again, my beloved *albiceleste* had been left on the side of the road, although this time we had ridden as far as the quarterfinals. But what we didn't know at the time was that we had just borne witness to Argentina's last great World Cup performance. At least, until today.

Four years later came the debacle in Japan and South Korea.

¡Ay! It hurts even to think about it.

PELÓN'S TRI

Toward the end of 1997, Bora Milutinovic qualified Mexico for the World Cup. But nobody was happy. Not the fans, and not the Federación. There was much to worry about. We had lost to Jamaica, and had gone through four straight tie games. And so . . . in order to right the ship and guarantee a solid performance in France, the top brass decided to make a coaching change.

Enter Manuel Lapuente, "El Pelón," or "Don Monolo," the top Mexican coach of the 1990s. He was kind, intelligent, and a three-time champion with Necaxa.

His team was based on the same player foundation as Bora's was, and it included several stars from the previous World Cup, including Jorge Campos, Claudio Suárez, Marcelino Bernal, Luis García, and García "El Beto" Aspe.

They were joined by a new *camada* (that is, "litter"—as they like to say in Mexico) of young talent, such players as Ramón Ramirez, Pavel Pardo, "Paco" Palencia, Braulio Luna, "El Chava" Carmona, "El Cabrito" Arellano, and three strikers just emerging into the primes of their careers: Cuauhtemoc "El Temo" Blanco, Ricardo Peláez, and "El Matador" himself, Luis Hernández.

The latter had himself the best World Cup. He scored four goals, equaling the efforts of both Ronaldo of Brazil and another "El Matador," Marcelo Salas of Chile.

For his part, "El Temo" Blanco wowed the entire world with his famous *"cuauhtemiña,"* his patented move wherein he gripped the ball between his own two feet and hopped over the challenges of two closing defenders. He brought it out on June 13th, in Mexico's opening match against South Korea, in Lyon. After being down early on, Peláez tied the match at 1–1 before Hernández added two of his own. Mexico went on to win 3–1, which was a lucky result considering it came on the thirteenth of the month!

The second encounter was in Bordeaux, and it was one for the ages. The Mexican press went so far as to dub it the best Mexican performance ever on European soil.

TRIVIA

Against what team did Cuauhtemoc Blanco utilize his famous *"cuauhtemiña"* move in a World Cup match?

They played Belgium, and the first half was simply unforgettable. They hit the crossbar on two separate occasions, Pavel Pardo was sent off, and Belgium was on top 2–0. But in the second, Pelón's boys showed renewed life, and clawed their way back into the match and onto the scoreboard. First came a penalty converted by "Beto" García Aspe, and then a goal by

Blanco, his first in World Cup play. Two goals apiece—so the game ended—and Mexico was alive and kicking.

Mexico's third match was against the powerful Dutch team of De Boer, Dennis Bergkamp, Marc Overmars, Edgar Davids, and their coach, Guus Hiddink, who also led South Korea in 2002 and will lead Australia in 2006.

For our presentation of this match, we invited our good friend Jorge Ramos from *Noticiero Univision* to our Miami studios so he could offer his perspective as a Mexican and as a lover of soccer.

By the 18th minute Holland was already up two goals to nil, and Mexico's hopes were slowly fading. They would need at least a tie in order to advance, and even then they would have to wait for the Belgium–South Korea match result, which was going on at the same time in Paris. Things began to look really grim for *los tri* when Belgium struck first there. Jorge was silent, not saying a word.

Once more, however, Don Manolo was able to inspire his squad at the break and make the necessary adjustments. He pulled two defenders in favor of "El Cabrito" Arellano and Peláez up front. Mexico took the field for the start of the second half, and set about making history.

First came the news that South Korea had evened the score with

With Mexican player Luis Hernández.

the Belgians, and then, after a grand play by "El Temo" Blanco, Peláez got his head on a ball that found the back of the net. Mexico's first goal.

Back in the studio, everyone began biting their nails. Everyone except Jorge Ramos, of course.

Mexico continued to press dramatically, and with only three minutes left in the game, they were met with misfortune: Ramón Ramírez was sent off. With only ten players left on the field and four minutes deep in injury time, Luís Hernández pulled what could be the greatest single play of his career out of his sleeve: falling away, he just managed to get a toe on the ball and poke it past the Dutch keeper for Mexico's second—and equalizing—goal.

Incredible!

In the studio, we stopped worrying our nails long enough to congratulate Jorge, who was finally beginning to show some emotion.

In Paris, Belgium and South Korea ended in a tie of their own, and both were out. Mexico was through to the second round, and Jorge gave me a gleeful hug.

¡Sí se pudo! Yes they could!

June 29th in Montpellier was the trial by fire—the rematch against the Germans, who had eliminated them on penalties back in Mexico '86. At the end of the first half, things were going well for Mexico. They were dominating play, and up on their opponents by a goal from "El Matador," his fourth of the World Cup.

TRIVIA
What country knocked Mexico out of France '98?

This time, the second half was a different sort of story. Lapuente made the poor decision of dropping back to protect their slim lead, and the Germans took advantage of their opportunity to attack. Klinsmann and Bierhoff each scored, and by the time Mexico had regrouped, it was already too late.

They lost 2–1, and were eliminated. In other words, *no se pudo más.*

It felt like the greatest fraud ever perpetrated in the history of Mexican soccer. How was it possible for them to play so well and yet lose so badly?

Their next opportunity would come four years later in Japan and South Korea, where once again *los tri* would suffer a staggering disappointment. This time, worse. You'll see.

BRASIL: GOING FOR "O PENTA"

think that the word was used for the first time in the history of soccer during that summer, 1998.

Everything in Brazil was *"o penta."* Songs, T-shirts, posters, publicity, commercials, everything and everyone was talking *penta*, referring, of course, to the fifth World Cup title that Brazil was going to win in France. And the rest of the world caught on. Even we non-Brazilian journalists were starting to use the word.

But in the end, it might have been overused. Too much hype can be hard on the luck.

They came in as runaway favorites, led by Mario "El Lobo" Zagallo, who had been given a second go-round as coach. Remember, he had also coached during the failure of '74, and he'd been Parreira's assistant in '94.

The new *"Scratch"* included a constellation's worth of new young stars, like Rivaldo, Cafú, Roberto Carlos, Sampaio, Aldair, and Ronaldo, who was the best player on earth at the time. They were rounded out by the veterans Taffarel, Dunga, and Bebeto. It was a heck of a roster.

They kicked off their quest in Paris on June 10th, against Scotland. After an own goal by the Scots (and surprisingly little effort by Brazil) they came away with a 2–1 victory. After that, they showed a bit of their beautiful game in a 3–0 win over Morocco, with goals coming from Ronaldo, Rivaldo, and Bebeto.

TRIVIA

Who was Brazil's coach in France '98?

Already qualified for the second round, they seemed lackadaisical in their third match, against Norway, and conceded a penalty in the final minute of play that resulted in a 2–1 defeat. The Brazilian press was up in arms.

The doubters and the critics were rising.

They would have to answer on the field of play. And in their following match, at Paris's Parc des Princes stadium, Chile would prove to be the sacrificial lamb. Ronaldo and Sampaio scored two goals apiece, and Brazil won handily 4–1.

In the quarterfinals they faced Denmark, which was flying largely under the radar through this year's tournament. Their only convincing win was 4–1 over Nigeria, and everyone expected Brazil to be dancing sambas around them all afternoon. They played in Nantes on July 3rd, but it was Brazil and not the Danes who were surprised. Brazil was saved by the grace of Rivaldo. He scored twice that afternoon, and it took all that Brazil had to emerge with a 3–2 victory.

Naturally, the Brazilian press was not happy. The critics were clamoring.

The semifinal was a rematch with the Dutch, which Brazil had eliminated in another semifinal, back

TRIVIA

In which match did Ronaldo score his first-ever World Cup goal?

in Dallas in 1994. This time the stage was Marseille, and the game play of both teams was dominated by a sense of caution. Ninety minutes ended 1–1, and that's the way the scoreboard remained until the penalties.

In that phase, Taffarel became the man of the match. He saved one from Cocu and another from De Boer. Brazil was—somewhat surprisingly—through to the Paris final, and the criticisms dropped in volume a bit. *"O penta"* was close at hand, and the team needed support.

But if they were to lose . . . well, you'll see!

"LES BLEUS" REACH THE FINAL

The boys in the blue jerseys—the heirs of Fontaine and Platini—had themselves a wonderful opportunity to erase the memories of some previous shortcomings by playing in a World Cup final on their home soil.

Their mission was placed in the hands of their new leader, the incomparable "Zizou," Zinedine Zidane. To many Frenchmen, he was a better player than Platini, but that's something you can decide for yourself.

In 1998, this extraordinary center midfielder—born in Marseille to Algerian parents—was all the rage of French soccer. His club, Juventus, had won every title imaginable, from the Italian league and European championships to an Intercontinental Championship in which they beat my beloved River, where his own idol, Francescoli, played.

But Zidane wasn't the only one. He was joined by other players on a team that was at once showy, solid, and efficient, and at times brilliant. I'm referring to Henry, Petit, Deschamps, Blanc, Trezeguet, Djorkaeff, Desailly, and Barthez.

The first sign that France's luck was about to change was their first-round group drawing.

They shared Group C with some lesser powers: South Africa, Saudi Arabia, and Denmark. Without much trouble, they won by scores of 3–0, 4–0, and 2–1, respectively. Henry and Trezeguet had themselves the first World Cup goals of their careers, and both are still playing today—looking better than ever. They should feature prominently in Germany '06.

And their good fortune persisted into the second round, where—as we've already seen—they downed a worthy Paraguay side on the first golden goal in World Cup history.

In the quarterfinals, they faced Italy once again, after having eliminated them back in the second round of Mexico '86. This time the match was taking place in St. Denis, and nothing happened. It was an incredibly boring game. It was goalless throughout, and went to penalties, where luck is as crucial as anything else. Proud France still had it, once again eliminating the Italians.

Of course, it was much more than luck, it was also the great performance of their keeper, Fabien Barthez, who saved a penalty after his countryman Bixente Lizarazú had failed in his own attempt. In the end, Italy's Dino Baggio missed, and France was through to the semifinals.

I'm not too sure that luck was a factor there. *Les bleus* were up against the surprise of the Cup, Croatia, and they did what they needed to do in order to win. Their defenseman Lilian Thuram was their hero that day with two goals, outpacing the eventual Golden Boot winner, Davor Suker, who had his fifth of the tournament that day. (He would get his sixth and final tally in the third-place match, leading his side over Holland 2–1.)

France had put themselves in the final.

Four days later, on that same field, they would face four-time world champions Brazil.

THE SECOND GRAND FINALE IN PARIS

The first time, it was Italy and Hungary, on June 19, 1938, in a stadium that was no longer standing.

Now it was Brazil and France, in another historic (though renovated) stadium, the Stade de France. It was the host's first appearance in a World Cup final, and Brazil's sixth.

The focus of the match would be the single combat between the two great players of the day, Ronaldo and Zidane. But everyone was also waiting with bated breath to see whether Brazil would be able to pull off *"o penta"* that all the world had been talking about.

For the French, it was a singular opportunity to wipe from their collective memory the pain of so many years of frustration. To forget about the beating that Brazil gave them in 1958, and the penalty shootout with the Germans in 1982.

And what do you think happened that day, July 8th?

Why, they did it!

Before the astonished eyes of the world, Brazil virtually disappeared from the field while France put on a veritable soccer clinic. Or rather, Zidane put on a clinic: a masterful demonstration of how to use your head inside the six-yard box. It was there that he scored two unforgettable goals, putting his team on the verge of a championship there in the first half. Petit added one more as a finishing touch, and France silenced the samba with a convincing 3–0 victory.

The country that gave birth to the World Cup of soccer had been crowned as champions for the first time in their history. Jules Rimet could finally rest in peace.

But you can imagine what was going on with the Brazilian press.

Their cries reached the heavens, and they were calling for Zagallo's head. They said everything that came into their heads: that Ronaldo was hurt and shouldn't have played; that he'd had an epileptic seizure before the match but his sponsor Nike forced him to play; that some of the players had been paid off . . . in the end, you name it, they said it.

But nobody could deny the merits of *les bleus*. Their stars demonstrated their true colors and their class, and their supremacy—or their good fortune—was never in question.

TRIVIA
How many goals did Zidane have in the '98 final?

Four years later, in Japan and South Korea, however, reality bit them with a new bit of history. Read on.

South Korea/Japan 2002: Ronaldo's World Cup

Actually, it was supposed to be South Korea's World Cup, but FIFA had a change of plans.

On the day of the announcement in 1996, the South Koreans had a giant festival in Seoul. FIFA had promised to place the first World Cup of the new millennium in Asia, and South Korea was the best candidate. They had successfully hosted the Olympics in 1988, so they had excellent infrastructure; also, they had the financial resources, and, above all, a great desire to do the job.

What they didn't know was that Havelange had already resolved that, for the first time in history, the World Cup would be hosted by two separate nations. South Korea and Japan would share the honors.

The news hit Koreans like a bucket of cold water in the face.

Japan? Why them? They were South Korea's political and economic archrival; they had even invaded and occupied their country for a time. Why did they have to share with *them*?

"Welcome to FIFA, baby!" was Havelange's response. (I'm kidding! He didn't say that!) But if he could place the World Cup in the earth's most potent economic power (read: the United States), then why not put it in the second?

And that's how the World Cup came to two nations at once.

To ensure a proper balance, FIFA decided that everything would

be evenly shared: the name, the groups, the number of games, the cities, the winnings, everything. The opening match would be in one place—South Korea—and the final would be in the other—Japan. The only particular concession that was made was that South Korea would get top billing on all official products. The event would be referred to as "South Korea/Japan 2002" and never the reverse.

Of course, in the wake of such odd beginnings, we shouldn't be surprised to find that some odd things happened along the way, too. First, teams like Germany, Brazil, and Mexico struggled mightily in the qualifying stages. Brazil wasn't even assured of a spot until after their final match, against Venezuela! Mexico had to change coaches at the last minute in order to salvage their chances and not be left out.

Once the tournament finally got under way, the surprises only continued. And not just a few. More than one world soccer power met with disaster that summer, and it started with the defending champions, France.

So let's take a look at the surprising and unique seventeenth FIFA World Cup of Soccer South Korea/Japan 2002. Even the mascots were odd.

Actually, this was the second time that a World Cup had more than one official mascot (Germany '74 had two, as well). South Korea/Japan had three, to be exact. They were extraterrestrials known as Atmoses, from the planet Atmoszone, and their names were Nik, Kaz, and Atos. The idea was to have something so nondescript that it wouldn't offend any one culture. But who would ever have worried about that? Havelange?

TRIVIA

What were the names of the three mascots for South Korea/Japan 2002?

EIGHT GROUPS, TWO NATIONS

To maintain the delicate balance, South Korea would take the first four groups and Japan would handle the latter four. Here is how it was all laid out:

Group A (South Korea): France, Senegal, Uruguay, Denmark
Group B (South Korea): Paraguay, South Africa, Spain, Slovenia
Group C (South Korea): Brazil, Turkey, China, Costa Rica
Group D (South Korea): South Korea, Poland, U.S.A., Portugal
Group E (Japan): Ireland, Cameroon, Germany, Saudi Arabia
Group F (Japan): Argentina, Nigeria, England, Sweden
Group G (Japan): Croatia, Mexico, Italy, Ecuador
Group H (Japan): Japan, Belgium, Russia, Tunisia

As you can see, there weren't many surprises among the participants: FIFA had pretty much rounded up the usual suspects.

The most glaring absence, so to speak, was Holland. Colombia and Chile were back home in South America. One of Africa's regulars—Morocco—was likewise absent.

But the most interesting thing about the absentees is that nearly all of them (the exception being Holland) will also be missing out on Germany '06.

In any case, the new faces that summer were Ecuador, Senegal,

China, and one of the brand-new European nations—Slovenia—part of the former Yugoslavia.

BORA'S FIFTH WORLD CUP

And since a World Cup without Bora wouldn't be much of a World Cup at all . . . the perennial coach was back, and leading yet another team.

He had promised the Chinese Soccer Federation (how would you say that in Chinese?) that he would get them to their first World Cup, and he delivered. South Korea/Japan was the fifth consecutive finals that the colorful coach participated in with a different team. Before this, you'll remember, there was Mexico in '86, Costa Rica in '90, the U.S.A. in '94, and Nigeria in '98.

Now he was with China, for whom results did not matter. Simply qualifying was reward enough. Their first match was against one of Bora's former clients, Costa Rica, who happened then to be led by his friend and former assistant coach, Alexandre Guimaraes. *Los ticos* defeated them 2–0.

TRIVIA
Which national team did Bora Milutinovic lead to South Korea/Japan '02?

After that, China fell to Brazil 4–0 and Turkey 3–0. They were shut out with nine goals against, but even so, they were quite satisfied with just having participated in the grand event.

And where might Bora be at this very moment? Surely he's looking for work for 2006 or 2010.

"LOS TICOS" COME UP SHORT

Speaking of Costa Rica, *los ticos* also reached Asia filled with enthusiasm. They were coming off an excellent qualifying round, finishing first in the CONCACAF hexagonal, and beating Mexico at the Azteca for the first time.

Their group didn't look overly daunting on paper, with the exception of Brazil, of course. Not much was expected of China, and Turkey was a virtual unknown, truly incognito. Nobody imagined that—like Croatia four years before—they would become the surprise of the tournament.

Guimaraes's *ticos* were led by their stars Paulo César Wanchope, Ronaldo Fonseca, Ronald Gómez, my good friend Mauricio Wright, and the cagey veteran Hernán Medford, who, at the tender age of thirty-four, was the last remaining holdover from the Italy '90 squad.

They opened in the South Korean city of Kwangju against Bora's China, and won handily, 2–0, on goals by Gómez and Wright. After that, they faced the unknown Turks, and things changed. It was a hard-fought match. Turkey got on the board first, and then dropped back into a defensive posture to guard against the Costa Rican attack, which finally managed to break through and find the equalizer with less than a minute to play. It came via Winston Parks, and the match ended 1–1.

Their third first-round game was more difficult: Brazil. If they tied, Costa Rica would advance. It was one of the best games of the first round, open and thrilling, and rife with goals...seven in all. After ninety supremely enjoyable minutes, Brazil had won 5–2, with goals coming from Rivaldo, Edmilson, Junior, and two from Ronaldo. Costa Rica's goals were thanks to Wanchope and Gómez.

TRIVIA

Which World Cup saw the debut of Paulo Wanchope?

Unfortunately, *los ticos* wouldn't be advancing into the second round. Turkey had edged ahead of them on goal differential. A shame, to be sure, because it was the best Costa Rican squad in recent memory.

Here's hoping they have better luck in Germany '06.

LIFE'S LITTLE SURPRISES!

The surprises of life—or of World Cups, I should say! We've already established that South Korea/Japan '02 was the World Cup of surprises. But, seriously, folks, there are surprises and then there are . . . *surprises*!

It's to be expected that some team will just have a bad run. But for three world powerhouses to bow out in the first round—including the defending world champions—is unheard of. You wouldn't even see such a thing in the movies!

But that summer we did. Right there on the field.

The first real shock was felt by France in their opening game. Maybe we should call it Senegal's opening game. Playing well and in excellent physical form, they tripped up the defending champions and left them in the dust, shaken and beaten. The excuse given was that Zidane was playing hurt. Perhaps. But the fact remains that the victory took the entire world by surprise, including the Senegalese fans watching on TV.

France then drew Uruguay 0–0 and fell 2–0 to Denmark, thus becoming the first defending champions forced to exit after the first round. What an embarrassment!

But that was only the first surprise. The second has to do with South Korea.

SURPRISE #2

Despite being the home team, and having the former Dutch international Guus Hiddink at the helm, nobody was expecting much from South Korea. Poland must have been thinking the same thing, because in the first Group D match, they were taken completely by surprise and suffered a 2–0 defeat.

After the rest of the round had played out, Poland was heading home while the Koreans were advancing for the first time in their history, after drawing with the United states (1–1) and toppling Portugal (1–0).

Their success continued all the way to the quarterfinals, after they had eliminated both Italy and Spain in controversial matches filled with dubious refereeing. But in any case, they had an entire country in the throes of World Cup fever.

SURPRISE #3

The third big surprise of the tournament was doled out by the United States the following day, on July 5th. They were facing Portugal, which counted four of the world's top players among its roster: Fernando Couto, João Pinto, Rui Costa, and former FIFA World Footballer of the Year, Luis Figo.

The Americans and their coach, Bruce Arena, arrived in Asia ready to erase the stinging memory of their performance in France '98. And they also had the services of a new crop of players, including Pablo Mastroeni, Clint Mathis, Josh Wolff, DaMarcus Beasley, and one who simply looked like a great player, Landon Donovan. And they were held together by their captain, a skilled veteran who was finally injury-free and ready to take his spot in the starting lineup. I'm talking, of course, about Claudio Reyna, who was more ready than he had ever been!

The game took place on the field at Suwon, not far from Seoul. And what a surprise it was to find the first half end with the United States on top 3–1. In the second, the Portuguese emerged from their state of shock and sought urgently to catch up. But the U.S. defense was more than equal to the task, and Portugal was held to just one other goal and a 3–2 loss. After that, Portugal downed South Korea 1–0 but nevertheless was summarily bounced from the competition.

The United States would continue on. They had tied with South Korea and lost to Poland, but they had reached the second round for the first time in their history. There they ousted Mexico, and very nearly took out Germany in the quarterfinals.

TRIVIA

Who was the coach of the United States team in the 2002 World Cup?

It was the best performance the United States had ever given in World Cup competition, and it served to vault them into the top ten of the FIFA World Rankings.

Not bad!

SURPRISE #4

As if that weren't enough, Mexico and Croatia also offered up a surprise. Not because Mexico won a valuable 1–0 victory, but rather because Croatia lost. They were still the revelation of the '98 Cup, and much was expected of them in South Korea and Japan. In the end, however, Croatia was eliminated in the first round while Mexico claimed first place in Group G, ahead of the Italians.

So, as you can see, the tournament was off to a dramatic start. And there were plenty of surprises yet to come.

"OS TETRAS" GOING FOR "O PENTA"

Though you might not believe it, Brazil was not the favorite heading in to the 2002 World Cup.

It was the first time in their storied history when this was the case. From the outset, they were just one more team hoping to put on a good show, but not necessarily thinking about winning it all.

This approach proved effective.

Luiz Felipe Scolari—"Felipão" or "Big Phil," as he was known—was the squad's new coach, and he was able to do his job without much pressure, for rarely had so little been expected of a Brazilian squad.

As I mentioned earlier, they had struggled even to qualify. A number of their stars were in the latter stages of their careers (with no new young talent in the wings), and their primary offensive threat, Ronaldo, had spent the previous two years battling a knee injury that saw him off the field more often than on it.

But Brazil being Brazil, the surprises were not long in coming.

Ronaldo opened against Turkey and looked to be in fine form, scoring once. Rivaldo—like Cafú and Roberto Carlos—proved that maybe he wasn't as old as previously thought, and one of the younger players, Ronaldinho, showed that he was *o filho do samba* through and through.

In the first round of play, Brazil dispatched Turkey (2–1), China (4–0), and Costa Rica (5–2). In other words, they scored eleven goals in three matches. Ronaldo and Rivaldo had scored in each of them, and Roberto Carlos and Ronaldinho had

TRIVIA
What was the name of the Brazilian star who came into the limelight during the 2002 World Cup?

one goal apiece. Clearly, the boys from Brazil were as good as ever.

For their first match of the second round, they traveled to Kobe, Japan, where they faced Belgium. Once again, Ronaldo and Rivaldo provided the offense, and Brazil won 2–0. Next up was England, in Shizuoka (also in Japan), and it proved to be one of the greatest games of the summer. Ronaldinho fooled the English keeper David Seaman badly with a looping shot, and Rivaldo scored a goal in his fifth straight match. The match—and the English hopes—ended 2–1.

In the semifinals, Brazil again had to face Turkey, whom they'd struggled to beat in group play, and who had become the "Croatia," so to speak, of the 2002 World Cup. Ronaldo rose to the occasion yet again, scoring the only goal of the match, his sixth overall. Once again, Brazil escaped with a win against the game Turks, and were on to another World Cup final: the seventh of their storied history.

What a record!

SURPRISE #5

Don't think I forgot the fact that Argentina also shocked the world during the summer of 2002. It's just that it pains me to remember it.

I'll be brief: they beat Nigeria 1–0 (goal by Batistuta) . . . lost to England 1–0 (goal by Beckham) . . . tied Sweden 1–1 . . . and were left out of the second round.

Any questions?

Yes, of course. They had a powerful team filled with stars shining at the zenith of their careers. Stars like Verón, Crespo, Ortega, López, Zanetti, Gallardo, Simeone, Aimar, González, and, of course, Batistuta.

Anything else?

Sure. It was my country's worst performance ever in a World Cup, one from which they have yet to fully recover, though we were able to erase a bit of the sting with the 2004 Olympic gold medal in Athens.

Say what?

Basically, we will slit our collective wrists if something similar happens in Germany '06. You can be sure of that.

Done?

Thanks very much.

VASCO'S "EL TRI"

He swept in like a paramedic offering first aid. Ready to resuscitate the dead. He was the savior of a nation, their guardian angel; in short, he was "El Vasco," Javier Aguirre, the man who brought Mexico back from the edge of the abyss.

It all started back in the qualifying stages. "El Ojitos" Meza was handed the reins by "El Pelón" Lapuente with high hopes. His credentials as coach included winning three championships with the club Toluca. And being the simple, serious, and intellectual man that he was, all of Mexico was expecting him to lead *los tri* to the promised land in 2002.

But they almost didn't even make it out of the desert!

For reasons nobody can explain, "El Ojitos" was a disaster. If it wasn't him, it was his roster. They lost to the United States in Columbus, to Costa Rica in the Azteca, to Honduras in San Pedro, and before he could lose any more, the Federación showed him the door. *Gracias.*

Enter "El Vasco," a member of the '86 squad and a winning coach with Pachuca. He was a man with a wonderful personality, kind, charismatic, sure of himself, and—apparently—quite a good coach. He saved *los tri* and qualified for the World Cup as the third best team in CONCACAF.

¡Uff!

TRIVIA

Who brought Mexico back from the brink of disaster to qualify for South Korea/Japan '02?

He made up his roster with the best that Mexico had at that particular moment. Good players who had fallen off their form were left behind. Even a naturalized Mexican born in Argentina was brought in to shore things up (Gabriel Caballero, one of his midfielders with Pachuca).

He called upon several veterans from France '98, including "El Conejo" Pérez, "El Cabrito" Arellano, Braulio Luna, "Paco" Palencia, "Chava" Carmona, and Cuauhtemoc Blanco. To that mix, he added a dash of new talent: Rafa Márquez, Gerardo Torrado, Jared Borgetti, and Ramoncito Morales.

It turned out to be an effective combination. It wasn't the best ever, but it may have been the most well organized. "El Vasco" knew how to do his job, and his team was a scrappy one. That became readily apparent in Niigata (Japan), on June 3rd, in their first match, opposite Croatia. Showing extraordinary mettle and a serenity never before seen from *los tri*, they clearly dominated their opponents and came away with a 1–0 win on a penalty-shot goal by Blanco.

Their second contest was against first-timers Ecuador, in Miyagi (Japan). Mexico was down by a goal early on, but they stormed back with goals from Borgetti (the first of his World Cup career) and Torrado (a cracker from outside the area). Final score: Mexico 2, Ecuador 1.

After that came Italy, and "El Vasco's" pupils again demonstrated their organized style of play. They largely shut down the Italians, and scored a goal of their own on a sensational header by Borgetti. They maintained that margin nearly throughout, until Alessandro del Piero tied things up in the 85th minute.

And that's how it ended, a 1–1 draw, but Mexico was advancing as the first-place team in their group. Excellent!

But that's as far as the dream would go. It was time for the nightmare to begin.

And the nightmare was called the United States of America. How many times had Mexico beaten them? Perhaps an easier question would be, how many times had *los gringuitos* beaten *los tri*?

They faced off in Jeonju, South Korea. It was Mexico's first match in that country, as they had played their first three games in Japan. And all of the composure and efficiency they had demonstrated during group play disappeared into thin air. The Americans shut them down like they never had before. Eight minutes into the match, they had their first goal: an amazing ball by Claudio Reyna that Brian McBride terminated with extreme prejudice. It seemed as if it had been drawn up in a laboratory.

TRIVIA

Against which team did Jared Borgetti's first-ever World Cup goal come?

Mexico made some changes and sought for solutions, but the U.S. team was unperturbed. They refused to let down their guard, and then—when Mexico least expected it—they had themselves their second, a great strike by Landon Donovan. The U.S. finished off a 2–0 victory, and Mexico's golden dream had come to an abrupt end.

TRIVIA

Who eliminated Mexico from the 2002 World Cup?

Once again, *no se pudo*. They just weren't able.

But this time, the pain was unbearable. Being ousted from the World Cup is bad enough, but to be knocked out by the United States is much, much worse. Inconceivable. A powerful and fatal blow.

In Germany '06 we'll see whether Mexico has recovered.

"CHARRÚAS" AND "GUARANÍES"

One was a return, the other a reappearance.

For the Uruguayan *celeste*, South Korea/Japan '02 meant their return to the World Cup after a twelve-year absence dating back to Italy '90. That team of Francescoli and the two Rubéns, Paz and Sosa, reached the second round, but suffered a quick loss to Italy. This squad was missing "El Príncipe" and his court, but they did have some new blood: Diego Forlán, Paolo Montero, Alejandro Lembo, Alvaro "El Chino" Recoba, Darío Silva, and our beloved Sebastián "El Loco" Abreu, reaping success of late on the fields of Mexico.

For their part, Paraguay's *guaraní* squad was reappearing on the heels of their excellent performance at France '98, in which it took history's first "golden goal" by the hosts (and eventual champions) to knock them out. José Luis Chilavert, Carlos Gamarra, and Celso Ayala were still the veteran leaders of the bunch, and they were joined by the new face of Paraguay's future who was honing his skills in the German league, Roque Santa Cruz, and the top goalscorer in the Mexican league and another good friend, José Saturnino Cardozo.

Uruguay had somewhat backed into the World Cup, after being forced to win a home-and-away play-off against Australia for the right to compete. Ironically, they lost a rematch of that very play-off, thus keeping them out of Germany '06.

The draw had Uruguay in Group A with France, Senegal, and Denmark. In theory, it wasn't overly difficult. They should advance, along with France. But now, of course, we know that this was the group of big surprises. Neither they nor France were able to make it out alive. Uruguay lost to Denmark before settling for a goalless draw with France and a 3–3 draw with Senegal. This latter match was simply unforgettable—one of the most emotional of the first round—and it featured Forlán scoring what many remember as the best goal of that entire summer. He played the ball down with his chest inside the area before unleashing a cannon-like shot just inside the far post. *Boom!* An instant classic!

Paraguay had qualified rather more comfortably—second place in the South American standings, behind Argentina—and they were led by their Italian coach, Cesare Maldini, father of Paolo.

In their first Group B appearance, South Africa surprised them with a penalty in the final minutes of the match, resulting in a 2–2 draw. Chilavert had been suspended for that game, in which Santa Cruz had his first World Cup goal. "El Chila" returned for their second match, against Spain, in Jeonju (South Korea). It was a disaster. Spain exacted revenge for the tie that finished them in '98 and steamrolled their way to an undisputable 3–1 win. Fernando Morientes had two that night, and Fernando Hierro added the third. An inauspicious debut for Chilavert, who was beginning to show his age. He just wasn't the same between the posts.

TRIVIA

Who coached Paraguay in 2002?

Their third match was against newcomers Slovenia, and Paraguay got their ticket punched to the second round with a 3–1 victory.

That led them to an appointment with Germany in Seogwipo (South Korea). The Germans had thrashed Saudi Arabia 8–0, tied Ireland 1–1, and downed Cameroon 2–0. They were getting great things from a young player by the name of Michael Ballack, who should be their star attraction this summer, as well.

It was a tight and complicated match, though largely lacking in emotions. Both teams focused their efforts on defense, but just when it seemed as if the game was heading for overtime, Oliver Neuville knocked one past "El Chila" in the 88th minute for a 1–0 German victory.

Paraguay was following Uruguay back to South America, and Chilavert bid farewell to both the World Cup and the national team.

For their part, Germany continued to win, reaching as far as the final match. They did so thanks to opportune goals by Ballack against the United States (1–0) in the quarters and South Korea (1–0) in the semifinals.

THE SOUTH KOREAN SHOW

Defying the doubters, Japan and South Korea managed to light a fire of soccer interest in their people. Perhaps the latter nation more, because their team advanced deeper into the Cup, but the Japanese also felt the emotions of a World Cup summer.

I already mentioned South Korea's surprising start. Japan had one, as well. They advanced to the second round for the first time in their history, and they did so as the first-place team in their group. To gain that place they tied Belgium 2–2 before beating Russia 1–0 and Tunisia 2–0.

In all of their games, Japan showed off the broad extent of their soccer evolution, and their players displayed both class and talent. These included Junichi Inamoto (star of Arsenal and Fulham), Shinji Ono (with Holland's Feyenoord), and their biggest player of all, Hidetoshi Nakata (star of Perugia, Roma, and Parma).

Unfortunately for them, they opened the elimination round against another of the big surprises of the summer, Turkey, and fell to them 1–0.

The South Koreans' luck would last a little longer. They started off the second round with one of the most intense matches of the summer, against Italy, and in front of some 38,000 Korean fans all decked out in red. Another five million were gathered in front of giant-screen televisions set up all over the country. Christian Vieri had opened the scoring in the 18th minute, and from that moment onward, the Koreans were forced into a seemingly impossible mission: break down the Italian defense and win the match for the hosts.

And they did it—though with a little help from the Ecuadorian referee Byron Moreno.

One of South Korea's best players, Ki Hyeon Seol, scored the equalizer in the 88th minute, and then—with three minutes left in overtime, before penalties—their star, Jung Hwan Ahn, eliminated the Italians with a historic goal.

It was simply tremendous.

After that they faced Spain in the quarterfinals, and once again they had the help of an official—Egypt's Gamal Ghandour, who inexplicably disallowed a clear Spain goal—during a tight match. After ninety scoreless minutes, they went into overtime, and then penalties. There the Koreans' touch was more true. They eliminated *la furia* in front of the astonished eyes of the world and the red-clad Koreans who had gathered in the main plazas of every city in the country. It truly was a "Red Tide," as someone famously put it.

Never before had a World Cup awakened so much new interest in the host nation's populous.

The Korean party would end in the semifinals, where the Germans crashed the event with a 1–0 win thanks to a Michael Ballack goal in the 75th minute. The hosts were graciously bowing out and the Germans were on to the final. The nation of South Korea returned to its daily life, but even so, it was with a smile.

THE FINAL IN YOKOHAMA

Brazil had begun quietly, without much in the way of grand expectations. But by the end they were all smiles, and proud to be the favorites once more.

Germany, on the other hand, started this World Cup as just one more strong squad, and by the final match, they were . . . just one more strong squad! They had demonstrated the old adage that sometimes it is better to be lucky than good. But arrive they had, regardless of whether or not they could stand up to the two-headed monster of Ronaldo and Rivaldo.

The scene was set on the thirtieth of June, there at Yokohama's majestic International Stadium, packed with over 90,000 fans. Another billion people were watching on televisions across the globe.

For those of you who are keeping track, this was the seventeenth World Cup final, some seventy-two years after the first final in Montevideo. It was also the seventh appearance in the final match for each of the two sides. The only difference was that Brazil had taken home the trophy in four of their seven trips to the final, while Germany had done so on but three occasions.

And another bit of rather unbelievable trivia: this was the first time these two world powers had ever played against each other in a World Cup match at any level. It was simply amazing to think that they had never met in all these years. Destiny, perhaps.

The game started off not unlike a boxing match, with both opponents showing caution, trying to feel the other out. But bit by bit, Brazil began to control the pace of the match, and twice they tested the great German goalkeeper and team hero, Oliver Kahn. But in general, the first half was rather discreet, without much emotion, and it ended without any goals.

But the samba began to rise up in volume during the second half.

In the 67th minute, with Brazil seemingly running at will, Ronaldo broke free and opened the scoring.

> **TRIVIA**
>
> Where was the final match of South Korea/Japan '02 played?

Twelve minutes later, Kleberson made a run up the right-hand wing before snaking a cross toward the center of the field. Rivaldo dummied the ball and allowed it to continue on to the feet of Ronaldo. With a cold precision, the great striker gathered the ball in before firing it toward the opposite post, far from Kahn.

Brazil 2, Germany 0.

And that's how it remained. There was no more scoring.

With what seemed like relative ease, Brazil had finally achieved the much-hyped and much-expected *"penta,"* their fifth World Cup championship. Ronaldo was crowned as the best player on earth, as well as being awarded the Golden Boot for his eight goals.

Once again, Germany had reached a World Cup final only to lose. It evoked memories of 1966 against England, '82 against Italy, and '86 against Argentina. Their luck had just run out.

> **TRIVIA**
>
> Who was the top goalscorer from South Korea/Japan 2002?

Will they have it back in 2006?

Place your bets. We'll soon see.

**Germany
2006**

One: The Thirty-two Teams and Their Stars

So we're finally here at the new, the next, the immediate: the eighteenth FIFA World Cup of Soccer Germany 2006! (The official name is still too long.)

Before delving into the details of who will be competing this summer and where they come from, let's review a few basic facts:

- A total of 17 World Cups have taken place since 1930.
- Nine have taken place in Europe, 4 in South America, 3 in North America, and 1 in Asia.
- Four countries have hosted the event twice: Mexico, France, Italy, and now Germany.
- Brazil has won the most World Cup titles, with 5.
- Germany and Italy have won 3 titles each, Argentina and Uruguay have each won twice, and France and England have each won once.
- The top goalscorer in World Cup history is France's Just Fontaine, with 13.
- The top goalscorer in a single World Cup match is Russia's Oleg Salenka, who had 5 goals in Russia's 6–1 win over Cameroon in U.S.A. '94.
- The only player to have won 3 World Cup titles is Pelé.
- The players with the most World Cup appearances are Antonio Carbajal of Mexico and Lothar Matthaeus of Germany, with 5 apiece.
- The highest-scoring single match of all time was Austria 7, Switzerland 5, during the 1954 Cup.
- The biggest margin of victory in a World Cup match was Hungary's 10–1 defeat of El Salvador in Germany '74.
- The only nation to have appeared in every single World Cup is Brazil.

The great unknown about the next World Cup is whether any of these records will be broken. What do you think? Who will win the Golden Boot? Who will have the best goal? We'll see. Just don't get lost in the Cup!

THE 32 CLUB

Once again, the World Cup will feature thirty-two teams, keeping in line with the standard set in France '98.

These privileged countries represent the five continents. Fourteen come from Europe (including the host), five from Africa, four from South America, four from Asia, four from North and Central America and the Caribbean, and one from Oceania. This will be the first World Cup in history to feature teams from truly every corner of the globe.

Here is the list, broken down by continent and in alphabetical order:

EUROPE	AFRICA	ASIA
Croatia	Angola	Iran
Czech Republic	Ghana	Japan
England	Ivory Coast	Saudi Arabia
France	Togo	South Korea
Germany	Tunisia	
Holland		**NORTH & CENTRAL**
Italy	**SOUTH AMERICA**	**AMERICA AND**
Poland	Argentina	**THE CARIBBEAN**
Portugal	Brazil	Costa Rica
Serbia and Montenegro	Ecuador	Mexico
Spain	Paraguay	Trinidad and Tobago
Sweden		United States
Switzerland		
Ukraine		**OCEANIA:**
		Australia

FIVE NEWCOMERS

The previous list includes, for the first time, five African nations, and four of them are newcomers (another record): Angola, Ghana, Ivory Coast, and Togo.

The CONCACAF region was also sending someone new: Trinidad and Tobago.

From Europe there was one new country and two others with new names. The former is Ukraine (part of the former Soviet Union), and the latter two are the Czech Republic (formerly Czechoslovakia) and Serbia and Montenegro (which had formerly shared a name with Yugoslavia). In other words, Germany '06 will see the debuts of six nations. It is the largest number of newcomers since the World Cup's Modern Age began in 1950.

In a way, too, Ecuador, Australia, and Iran are borderline newcomers. They're each playing in only their second World Cup ever. Ecuador made their true debut in South Korea/Japan, while Iran did so in France '98 and Australia in Germany '74.

Among the major players returning to the stage this summer is Holland, back for the first time since '98. Switzerland—which isn't considered in the upper echelon, but was the host back in '54—is making its first appearance since U.S.A. '94. As such, welcome back to both.

The notable absences will be Belgium, Morocco, Cameroon, and, of course, Bulgaria and Romania, who have so often been stumbling blocks for other teams en route to the final. This time, however, they won't be.

But of all the absentees, the ones I'll miss the most (for personal, sentimental reasons) will be Colombia, Chile, and Uruguay.

THE FORMAT

The format of Germany '06 will remain the same as it was four years ago: eight groups of four teams, from which the top two in each will advance to the second round of single elimination.

The matches will take place in twelve different German cities: Munich, Stuttgart, Nuremberg, Frankfurt, Hanover, Kaiserslautern, Cologne, Gelsenkirchen, Dortmund, Hamburg, Leipzig, and Berlin.

The drawing was held on December 9, 2005, in Leipzig, and the groups fell out in the following manner:

> **Group A:** Germany, Costa Rica, Poland, Ecuador
> **Group B:** England, Paraguay, Trinidad and Tobago, Sweden
> **Group C:** Argentina, Ivory Coast, Serbia and Montenegro, Holland
> **Group D:** Mexico, Angola, Iran, Portugal
> **Group E:** Italy, Ghana, U.S.A., Czech Republic
> **Group F:** Brazil, Croatia, Australia, Japan
> **Group G:** France, Switzerland, South Korea, Togo
> **Group H:** Spain, Ukraine, Tunisia, Saudi Arabia

I should mention, of course, that this is the first World Cup where the defending champion was *not* given an automatic place in the finals.

Brazil had to qualify just like everybody else, with the exception, however, of the hosts, Germany.

"A TIME TO MAKE FRIENDS"

Sounds good to me!

That's the official slogan of this summer's World Cup, and, if memory serves me correctly, it's also the first World Cup to have such a thing.

Speaking of official things, the mascot this time around will be a lion cub named "Goleo," something much more recognizable and realistic than the three weird aliens from South Korea and Japan. Another new development is the fact that this time around, the mascot will have his own theme song.

Marketing, baby. Marketing!

THE OPENING CEREMONIES

Germany '06 will be trying something else new, as well: it will mark the first time that the opening ceremonies will be held *two days* before the opening match, on Wednesday, the seventh of June. Traditionally, the two things occur on the same day.

I imagine the reason is so that they can hold a bigger and more spectacular production. You all know how much the Europeans like to put on a show ... and to drive up ticket prices—which run from $125 to $900!

The event's organizers are describing the ceremony as "spectacular" and a "sensual extravaganza" that combines elements of music, dance, and special effects.

According to them, it will be an event unlike any other on earth, one

With the world-renown artist Romero Britto, who very kindly gave me a painting representing his vision of the 2006 World Cup in Germany.

that will make use of pyrotechnics and the latest technology in lighting effects in order to communicate "the emotional power of soccer."

Sweet!

The director of the event will be the Austrian artist André Heller. I don't know him, but they say he's a famous audiovisual artist. His team of assistants includes other artists, choreographers, designers, decorators, and illuminators. During the show, some 7,000 volunteers will be active in masks and costumes. Another 1,500 are working on the production itself.

In other words, Berlin's historic Olympic Stadium will light up, shine, explode, and resound like never before.

Not even Hitler put on a show of this magnitude during the '36 Olympics!

SPEAKING OF MONEY . . .

Yes sir, we're talking about the stuff that drives the World Cup (apart from passion, that is): cash, loot, dough, smackers, *lana, chavos, muna* . . .

The Organizing Committee for Germany '06 will be spending some $513 million to mount the show. This investment should be mitigated via ticket sales, food and beverage sales, and other commercial interests. But even that won't be enough. The rest will come from FIFA's coffers, some $200 million in all.

But that's nothing to the powerful organization. By some calculations, the World Cup is expected to generate the modest sum of—are you ready for this?—$2 billion!

Ka-ching, ka-ching!

More than half of that—$1.4 billion—comes from television rights. The rest will be coughed up by the official sponsors of the event, who range from McDonald's to Fuji, Budweiser, Adidas, and so on . . .

In the end, after all the accounts have been paid, FIFA will have made some $130 million. Not bad for an event that lasts just one month!

THE PRIZE

Okay, now what do you think the world champions will win? Besides the honor and prestige that comes with lifting the Cup, there is a cash prize of—*ka-ching!*—$19 million! Almost a million per player, right? They wish! Actually, the Federation will pay a premium to the players, but it won't be quite that much.

In the case of Germany, for example, we know that the Federation has promised to pay each player $350,000 if they win it all, $175,000 if they are the runner-up, $117,000 if they reach the semifinals, and $58,000 if they reach the quarters.

The runner-up will also be receiving money. Seventeen million dollars, to be precise. Sixteen million will go to both the third- and fourth-place teams. In other words, once you reach the semifinals, your team is guaranteed a premium of at least $16 million.

And there's even something for the losers. So, don't worry.

The four teams that reach the quarterfinals but wind up eliminated there will go home with some $9 million in their collective pockets. And the eight teams that are eliminated right at the start of the second round will have some $6 million to take home. In other words, simply advancing out of group play guarantees your team *at least* $6 million.

Finally, those poor squads who are eliminated in the first round will at least be going home not quite as . . . well . . . poor. FIFA pays everyone a minimum of $4.5 million just to participate.

Now you see why everybody wants in!

WHO'S WHO IN GERMANY '06

Okay, then. Now it's time to take a look at the thirty-two teams that will be participating in the 2006 World Cup.

We'll go country by country, and continent by continent. We'll begin with the Americas before going on to Europe, Africa, Asia, and Oceania.

I'll give you some basic information about each country and their team, but not so much (I hope) that you get bored with me.

I'll include the country's FIFA World Ranking (as of December 2005) and how they qualified; their World Cup history; the group they'll be playing in and their rivals; the name of their coach and his experience; their star players with their positions, and, when appropriate, the club they play for, young players you should keep an eye on; and—finally—a general description of the team and my own personal thoughts on them. (Note: the information I'm giving is current as of the time of this book's writing. We should all bear in mind how things can change from day to day in the world of competitive soccer.)

Ready?

We'll start with South America, and the country that will eventually be crowned champion—and it has nothing to do with the alphabet.

ARGENTINA

FIFA WORLD RANKING 4

HOW THEY QUALIFIED Second in South America.

HISTORY Fourteenth World Cup. World Champions in Argentina '78 and Mexico '86. Runners-up in Uruguay '30 and Italy '90. Hosts in 1978.

LAST APPEARANCE South Korea/Japan '02. Eliminated in the first round. (*¡Ay Dios mio!*)

2006 RIVALS Group C—Ivory Coast, Serbia and Montenegro, Holland.

COACH José Pekerman, coach since 2004. Won three World Youth Championships with Argentina.

STARS They're *all* stars, but . . .
- Hernán Crespo (striker, Chelsea, seven goals in qualifying)
- Juan Pablo Sorín (defender, Villareal)
- Pablo Aimar (midfielder, Valencia)
- Juan Román Riquelme (midfielder, Villareal, first World Cup)
- Carlos Tévez (striker, Corinthians, first World Cup)

WATCH OUT FOR THIS GUY LIONEL MESSI: At nineteen years old, he is already an excellent midfielder for Barcelona. He was the best player and top goalscorer during the World Youth Championships in Holland in 2005. He made his debut with the full national team toward the end of qualifying and immediately made his mark. He was much praised by the Argentine press. He's no Maradona, but he is better than Tevéz, who is quite a player himself. According to Pekerman, "He's a phenom, a joy. He's going to show us some wonderful things." Don't let him out of your sight.

COMMENTARY My beloved *albiceleste* will win the championship because the final falls on my birthday. It's the only present I want, and I think we have what we need to accomplish the task: namely, a

great coach in charge of a team evenly balanced between veterans (Ayala, Zanetti, Sorín, Crespo, Aimar) and young talent (Messi, Tévez, Riquelme, Rodríguez, Demichellis, Cambiasso, Mascherano). What more could you ask for? Ah . . . good luck, I suppose. I don't know how much of that we'll have. Our group may be the second most difficult in the draw, but we'll see. Nobody will stop us until July 9th, the day of the Berlin final. Not even Brazil, whom we owe a bit of revenge after the Copa América and Confederations Cup results. *¡Vamos Argentina, carajo!*

BRAZIL

FIFA WORLD RANKING 1

HOW THEY QUALIFIED First in South America. It
was the first time in World Cup history that the
defending champion had to go through qualifying.

HISTORY Eighteenth World Cup. Only nation to qualify for every
World Cup. Five-time champions: Sweden '58, Chile '62, Mexico '70,
U.S.A. '94, South Korea/Japan '02. Runners-up in Brazil '50 and
France '98. Third place in France '38 and Argentina '78. Hosts in 1950.

LAST APPEARANCE South Korea/Japan '02. Champions.

2006 RIVALS Group F—Australia, Japan, Croatia.

COACH Carlos Alberto Parreira. Coach since 2002. His fifth World
Cup. Led Brazil to the '94 championship, and also led Kuwait in
Spain '82, United Arab Emirates in Italy '90, and Saudi Arabia in
France '98.

STARS Where to begin?
- Ronaldo (striker, Real Madrid, ten goals in qualifying, fourth World Cup, alternate on the '94 team)
- Ronaldinho (striker, Barcelona, second World Cup)
- Roberto Carlos (defender, Real Madrid, fourth World Cup)
- Cafú (defender, Milan, fourth World Cup)
- Kaká (striker, Milan, second World Cup, first time as a starter)

WATCH OUT FOR THIS GUY ADRIANO: We already know him from the Copa América, the Confederations Cup, and from Inter Milan. Already a formidable goalscorer at twenty-four years of age, he is tall, strong, and a cannon-like shot with either leg. He had six goals in qualifying. He may not contend for the Golden Boot award because of all the competition (even from his own teammates), but we can expect at least a couple of outstanding goals. Don't lose sight of him, and keep your VCRs ready!

COMMENTARY The five-time champions are the undisputed favorites. Ronaldinho is the best player in the world at the moment, and there are several young players hungry for glory of their own. But be careful! Every time this happens, they fail to win it all. It happened in Spain '82, Mexico '86, Italy '90, and France '98. On the other hand, the 2002 squad was not among the pretournament favorites, and we all know what happened there. They have drawn a comfortable group and should advance without any trouble. But—as Pelé himself has said—"Beware of complacency!"

ECUADOR

FIFA WORLD RANKING 37

HOW THEY QUALIFIED Third place in South America, after Brazil and Argentina.

HISTORY Second World Cup.

LAST APPEARANCE South Korea/Japan '02. Failed to advance to the second round. Defeated Croatia but lost to Italy and Mexico.

2006 RIVALS Group A—Germany, Costa Rica, Poland.

COACH Luis Fernando Suárez. Coach since 2004. Former Colombian player. Former assistant to Pacho Maturana. Former coach of Pereira, Cali, Tolima, and champion with Medellín's Nacional. In Ecuador, he led Quito's Aucas, and the Copa América squad in 1997.

STARS
- Ivan Hurtado (Captain, defender, Al Arabi de Qatar)
- Agustín "Tin" Delgado (striker, Barcelona (Ecuador), five goals in qualifying)
- Ulises de la Cruz (defender, Aston Villa)
- Edison Méndez (striker, five goals in qualifying)

WATCH OUT FOR THIS GUY CHRISTIAN LARA: He inherited the number 10 jersey from Alex Aguinaga, which carries with it equal portions of pressure and honor. He made his national team debut in the qualifying match against Argentina, where he scored his first goal

and set up the team's second. At twenty-six years of age, he is already the star of his club team, El Nacional, where he's known as "Larita" and compared with Robinho on account of his size (5'4"). He is intelligent, quick, and creative. His dream is to succeed in Argentina, Mexico, or Europe. Taking advantage of the World Cup stage would help him in that regard.

COMMENTARY The altitude of Quito helped them to qualify—they were undefeated at home, including wins over both Brazil and Argentina. It remains to be seen whether they can succeed at sea level, in Germany. Their team is fast, they run freely, and they defend well, and they moved ahead of Colombia, Uruguay, and Chile in the rankings. Their four major players—Hurtado, de la Cruz, Méndez, and Delgado—already have World Cup experience, and will not be intimidated by anyone. They are joined by the prospects Luis Valencia, Franklin Salas, and "Larita." They are in a difficult draw where anything could happen. But they can surprise opponents with their joyful style of play, which has improved quite a bit in the past five years.

PARAGUAY

FIFA WORLD RANKING 30

HOW THEY QUALIFIED Fourth place in the South American zone.

HISTORY Seventh World Cup. Reached the second round in both France '98 and South Korea/Japan '02.

LAST APPEARANCE South Korea/Japan '02. Reached the second round, where they were defeated by Germany, 1–0.

2006 RIVALS Group B—England, Sweden, Trinidad and Tobago.

COACH Aníbal "Maño" Ruíz. Coach since 2002. Uruguayan. Formerly the coach of El Salvador, Olimpia (Paraguay), Nacional (Uruguay), and Necaxa, Tecos, Veracruz, Puebla, León, and Correcaminos (all in Mexico).

STARS
- José Saturnino Cardozo (striker, San Lorenzo, third World Cup, seven goals in qualifying)
- Carlos Gamarra (defender, Palmeiras, third World Cup)

- Roberto Acuña (midfielder, La Coruña, third World Cup)
- Roque Santa Cruz (striker, Bayern Munich, second World Cup)

WATCH OUT FOR THIS GUY NELSON HAEDO: This twenty-three-year-old striker is the promising future of Paraguayan soccer. At eighteen he was picked up by Germany's Werder Bremen, where he plays to this day. He was the star of the *guaraní* team in the 2003 World Youth Championships. He is very fast, and all the experts say he has a real nose for the goal. He was given a chance to prove himself with the full national squad toward the end of qualifying, and he surprised everyone. Remember his name: Haedo.

COMMENTARY Paraguay's *albiroja* squad is seeking to improve upon their previous two World Cup performances, in which they advanced,

both times, to the second round only to lose by one goal. They finished fourth in South American qualifying, thanks to a combination of veteran players and young talent, including a couple of excellent midfielders who led Paraguay to the silver medal at the Athens Olympics, Julio Dos Santos and Edgar Barreto. The cagey old veteran "Maño" is going to need all his *mañas* (skills) to get them out of group play. And since Pepe Cardozo is playing in his final World Cup, he will be eager to end on a positive note. Hopefully his aim will be true. Watch out for Paraguay!

NORTH AND CENTRAL AMERICA AND THE CARIBBEAN

COSTA RICA • UNITED STATES
MEXICO • TRINIDAD AND TOBAGO

COSTA RICA

FIFA WORLD RANKING 21

HOW THEY QUALIFIED Third in the CONCACAF region, behind the United States and Mexico.

HISTORY Third World Cup. Advanced to the second round of Italy '90, where they were eliminated by Czechoslovakia 4–1.

LAST APPEARANCE South Korea/Japan '02. Eliminated in the first round.

2006 RIVALS Group A—Germany, Ecuador, Poland.

COACH Alexandre Guimaraes. Coach since 2005. Also led Costa Rica during South Korea/Japan '02. Has also coached Saprissa and Irapuato and Dorados in Mexico. Born in Brazil. Played for Costa Rica in Italy '90.

STARS

- Paulo César Wanchope (striker, top goalscorer on the team, eight goals during qualifying, participating in his final World Cup)
- Dany Fonseca (midfielder, first World Cup)
- Ronald Gómez (striker, Saprissa, second World Cup)
- Walter Centeno (midfielder, Saprissa, second World Cup)

WATCH OUT FOR THIS GUY ALVARO SABORIO: A twenty-four-year-old natural-born goalscorer who plays his club soccer with Saprissa, he was the leading scorer during the 2004 Costa Rican club season, with twenty-five tallies. In 2005 he added fifteen more. In his five years as a professional, he has scored one hundred times. After Wanchope,

he is the best striker that Costa Rica has produced in recent memory. He had three during qualifying. Germany will be his first World Cup, and much is expected of him. The pressure, however, shouldn't affect him, as he has already appeared in the Athens Olympics and the 2005 World Club Championship. Pay attention, because he's going to go far.

COMMENTARY The goal for *los ticos* is to repeat their performance of Italy '90, where they were a huge surprise in their first World Cup, defeating Scotland and Sweden and advancing to the second round. In South Korea/Japan '02, they continued to impress

people with their fast and organized style of play. They failed to advance, finishing just behind Turkey (the eventual third-place finishers in the whole tournament) on goal differential. Their group is fairly stacked, but with Wanchope playing in his final World Cup—and with Fonseca, Gómez, Centeno, and Saborio showing the best form of their careers—I believe that *los ticos* will be inspired enough to repeat their performance of Italy '90. Much luck, and . . . ¡pura vida!

UNITED STATES

FIFA WORLD RANKING 8

HOW THEY QUALIFIED First place in CONCACAF, ahead of Mexico, Costa Rica, and Trinidad and Tobago.

HISTORY Eighth World Cup. Reached the semifinals of Uruguay '30 and the quarterfinals of South Korea/Japan '02. Hosts in 1994.

LAST APPEARANCE South Korea/Japan '02. Reached the quarterfinals by defeating Mexico. Were eliminated by runners-up, Germany.

2006 RIVALS Group E—Italy, Czech Republic, Ghana.

COACH Bruce Arena. Coach since 1999. Former coach of DC United, where he was twice MLS champions. This will be his second World Cup.

STARS
- Claudio Reyna (Captain, midfielder, Manchester City, third World Cup)
- Landon Donovan, (striker, L.A. Galaxy, second World Cup)
- Brian McBride (striker, Fulham, third World Cup)

- DaMarcus Beasley (striker, PSV Eindhoven, second World Cup)
- Kasey Keller (goalkeeper, Borussia Mönchengladbach (Germany), fourth World Cup, only starter remaining from the France '98 squad)

WATCH OUT FOR THIS GUY

OGUCHI ONYEWU: Has Nigerian blood and a steely resolve. Defender for Belgium's Standard Liege. Twenty-four years old, standing 6'4" in height, he plays with a calmness and a composure unusual for one so young. He broke out with the US U-17 and U-20 teams. In 2002 he was signed by Metz of France, and in 2004 he was transferred to Belgium, where he is one of the top defenders in their first division. "Gooch" (as he is known) has caught Arena's attention, and was a starter during the 2005 Gold Cup. He will likely start in Germany as well. Keep an eye on him.

COMMENTARY This will be the fifth consecutive World Cup appearance for the United States. And perhaps the fifth time will be a charm. If it's better than their fourth appearance—where the U.S. just came up short against Germany in the quarterfinals—then this World Cup will have historic significance. Twelve years ago, they didn't even have their own professional league, and now they're among the ten best teams on the planet! The MLS is gaining strength every year, and many U.S. stars play in Europe (Reyna with Manchester City, Lewis with Leeds United, Beasley with PSV Eindhoven, McBride and Bocanegra with Fulham, Keller with Borussia). Their group is a tough one, but it seems that there is nothing the U.S. team puts its mind to that it cannot achieve. Italy and the Czech Republic had better watch out. Go U.S.A.!

MEXICO

FIFA WORLD RANKING 7

HOW THEY QUALIFIED Second place in the CON-CACAF region.

HISTORY Thirteenth World Cup. Reached the quarterfinals of Mexico '70 and Mexico '86. Hosts in '70 and '86.

LAST APPEARANCE South Korea/Japan '02. Eliminated in the first match of the second round by the United States.

2006 RIVALS Group D—Iran, Angola, Portugal.

COACH Ricardo Lavolpe. Coach since 2003. Argentine by birth. Former coach of Toluca, Chivas, América, Puebla, Atlas, and Atlante. As a player, was the goalkeeper for Atlante and was a member of the Argentine World Cup team in 1978.

STARS
- Rafa Márquez (defender, Barcelona)
- Oswaldo Sánchez (keeper, Chivas, first World Cup as a starter)
- Jared Borgetti (striker, Bolton, fourteen goals in qualifying)

- Cuauhtemoc Blanco (striker, América, third World Cup)
- Guille Franco (striker, Monterrey, born in Argentina)

WATCH OUT FOR THIS GUY JAIME LOZANO: Despite playing injured, he made his mark during the qualifying stages. "El Jimmy" is twenty-seven years old and plays midfield for the Tigres of Monterrey, where he demonstrates a sense of class and freedom, not to mention a lethal free kick. He scored eleven goals, second best on the team. He is in Lavolpe's good graces, and was named as a starter for the Copa América and the Confederations Cup, where he really took flight. That experience should help him to soar to even greater heights in Germany.

COMMENTARY Lavolpe promised to take *los tri* to the World Cup, and he delivered. But it wasn't without suffering a number of controversies that many would like to forget (I'm thinking of Hugo Sánchez, who was the main opponent to having a foreign-born coach). Lavolpe considered the best players he had access to, including younger talent and naturalized citizens, and has put together the best team possible. They scored twenty-two goals in qualifying, and finished just behind the United States in CONCACAF (though with the same record). And at the time of the draw, FIFA gave them one of the coveted number-one seeds, assuring them of a favorable group. Mexico will advance out of the first round without problems as long as they take care of business on the field and do not get waylaid by confidence. Otherwise, Hugo will have a field day.

TRINIDAD AND TOBAGO

FIFA WORLD RANKING 51

HOW THEY QUALIFIED Won the play-off against
Bahrain (Asia).

HISTORY First World Cup.

LAST APPEARANCE N/A

2006 RIVALS Group B—England, Paraguay, Sweden.

COACH Leo Beenhakker. Coach since 2004. Previously coached
Holland at Italy '90 and Saudi Arabia leading up to U.S.A. '94. Also
coached at Ajax, Feyenoord, Real Madrid, Real Zaragoza, América,
and Chivas.

STARS
- Dwight Yorke (Captain, striker, Sydney FC (Australia), has
  played with Manchester United, Aston Villa, and Birmingham
  City)

- Russell Latapy (midfielder, thirty-eight years old, Falkirk (Scotland), played with Porto and Boavista (Portugal) and Glasgow Rangers, had retired from international competition before being convinced to return to the national team)
- Stern John (striker, Coventry City (England), has played with the Columbus Crew of the MLS, and led the league in scoring in 1998, scored twelve goals in qualifying, behind only Borgetti)

WATCH OUT FOR THIS GUY CHRIS BIRCHALL: A twenty-two-year-old midfielder who plays his club ball with Port Vale of the English second division. Born in England to a Trinidadian mother, he is the only Caucasian player on the team. He plays well along the right wing, and has a good long-range shot. He's already scored several goals in such a manner since getting his first cap back in 2005, and one of them was the equalizer against Bahrain in the first leg of their play-off.

COMMENTARY Beenhakker will be adored in this Caribbean nation for the rest of his life. He achieved the impossible: qualifying for the World Cup. It wasn't cheap, but it was worth it. They finished fourth in the CONCACAF region, thus earning the right to a play-off against one of the Asian teams (Bahrain), whom they defeated to earn their ticket. And you can imagine the Carnival that broke out on the streets of Trinidad and Tobago. It's still going on, because for them, this World Cup will be exactly that: a Carnival. They have nothing to lose and everything to gain. And they may even be able to surprise England or Sweden (though I doubt they'll sneak up on Paraguay).

EUROPE

**CROATIA • CZECH REPUBLIC • ENGLAND
FRANCE • GERMANY • HOLLAND • ITALY • POLAND
PORTUGAL • SERBIA AND MONTENEGRO • SPAIN
SWEDEN • SWITZERLAND • UKRAINE**

CROATIA

FIFA WORLD RANKING 20

HOW THEY QUALIFIED Won Group 8 (ahead of
Sweden, Bulgaria, and Hungary).

HISTORY Third World Cup. Made their first
appearance in France '98 and finished third. Their star, Davor Suker,
won the Golden Boot.

LAST APPEARANCE South Korea/Japan '02. Failed to advance out of
the first round, losing to Mexico and Ecuador.

2006 RIVALS Group F—Brazil, Australia, Japan.

COACH Zlatko Kranjcar. Coach since 2004. Former player for the former Yugoslavia. Making his first appearance as a World Cup coach.

STARS
- The brothers Niko (Captain, midfielder, Hertha Berlin) and Robert Kovac (defender, Juventus, both born in Germany)
- Dado Prso (striker, Rangers)
- Josip "Joe" Simunic (sweeper, Hertha Berlin)
- Igor Tudor (defender, Siena)

WATCH OUT FOR THIS GUY DARIJO SRNA: You've heard of him, right? Twenty-three years old, right winger, creates problems for the defense, scores goals. Five, to be exact, in qualifying. Reminiscent of Roberto Carlos in that regard. Plays in Croatia's league, with Shakhtar Donetsk. Don't forget his name.

COMMENTARY The team with the checkered jerseys isn't as good as it was in France '98, when it had Sukor at the helm, but they were

unbeaten in Europe's Group 8, which leads me to believe they will improve upon their 2002 performance. Their best attribute is their defense. Coach Kranjcar, who is very well liked and respected throughout Croatia, took over the team in the wake of their disastrous 2004 European Championships, and he led them to the World Cup. His son, the midfielder Niko Kranjcar, also plays for the team. They play in a tough group, but they should advance, if not very far.

CZECH REPUBLIC

FIFA WORLD RANKING 2

HOW THEY QUALIFIED Eliminated Norway in a repechage. Finished second in Group 1, behind Holland but ahead of Romania and Finland.

HISTORY First World Cup, after appearing eight times as Czechoslovakia. Were runners-up in France '38 and Chile '62.

LAST APPEARANCE It is their first appearance as the Czech Republic. As Czechoslovakia, they reached the quarterfinals of Italy '90.

2006 RIVALS Group E—Italy, Ghana, United States.

COACH Karel Bruckner. Coach since 2002. Was formerly the coach of Poland during the Sydney Olympics (2000), and coach of the U-20 team.

STARS
- Pavel Nedved (midfielder, Juventus, superstar of the team)
- Jan Koller (striker, Borussia Dortmund, top goalscorer on the team with more than forty in his career)

- Tomas Rosicky (midfielder, Borussia Dortmund, twenty-six years old, seven goals in qualifying)
- Jan Polak (midfielder, Norimberk (Germany), twenty-five years old, four goals in qualifying)
- Peter Cech (goalkeeper, Chelsea, twenty-four years old, named the best keeper in Europe's Champions League in 2004)

WATCH OUT FOR THIS GUY MILAN BAROS: A sensational twenty-five-year-old striker for Aston Villa. Played with Liverpool for a spell before moving to Aston Villa for an $8 million transfer fee. Has the look of a prime goalscorer. Scored five times in qualifying, and was the top goalscorer in the 2004 European Championships. Two of them came against Denmark in a two-minute span! Don't lose sight of him.

COMMENTARY This is one of the most dangerous European squads. They have scored thirty-five goals in twelve qualifying matches, equaling the total of Portugal. Five of their stars have at least four goals to their name. Jan Koller was the second-highest scorer in all of Europe, with nine tallies. Rosicky had seven, Baros five, Vratilslav Lokvenc five, Jan Polak four. It's not without reason that FIFA has them ranked second in the world. They should prove to be a huge headache in Germany, especially in their first-round group. I think they'll go quite far. Not quite to the final, but they will be in the quarters at least. You can quote me on that.

ENGLAND

FIFA WORLD RANKING 9

HOW THEY QUALIFIED First in Group 6, ahead of Poland, Austria, and Ireland.

HISTORY Twelfth World Cup. Winners at England '66, fourth at Italy '90. Hosts in 1966.

LAST APPEARANCE South Korea/Japan '02. Eliminated in the quarterfinals, 2–1, against Brazil.

2006 RIVALS Group B—Paraguay, Trinidad and Tobago, and Sweden.

COACH Sven-Goran Eriksson. Coach since 2001. Swedish. Former coach of Benfica, Roma, Fiorentina, Sampdoria, and Lazio. Second World Cup as coach.

STARS
- David Beckham (Captain, midfielder, Real Madrid)
- Michael Owen (striker, Newcastle)
- Rio Ferdinand (sweeper, Manchester United)
- Frank Lampard (midfielder, Chelsea, five goals in qualifying)

WATCH OUT FOR THIS GUY
WAYNE ROONEY: It's no secret that this twenty-one-year-old striker from Manchester United is the real deal. Ever since he first cracked the ranks of the national team in 2003 at the age of seventeen, he has at times been as sensational as Pelé, who was the same age in Sweden '58. He is strong, explosive, and a powerful finisher, as well as being the youngest player ever to appear on England's full national team. He had four goals in the 2004 European Championships.

If all goes well, this World Cup will be his coronation as the biggest star of British football.

COMMENTARY With Rooney and Owen up front, Lampard in the middle, and Ferdinand in the back—and if Beckham has enough juice left in him—England has enough to win it all. However, it will take some luck as well. Eriksson, who will be facing the country of his birth in the first round, has reinvigorated the team with some young talent like John Terry (26), Joe Cole (25), and Jermain Defoe (24). As a result, they qualified first in their group. But we all know how demanding the British press can be. In their minds, since England invented soccer, then England should be the best at it. But of course it's not that simple. For the Brits, it never has been. But this time will be different. They have a favorable draw, and I believe this time their luck will change . . . unless they have to play Brazil or Argentina, of course!

The Thirty-two Teams and Their Stars

FRANCE

FIFA WORLD RANKING 5

HOW THEY QUALIFIED Won Group 4, ahead of Switzerland, Israel, and Ireland.

HISTORY Eleventh World Cup. Winners at France '98. Hosts in both 1938 and '98.

LAST APPEARANCE South Korea/Japan '02. Eliminated in the first round without a win and without a goal. An utter disaster!

2006 RIVALS Group G: Switzerland, South Korea, and Togo.

COACH Raymond Doménech. Coach since 2004. Former star and former coach of Olympique of Lyon. First World Cup as coach.

STARS
- Zinedine Zidane (Captain, midfielder, Real Madrid)
- Claude Makelele (midfielder, Chelsea)
- David Trezeguet (striker, Juventus)
- Thierry Henry (striker, Arsenal)

WATCH OUT FOR THIS GUY JEAN-ALAIN BOUMSONG: Considered the heir of the great captain and central defender Marcel Desailly.

Born in Cameroon, this twenty-seven-year-old made his debut at the 2004 European Championships and currently plays for Newcastle in England. He is strong, agile, and elegant. A natural stopper. He won his spot as a starter toward the end of the qualifying campaign. The World Cup stage should inspire him to greatness.

COMMENTARY *Les bleus* both want and simply have to redeem themselves in the eyes of their public after what happened in 2002. The 2006 team is a mix of veterans (Zidane, Vieira, Makelele, Thuram, Henry, and Trezeguet) and new faces, like William Gallas (Chelsea), Jean-Alain Boumsong (Newcastle), Willy Sagnol (Bayern Munich), Vikash Dhovasoo (Milan), and Florent Malouda (Lyon). All are seeking to add another chapter to the glorious history of Gallic soccer. After all, France is the birthplace of the World Cup. They were unbeaten in their qualifying rounds, though they did have a number of ties (five) and not many goals (fourteen in ten matches) in a relatively weak group. Their two main goalscorers, Henry and Trezeguet, are quite prolific on their respective club teams, but seem to lose their touch when they play for the national team. Will they come around in Germany? They had better, if they don't want to repeat the failures of South Korea/Japan. France is depending on them.

GERMANY

FIFA WORLD RANKING 16

HOW THEY QUALIFIED As hosts.

HISTORY Sixteenth World Cup. Three-time champions: Switzerland '54, Germany '74, and Italy '90. Runners-up in England '66, Spain '82, Mexico '86, South Korea/Japan '02. Hosts in 1974.

LAST APPEARANCE South Korea/Japan '02. Runners-up, losing to Brazil 2–0 in the final.

2006 RIVALS Group A—Costa Rica, Poland, and Ecuador.

COACH Jürgen Klinsmann. Coach since 2003. Former star striker for the team. Making his first appearance as a World Cup coach.

STARS
- Michael Ballack (Captain, midfielder, Bayern Munich)
- Lukas Podolski (striker, FC Cologne, Polish and German)
- Miroslav "Miro" Klose (striker, Bremen, Polish and German)

WATCH OUT FOR THIS GUY BASTIAN SCHWEINSTEIGER:
Nicknamed "Basti," this supremely talented twenty-year-old midfielder for Bayern Munich is very popular across Germany. He had a
successful debut run at the 2004 European Championships, and
showed more class at the 2005 Confederations Cup. Keep an eye on
him, for he should do very good things playing at home.

COMMENTARY This year's Germany isn't the Germany of '74, '86, or
'90, when they were World Cup champions. Their new players just
don't compare with the Beckenbauers, the Müllers, the Sellers, or the
Rummenigges of years past. Plus, they are playing under tremendous
pressure from the public and the press, neither of which is convinced
of their strength as a side. But we have to remember that Germany is
Germany, and it will be difficult to beat them in their own house,
especially in the first round. So . . . can they win it all? The champion
will need luck, and the Germans have always had it. I wouldn't count
them out just yet.

HOLLAND

FIFA WORLD RANKING 3

HOW THEY QUALIFIED Winners of Group 1, ahead of the Czech Republic, Romania, and Finland.

HISTORY Eighth World Cup. Runners-up in Germany '74 and Argentina '78. Fourth in France '98.

LAST APPEARANCE France '98. Finished fourth, losing to Croatia 2–1 in the consolation match.

2006 RIVALS Group C—Argentina, Ivory Coast, and Serbia and Montenegro.

COACH Marco van Basten. Coach since 2004. Former star of the national team, Ajax, and AC Milan. Several times honored as the best player in both Europe and the world. This is his first World Cup as coach.

STARS

- Ruud van Nistelrooy (striker, Manchester United, seven goals in qualifying)

- Edgar Davids (midfielder, Tottenham)
- Roy Makaay (striker, Bayern Munich)
- Phillip Cocu (defender, PSV Eindhoven)

WATCH OUT FOR THIS GUY RAFAEL VAN DER VAART: This versatile twenty-three-year-old playmaker is one of the best Dutch prospects at this time. He cut his teeth in the ranks of Ajax, where he was compared to both Cruyff and Bergkamp. He's a favorite of Marco van Basten (along with Robin van Persie, the striker from

Arsenal), and forms a dangerous attacking force with superstar Ruud van Nistelrooy.

COMMENTARY The new "Clockwork Orange" arrives just as they did in France '98: needing to vindicate themselves in the eyes of the world after not qualifying for the previous World Cup. And to start things off, they went undefeated in a difficult qualifying group. They scored twenty-seven goals while conceding only three, the third-best average in all of European qualifying, after Portugal and Sweden. Van Basten has based his selection on young talent like Robin van Persie (Arsenal), Rafael van der Vaart and Khalid Boulahrouz (Hamburg), Wesley Sneijder (Ajax), and Arjen Robben (Chelsea). Holland is definitely one of the big favorites to win this World Cup. First, however, they will have to survive Group C, the toughest one, where they will once again face Argentina.

ITALY

FIFA WORLD RANKING 12

HOW THEY QUALIFIED Winners of Group 5, ahead of Norway, Scotland, and Slovenia.

HISTORY Sixteenth World Cup. Three-time champions: Italy '34, France '38, and Spain '82. Runners-up at Mexico '70 and U.S.A. '94. Hosts in 1934 and 1990.

LAST APPEARANCE South Korea/Japan '02. Eliminated in their first match of the second round on a golden goal by South Korea.

2006 RIVALS Group E—Ghana, United States, and the Czech Republic.

COACH Marcello Lippi. Coach since 2004. Former coach of Juventus, with five Italian league championships and one European and one Intercontinental Championship.

STARS
- Francesco Totti (striker, Roma)
- Alessandro Nesta (sweeper, Milan)

- Christian Vieri (striker, Milan)
- Alessandro del Piero (striker, Juventus)

WATCH OUT FOR THIS GUY
LUCA TONI: He's not
exactly a boy. He's twenty-
nine years old, but he has
never played in a World
Cup before. And he's the
top Italian goalscorer in a
league rife with foreigners.
At Fiorentina, he's com-
pared with Batistuta. And
like "Batigol" in '94, he
started off with goals
galore: thirteen in sixteen
matches. On the strength of
that, he was paid ten million euros to transfer to
Palermo, where he scored
thirty in 2003. He had four
during qualifying, which
was best on the team. If he
gets hot, he could prove to
be another Rossi, Schillaci,
or Baggio, who all led Italy
to the final. Be ready in
case he proves to be another *miracolo*.

COMMENTARY The famed *azzurri* arrive—as they always do—among
the favorites. Up front, they have the veterans Totti, Vieri, and del
Piero, to say nothing of Luca Toni and two young stars with excellent
futures: Antonio Cassano (twenty-four years old, Roma) and Alberto
"Il Gila" Gilardino (twenty-four, Milan). Their defense continues to be
strong, as is Italy's tradition, and in the midfield they have a spirited
young colt, born in Argentina, by the name of Mauro Camoranesi, who
played for Cruz Azul and now Juventus. Lippi's triumphant spirit
will be tested in Germany, especially during the first round in their
difficult group. Will they prevail? I think so. Italy is going to put on
a great show in search of their fourth World Cup title.

POLAND

FIFA WORLD RANKING 23

HOW THEY QUALIFIED One of the two best second-place finishers in Europe. Behind England and ahead of Austria and Ireland in Group 6.

HISTORY Sixth World Cup. Finished third in Germany '74 and Spain '82.

LAST APPEARANCE South Korea/Japan '02. Eliminated in the first round.

2006 RIVALS Group A—Germany, Costa Rica, and Ecuador.

COACH Pawel Janas. Coach since 2002. Former national team player, including Spain '82. Was coach of Poland's Olympic squad in '92. First World Cup as coach.

STARS
- Maciej Zurawski (striker, Celtic, seven goals in qualifying)
- Tomas Frankowski (midfielder, Elche, seven goals in qualifying)
- Kamil Kosowski (midfielder, FC Kaiserslautern)
- Jerzy Dudek (goalkeeper, Liverpool)

WATCH OUT FOR THIS GUY EUZEBIUSZ SMOLAREK: "Ebi" for short. A twenty-five-year-old offensive midfielder who plays his club ball with Dortmund's Borussia. Highly experienced for a player of his age. Began his professional career in 2000 with Holland's Feyernoord, where he played for four seasons before transferring to Dortmund. His father, Wlodzimierz Smolarek, was also a player for Poland's national team, and he is the best young prospect on a team laden with veterans.

COMMENTARY Poland finished second in a difficult group, just one point behind the winners, England. But they were still able to qualify for the finals as one of the two best second-place teams in group play. They only lost two qualifying matches, and proved to be quite an offensive threat, scoring twenty-seven times in ten games. But since the days of players like Lato, who led Poland to a pair of third-place World Cup finishes, the team has not been the same. Their best players today are all around thirty years of age and don't compare favorably with the stars of their past. I doubt that Poland will make much of a splash in Germany. They won't make it out of Group A.

PORTUGAL

FIFA WORLD RANKING 10

HOW THEY QUALIFIED Undefeated winners of Group 3, ahead of Slovakia, Russia, and Estonia.

HISTORY Fourth World Cup. Finished third at England '66, where Eusebio was the tournament's top goalscorer.

LAST APPEARANCE South Korea/Japan '02. Eliminated in the first round, with losses to the United States (3–2) and South Korea (1–0).

2006 RIVALS Group D: Mexico, Iran, and Angola.

COACH Luiz Felipe Scolari, also known as "Felipão," or "Big Phil." Coach since 2003. Led Brazil to the 2002 World Cup title. Led Portugal to Runners-up at the 2004 European Championships.

STARS
- Luis Figo (midfielder, Inter Milan)
- Rui Costa (midfielder, AC Milan)

- Pauleta (Pedro Miguel Carreiro Resendes) (striker, Paris St. Germain, top goalscorer during European qualifying, with eleven tallies)
- Deco (Anderson de Sousa) (midfielder, Barcelona, born in Brazil)

WATCH OUT FOR THIS GUY CRISTIANO RONALDO: This twenty-one-year-old is good enough that Manchester United looked to him to replace David Beckham when he left for Real Madrid. He's a midfielder with great—sometimes spectacular—ball-control skills. He had seven goals during qualifying, which put him second on the team behind Pauleta. He really made a name for himself during the 2004 European Championships, and I think he'll do more of the same in Germany, continuing on his way to becoming the next great Portuguese star.

COMMENTARY Portugal was the top goalscoring team in all of European qualifying, with thirty-five goals in only twelve matches. And they only conceded five. Which you might expect from the team that really should have won the 2004 European Championships on its own soil, if it weren't for an inexplicable loss to Greece, who didn't even qualify for Germany '06. Felipão knows what it's like to play in—and win—a World Cup. His experience will prove quite useful this summer. If he can inspire his adopted team the way he inspired his fellow Brazilians four years ago, then Portugal will go quite far indeed. Perhaps not to the championship, but they will surprise some people. They will advance out of Group D along with Mexico and erase the memory of their failure four years ago. Of that you can be sure.

SERBIA AND MONTENEGRO

FIFA WORLD RANKING 47

HOW THEY QUALIFIED Undefeated winners of
Group 7. Ahead of Spain, Bosnia, and Belgium.

HISTORY First World Cup. As Yugoslavia, they appeared in nine, finishing fourth at Uruguay '30 and Chile '62.

LAST APPEARANCE France '98 (as the former Yugoslavia). Eliminated
by Holland in the second round, 2–1.

2006 RIVALS Group C—Argentina, Ivory Coast, Holland.

COACH Ilija Petkovic. Coach since 2001. The former assistant coach
with Yugoslavia at France '98 and South Korea/Japan '02. Former
player for Yugoslavia at Spain '82. First World Cup as coach.

STARS
- Savo Milosevic (striker, Osasuna)
- Mateja Kezman (striker, Atlético Madrid, five goals during
  qualifying)
- Darko Kovacevic (striker, Real Sociedad)
- Dejan Stankovic (Captain, midfielder, Inter Milan)

WATCH OUT FOR THIS GUY

ZVONIMIR VUKIC: Twenty-seven-year-old offensive midfielder from Portsmouth (England). He's not all that young, but the world has yet to take notice of him. This will be his first World Cup. He stands 6'1", and he's creative, athletic, and he knows how to find the goal. He scored four times in qualifying, and in the four years he spent playing for Belgrade, he scored fifty-three, including twenty-two in one season alone. This dangerous ability will surely make itself apparent in Germany.

COMMENTARY Starting in 2003, Yugoslavia began to play under the name of Serbia and Montenegro. And remaining unbeaten throughout qualifying has been their greatest accomplishment thus far. They did not participate in the 2004 European Championships, or in the Athens Olympics. Their best weapon is their defense, and it's among the best in Europe, only giving up a single goal in a 1–1 draw with Spain. The team is based around the veterans Milosevic, Kovascevic, and Kezman, as well as the newcomers Pedrag Ocokolijic (defense), Vukic (midfield), and Marco Pantelic (striker). They have a difficult draw—as difficult as their qualifying round was—which means they'll have to play well. I think they'll trip up a couple of teams . . . but I hope Argentina isn't one of them!

SPAIN

FIFA WORLD RANKING 6

HOW THEY QUALIFIED Winning a play-off against Slovakia. They finished second in Group 7, behind Serbia and Montenegro and ahead of Belgium and Bosnia-Herzegovina.

HISTORY Twelfth World Cup. Finished fourth at Brazil '50. Hosts in 1982.

LAST APPEARANCE South Korea/Japan '02. Eliminated in the quarter-finals by South Korea on penalty kicks.

2006 RIVALS Group H—Ukraine, Tunisia, Saudi Arabia.

COACH Luis Aragonés. Coach since 2004. Former player and former coach of Atlético Madrid, Real Madrid, Barcelona, Espanyol, Valencia, Real Betis, Sevilla, and Mallorca. First World Cup as coach.

STARS
- Raúl (Raúl González) (Captain, striker, Real Madrid)
- Carles Puyol (defender, Barcelona)
- Xavi Hernández (midfielder, Barcelona)
- Fernando Morientes (striker, Liverpool)
- Guti (José María Gutiérrez) (striker, Real Madrid)

WATCH OUT FOR THIS GUY FERNANDO TORRES: A twenty-one-year-old striker for Atlético Madrid, and the brightest Spanish prospect currently at that position. Quick, strong, intelligent, and skillful. He's right-footed but can use his left quite well indeed. Was the team's top goalscorer during qualifying, with seven to his name. As Aragonés himself says, "no two of his goals are alike." Keep an eye on him this summer, because he's sure to do something amazing.

Commentary: The *"Furia Roja"* barely qualified, despite not losing a single match (six wins and six ties). They were forced into a play-off with Slovakia in order to got their ticket punched, which they did in no uncertain terms, with a 5–0 win. One of their emerging stars, Luis García of Liverpool had a hat trick that day. According to Aragonés, Spain is going to Germany to win it all. Good luck! Which is something that they've never seemed to have at World Cup time and they'll need it, too. They'll also need Xavi to be fully recovered from knee surgery. Will this be Spain's year? I don't think so, but I do hope. All of Latin America would celebrate with pride. And things are already off to a good start: they have a favorable group.

SWEDEN

FIFA WORLD RANKING 14

HOW THEY QUALIFIED One of the two best second-place finishers in qualifying. They finished tied on points with the Group 8 winner, Croatia.

HISTORY Eleventh World Cup. Runners-up at Sweden '58. Third place at U.S.A. '94. Hosts in 1958.

LAST APPEARANCE South Korea/Japan '02. Won their group, ahead of Argentina and England. Eliminated in the second round by Senegal.

2006 RIVALS Group B—England, Paraguay, and Trinidad and Tobago.

COACH Lars Lagerback. Coach since 2004. Was also one of the coaches for the 2002 World Cup squad.

STARS
- Henrik Larsson (striker, Barcelona, five goals in qualifying)
- Fredrik Ljungberg (striker, Arsenal, seven goals in qualifying)
- Olof Mellberg (Captain, defender)

WATCH OUT FOR THIS GUY

ZLATAN IBRAHIMOVIC: A twenty-four-year-old striker for Juventus. He's the new sensation in Swedish soccer, one of the best strikers in recent memory, and one of the best prospects in all of Europe. With eight goals in qualifying, he was the third-highest scorer in the zone. He had a great one late in the match against Hungary, in Budapest, to give Sweden a 1–0 win. He's athletic, elusive, and he makes an excellent sidekick to the veteran Larsson. He was barely twenty years old when he appeared twice as a substitute in the 2002 World Cup, and this time around should be his international coming-out party. Remember the name: Ibrahimovic.

COMMENTARY Sweden is a young team, averaging only twenty-four years of age. Around the veterans Ljungberg, Mellberg, and Larsson is a fistful of young players who have cropped up in the past five years. Most of them are midfielders and strikers, such as Christian Wilhemsson, Johan Elmander, Markus Rosenberg, and—of course—Ibrahimovic. Sweden scored thirty goals in only ten games in a very difficult qualifying group, which gave them the best goals/game average in all of Europe. Coach Lagerback has a lot of confidence in his young team, and is betting that they will prove to be a very pleasant surprise indeed. I agree. Beware Sweden!

SWITZERLAND

FIFA WORLD RANKING 36

HOW THEY QUALIFIED Defeated Turkey in a home-and-away play-off, 2–0 in Bern, 4–2 in Istanbul. Finished second in Group 4, behind France yet in front of Israel and Ireland.

HISTORY Eighth World Cup. Reached the quarterfinals of Italy '34, France '38, and Switzerland '54. Hosts in 1954.

LAST APPEARANCE U.S.A. '94. Eliminated by Spain in the second round, 3–0.

2006 RIVALS Group G—France, South Korea, and Togo.

COACH Jakob "Kobi" Kuhn. Coach since 2001. Former star of FC Zurich and the Swiss national team. First World Cup as coach.

STARS

- Alexander Frei (striker, Stade Rennes)
- Raphael Wicky (midfielder, Hamburg)
- Marco Streller (striker, Stuttgart)

WATCH OUT FOR THIS GUY TRANQUILO BARNETTA: Only twenty-one years old, he represents another of the kids who should feel right at home this summer in Germany. He plays as an offensive midfielder for Bayern Leverkusen. Along with his teammate Philippe Senderos (defender for Arsenal), he started for the U-17 squad that won the European Championship in 2002. He's got quite a bit of class and poise for his age, and can flow freely and elegantly into space or away from a rival. The Swiss adore him, and expect him to go quite far as a player. So pay attention!

COMMENTARY The Helvetic selection proved to be quite the surprise in qualifying, as they eliminated the powerful Turks—who had fin-

ished third in 2002—from contention this time. They did not lose a single qualifying match, finishing second in their group. It's been eight years since Switzerland participated in a World Cup, and this year they will be looking to revive the success they had at U.S.A. '94, where they played well enough to reach the second round. Defense is their strong suit, with their veteran captain Johann Vogel, the young Senderos, and a keeper with a good deal of experience, Pascal Zuberbuhler. I expect them to repeat their success of U.S.A. '94 and reach the second round, but not any further than that.

UKRAINE

FIFA WORLD RANKING 40

HOW THEY QUALIFIED Winners of Group 2, ahead of Turkey, Denmark, and Greece.

HISTORY First World Cup.

LAST APPEARANCE N/A

2006 RIVALS Group H—Spain, Tunisia, and Saudi Arabia.

COACH Oleg Blokhin. Coach since 2003. Former star striker for the Soviet Union, and for Dynamo Kiev. Named Best European Footballer in 1975.

STARS
- Andriy "Sheva" Shevchenko (striker, Milan, six goals in qualifying)
- Andriy Voronin (striker, Bayern Leverkusen)
- Andriy Gusin (midfielder, Dynamo Kiev)
- Aleksandr Shovkovski (goalkeeper, Dynamo Kiev)

WATCH OUT FOR THIS GUY
ANDRIY RUSOL: A twenty-three-year-old sweeper and student of Blokhin's who was given the opportunity to prove himself on the national team. He's tall and strong, but very elegant in his style. And quite good in the air on corner kicks as well. He's already scored a pair of goals since making his full international debut in 2005. He plays his club soccer with Dnipro Dnipropetrovsk in his home country, and will surely be considering other offers after this summer is done.

COMMENTARY This team of many Andriys is a first-timer with a bit of a World Cup history. Several Ukrainian players have experience in the former Soviet Union. It was the first European nation to qualify, winning their group ahead of vaunted Turkey (whom they beat 3–0 in Istanbul) and Greece (whom they beat 1–0 in Athens). The team draws primarily from Dynamo Kiev and Dnipro Dnipropetrovsk; in other words, most of the players know one another well. Their defense is staunch and efficient, especially the goalkeeper Shovkovski, only giving up seven goals in twelve qualifying matches, including six shutouts. And the superstar Shevchenko isn't the only offensive threat on the team. He's accompanied by another Andriy—Andriy Voronin—who played in Germany for a number of years, and hence should feel right at home. Obviously, the Ukrainians are not among the favorites, but every World Cup produces a few surprises, and it wouldn't surprise me to see them be one in 2006.

AFRICA
ANGOLA · GHANA · IVORY COAST
TOGO · TUNISIA

ANGOLA

FIFA WORLD RANKING 62

HOW THEY QUALIFIED Winners of Africa's Group 4, ahead of Nigeria and Algeria.

HISTORY First World Cup.

LAST APPEARANCE N/A

2006 RIVALS Group D—Mexico, Iran, Portugal.

COACH Luis de Oliveira Gonçalvez. Coach since 2003. Was previously the coach for Angola's U-17 and U-20 teams.

STARS

- Fabrice "Akwa" Maieco (Captain, thirty-three years of age, born in Qatar)
- Bruno Mauro (striker, thirty-two years of age, plays in Portugal)
- Flavio Amado (striker, plays in Egypt)

WATCH OUT FOR THIS GUY PEDRO MANUEL "MANTORRAS" TORRES: Twenty-four-year-old striker for Benfica. By virtue of being a supremely skilled African, he is often compared to Eusebio: he has the same Afro-Latino style as the famous Portuguese striker. He was being brought up in Barcelona's system, but coach Louis van Gaal let him go in favor of more "community" (read: European) players. Don't lose sight of this one.

COMMENTARY The *"Palancas Negras"* finally achieved their dream of playing in a World Cup. And it was extraordinarily close. They were tied in first place with Nigeria, but with one less goal against. It took them four tries before qualifying for this World Cup. In '86 they were eliminated by Algeria, and the next three times after that it was Cameroon (who did not qualify this time around) who proved to be the thorn in their foot. They are not the best team in Africa, but they do carry a strong soccer influence from Portugal, their European colonizer. And they will meet them, as a part of Group D (along with Mexico). Their aim is to beat them however they can. If they do, all the waiting will have worth it. But one thing is for certain: they have the best names of any squad this summer, with players like Zé Kalanga, Lebo Lebo, Love, Loco, Jamba, and Lama.

GHANA

FIFA WORLD RANKING 50

HOW THEY QUALIFIED Winners of Africa's Group 2, ahead of South Africa, Congo, and Uganda.

HISTORY First World Cup.

LAST APPEARANCE N/A

2006 RIVALS Group E—Italy, United States, and the Czech Republic.

COACH Ratomir Dujkovic. Coach since 2004. Serbian by birth. Former coach of Rwanda. Speaks excellent Spanish, thanks to his years as a player for Valencia and as a coach in Venezuela.

STARS
- Michael Essien (midfielder, Chelsea, three goals in qualifying)
- Stephen Appiah (Captain, midfielder, Chelsea, four goals in qualifying)
- Sulley Ali Muntari (midfielder, Udinese)

WATCH OUT FOR THIS GUY MICHAEL ESSIEN: To understand just how good this twenty-four-year-old star really is, all you need to know is that Chelsea paid Olympique of Lyon—read this carefully— a $40 million transfer fee, making him the most expensive African player in the world! Good, right? He is the engine that drives his English club, along with his paisano Appiah. He can play defense or venture on the attack with equal ability. Chelsea's Portuguese coach, José Mourinho, describes him as being "multifunctional." It's not without reason that he commanded such a high transfer fee. Keep an eye on him when you see Ghana play.

COMMENTARY The Serbian coach, Dujkovic, was the fourth coach to lead the "Black Stars" of Ghana during the qualifying rounds. He had barely arrived in late 2004, and yet the first thing he did was to impose a sense of discipline. It was hard, but he got results. He took them to the Promised Land. Thanks to him—and the leadership of Essien and Appiah, and four goals from Asamoah Gyan—Ghana has reached their first World Cup since they started competing for spots back in 1962. They've already won three World Youth titles, and several African Cups, but never before have they reached the big dance. The only problem is that the floor is filled with better dancers. Their group is a tough one, and it will be very hard for them to advance. But this will not detract from their joy on the field, and they will put on quite a show.

IVORY COAST

FIFA WORLD RANKING 41

HOW THEY QUALIFIED Winners of Africa's Group 3, ahead of Cameroon and Egypt.

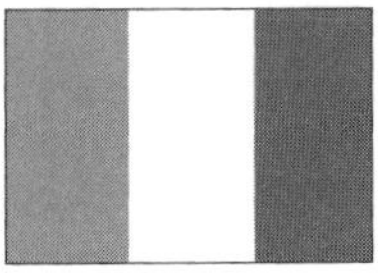

HISTORY First World Cup.

LAST APPEARANCE N/A

2006 RIVALS Group C—Argentina, Serbia and Montenegro, and Holland.

COACH Henri Michel. Coach since 2004. French by birth. Fifth World Cup. Led France at Mexico '86, Cameroon at U.S.A. '94, Morocco at France '98, and Tunisia at South Korea/Japan '02. Another Bora, you might say!

STARS
- Didier Drogba (striker, Chelsea)
- Kolo Touré (sweeper, Arsenal)
- Aruna Dindane (striker, Racing Lens (France))

WATCH OUT FOR THIS GUY DIDIER DROGBA: He is simply the best player in the history of Ivory Coast soccer. At twenty-eight years of age, he has a strong international reputation, especially in France, where he was named Player of the Year in 2004. Currently plays with Chelsea in the English Premiership, along with Hernán Crespo and some of the other top strikers on the planet. Along with Cameroon's Samuel Eto'o and Ghana's Essien (his Chelsea teammate), this sensational striker is considered one of the best African players working today. With his class, speed, and finishing touch, he's going to have an excellent World Cup. Remember the name Drogba.

COMMENTARY The Ivory Coast "Elephants" are the best African team at this year's World Cup, after Tunisia. With Michel at the helm and Drogba on the pitch, they may well repeat the success that Senegal found in South Korea/Japan. In qualifying, they beat out Cameroon by a single point—Cameroon had tied with Egypt on the final day of play—and achieved what they called "the divine classification." As they're in the "Group of Death," they are going to have to play the best soccer of their lives in order to advance. If they do—and I hope they don't do it at the expense of Argentina—they will be the surprise of the century. Of that you can be sure . . . as you can be of the fact that their country has the most difficult name in German: Elfenbeinküste!

TOGO

FIFA WORLD RANKING 56

HOW THEY QUALIFIED Winners of Africa's Group 1, ahead of Senegal and Congo.

HISTORY First World Cup.

LAST APPEARANCE N/A

2006 RIVALS Group G—France, Switzerland, and South Korea.

COACH Stephen Keshi. Coach since 2004. Nigerian by birth. Was an assistant coach for Nigeria, and an Olympic champion in Atlanta '96. Also was the captain of the Nigerian national team for their U.S.A. '94 campaign.

STARS
- Kossi Agassa (goalkeeper, Paris St. Germain)
- Mamam Cherif Touré (midfielder, Metz (France), three goals in qualifying)
- Eric Akoto (defender, plays his club soccer in Austria)

WATCH OUT FOR THIS GUY EMMANUEL ADEBAYOR: This twenty-two-year-old striker for Monaco is of Nigerian stock. Led all of Africa with eleven goals during qualifying, which has made him into the biggest figure in Togo soccer. When he was only eighteen years old, he was signed by the French club Metz, the team with which he ascended into the first division. In 2003 he was sold to Monaco for a $4 million transfer fee, and there he has played alongside other such greats as Javier Saviola, Fernando Morientes, and Rafa Márquez. Tall and spindly, he is excellent in the air. His knack for the goal should follow him to Germany.

COMMENTARY The arrival of the "Falcons" was the biggest surprise in all of qualifying ... not just in Africa, but the world over. Nobody expected this small nation of barely five million inhabitants to eliminate Senegal, the surprise team of South Korea/Japan '02. In the final match of the qualifying group, Senegal needed a win for themselves and for Togo to lose or draw their match with Congo. And what do you think happened? Senegal won ... and Togo did as well, 3–2, with a goal from Abebayor and two from Abel Coubadja. The miracle had arrived, and the team led by the Nigerian coach Keshi were on to the World Cup. Playing in the most difficult group of the draw will make it very hard to advance. But these Falcons fly high, and don't forget all the noise Senegal made four years ago. Will history repeat itself?

TUNISIA

FIFA WORLD RANKING 28

HOW THEY QUALIFIED Winners of Africa's Group 5, one point ahead of Morocco.

HISTORY Fourth World Cup. Participated in, but did not advance at, Argentina '78, France '98, and South Korea/Japan '02.

LAST APPEARANCE South Korea/Japan '02. Failed to advance to the second round.

2006 RIVALS Group H—Spain, Ukraine, and Saudi Arabia.

COACH Roger Lemerre. Coach since 2003. With Tunisia, won the 2004 African Nations Cup. Former coach of France. Won the European Cup in 2000 and the Confederations Cup in 2001. Was an assistant at France '98. Resigned after South Korea/Japan '02.

STARS
- Karim Saidi (defender, twenty-three years of age, Feyenoord (Holland))
- Silva dos Santos (striker, born in Brazil, plays in France, six goals during qualifying)

- Jose Clayton (defender, born in Brazil, third World Cup with Tunisia)

WATCH OUT FOR THIS GUY

HAYKEL GUEMAMDIA: This twenty-four-year-old center forward made his national team debut during qualifying, where he scored three goals. He was the second-highest scorer on the team, and he converted a penalty against Argentina in the 2005 Confederations Cup (Tunisia lost 2–1). In just a short amount of time, he has become a national idol. He is a natural goalscorer, quick and versatile, and can finish well with either foot. He has a brilliant future and will surely be fielding offers once his World Cup summer has concluded.

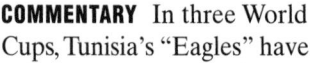

COMMENTARY In three World Cups, Tunisia's "Eagles" have only won one match. That was a 3–1 victory at Argentina '78. And do you remember their victim? Mexico! But since then, they haven't been able to win a second. Their aim is to reverse that trend in Germany. And they have what they need. Their French coach, Lemerre, is a good strategist, and the influence of two naturalized Brazilian players gives them a dynamic unlike that of the other African squads. Which is why they are the Continental Champions and the highest-scoring team in the zone, with twenty-five goals. They have a balanced draw and could surprise some people. At the very least, they should achieve their objective of winning a second World Cup match. Who will be the victim this time?

ASIA

IRAN · JAPAN · SAUDI ARABIA · SOUTH KOREA

IRAN

FIFA WORLD RANKING 19

HOW THEY QUALIFIED Second place in Asia's Group 2, behind Japan.

HISTORY Third World Cup. Never advanced out of the first round. Has one win and one tie.

LAST APPEARANCE France '98. Eliminated in the first round. Defeated the United States 2–1.

2006 RIVALS Group D—Mexico, Angola, and Portugal.

COACH Branko Ivankovic. Coach since 2002. Croatian by birth. Former assistant to Croatian coach Ciro Blazevic at France '98. Former coach of Hanover '96. Has a Ph.D. in physical education.

STARS

- Ali Daei (Captain, striker, top goalscorer in the region, with nine goals, has played for Bayern Munich, Hertha Berlin, and at France '98)
- Vahid Hashemian (striker, Hannover 96, four goals during qualifying, played for Bayern Munich)
- Mehdi Mahdavikia (defender, Hamburg, played at France '98)
- Ali Karimi (striker, Bayern Munich, "The Wizard of Tehran" was Asian Footballer of the Year in 2004)

WATCH OUT FOR THIS GUY ARASH BORHANI: This twenty-two-year-old striker plays his club ball with Pas in Tehran. Everyone expects him to be the next big Iranian star. He is fast and very skillful, and he distinguished himself with the Olympic team. Toward the end of the qualifying stages, he was called up to the full national team, where he scored two crucial goals. Keep him in mind when Iran makes its debut against Mexico on June 11th in Nuremberg.

COMMENTARY After Japan, Iran is the best Asian team, as ranked by FIFA. Their Croatian coach has been with the team for four years, and he has improved their rhythm of play, giving it speed and precision. And he has at his disposal five very talented "German" players; that is, they all play in the Bundesliga. Besides Karimi, Hashemian,

and Mahdavikia, they include Ferydoon Zandi (Keiserslautern) and Moharram Navidkia (Bochum). The team captain, the legendary goalscorer Daei, also played in Germany for several years. This European influence will serve the Iranians well, and they should make life very difficult for someone—either Mexico or Portugal—in Group D.

JAPAN

FIFA WORLD RANKING 15

HOW THEY QUALIFIED First place in Asia's Group 2, ahead of Iran.

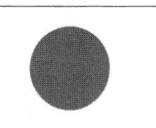

HISTORY Third World Cup.

LAST APPEARANCE South Korea/Japan '02. Advanced to the second round, where they were eliminated by Turkey.

2006 RIVALS Group F—Brazil, Australia, and Croatia.

COACH Zico. Coach since 2003. Former player and coach of Kashima in Japan. Before that, he was Brazil's minister of sports and the star of Flamengo. Mainstay of the Brazilian national team at Spain '82 and Mexico '86.

STARS
- Hidetoshi Nakata (striker, Bolton Wanderers, has also played for Fiorentina, Parma, Roma, Perugia, and Bologna)
- Shunsuke Nakamura (midfielder, Celtic)

- Junichi Inamoto (midfielder, West Bromwich, has also played for Arsenal and Fulham)
- Shinji Ono (midfielder, Feyenoord)

WATCH OUT FOR THIS GUY YOSHITO OKUBO: This twenty-three-year-old striker with Mallorca is the best offensive threat that Japan has produced in recent years. He is small but very strong, with a cannon for a right leg, and was the star of Japan's U-20 squad. Zico

called him up to the full national roster at the start of qualifying, and he has not disappointed. Don't forget his name: Okubo.

COMMENTARY Since Zico took over the reins, Japan has won the Asian Cup and the Kirin Cup in 2004, and had a fine showing at the 2005 Confederations Cup, where they beat European Champions Greece and tied with Brazil. He has become an idol in the Land of the Rising Sun. But this summer in Germany will be a trial by fire. They face his compatriots, Brazil, in addition to Australia and the game, enthusiastic Czechs. But Zico has an excellent team filled with young talent that he has personally recruited and culled from all across Japan—players like the twenty-two-year-old Tatsuya Tanaka. Their goal is to improve upon their previous World Cup performance and reach the quarterfinals.

SAUDI ARABIA

FIFA WORLD RANKING 32

HOW THEY QUALIFIED Winners of Asia's Group 1, ahead of South Korea.

HISTORY Fourth World Cup. Reached the second round at U.S.A. '94.

LAST APPEARANCE South Korea/Japan '02. Eliminated in the first round, including an 8–0 thrashing at the hands of Germany.

2006 RIVALS Group H: Spain, Ukraine, and Tunisia.

COACH Gabriel Calderón. Coach since 2004. Argentine by birth. Former player for the *albiceleste* at Spain '82 and Italy '90. World Youth Champion at Japan '79 alongside Maradona. Has played for Racing, Independiente, Real Betis, and Lausanne (Switzerland).

STARS

- Sami al-Jaber (center forward, thirty-four years of age, fourth World Cup, superstar of Saudi soccer, Calderón coaxed him out of retirement)
- Ibrahim al-Shahrani (midfielder, thirty-one years of age, third World Cup, three goals during qualifying)

WATCH OUT FOR THIS GUY

MOHAMMAD AL-SHLHOUB: This twenty-six-year-old midfielder is small in stature but plays very big with the ball. He scored three goals during qualifying. They call him "Baby Maradona," and he wears the number 10 jersey. The best player at the 2000 Asian Cup, he played sparingly during South Korea/Japan '02, but will make an impact as a starter this summer.

COMMENTARY

This is the fourth World Cup for the "Sons of the Desert." But ever since their debut at U.S.A. '94 (where they advanced to the second round), their perform-ance has deteriorated every time. At France '98, they failed to win a single match, and in South Korea/Japan '02 they were humiliated by Germany 8–0. To stop this downward spiral is their aim for the summer, and their new coach has focused his attention on the things the team has been lacking in: discipline and physical conditioning. Their group is a daunting one and they cannot be expected to advance, but that does not mean that they won't steal a point from someone.

SOUTH KOREA

FIFA WORLD RANKING 29

HOW THEY QUALIFIED Finished second in Asia's Group 1, behind Saudi Arabia.

HISTORY Seventh World Cup. Semifinalists in 2002.

LAST APPEARANCE Reached the semifinals of South Korea/Japan '02, where they were eliminated by Germany.

2006 RIVALS Group G—France, Switzerland, and Togo.

COACH Dick Advocaat. Coach since 2005. Dutch by birth. Former coach of Holland at U.S.A. '94 and the 2004 European Championships. Led United Arab Emirates to the World Cup as well. Former coach of PSV Eindhoven and Scotland's Rangers. Assistant to Rinus Michel, the father of Holland's "total football" at Germany '74.

STARS
• Lee Young-Pyo (midfielder. Tottenham Hotspur, second World Cup)

- Ahn Jung Hwan (striker, Metz (France))
- Lee Dong Gook (striker, Werder Bremen, five goals during qualifying)

WATCH OUT FOR THIS GUY PARK JI-SUNG: This creative, twenty-five-year-old midfielder is the new star of Korean soccer. In 2005 he transferred from PSV Eindhoven to Manchester United at the suggestion of South Korea's former coach, Guus Hiddink. He appeared as a substitute during the 2002 World Cup, and scored the pivotal goal in a 1–0 win over Portugal that got them into the second round.

COMMENTARY Was their performance in the 2002 World Cup the result of ability or luck? That is the question the "Red Devils" will have to answer this summer in Germany. As one of the hosts of the previous World Cup, the Koreans wowed the world under the direction of their Dutch coach Guus Hiddink. They defeated Portugal, Italy, and Spain, reaching the semifinals. But there have been many changes since then. Hiddink has left, and they only managed to finish in second place in their qualifying group. They even lost at home, prompting the resignation of then-coach Jo Bonfrère. Their group this summer should be won by France; in other words, South Korea will be battling with Switzerland for second place. Will there be another miracle a la 2002?

OCEANIA
Australia

AUSTRALIA

FIFA WORLD RANKING 49

HOW THEY QUALIFIED Defeated Uruguay in a home-and-away play-off that came down to penalties.

HISTORY Second World Cup.

LAST APPEARANCE Germany '74. Eliminated in the first round.

2006 RIVALS Group F—Brazil, Croatia, and Japan.

COACH Guus Hiddink. Coach since 2005. Former coach of South Korea for the 2002 World Cup, and of his native Holland at France '98. Has also held the reins at PSV Eindhoven, Valencia, Real Madrid, and Real Betis.

STARS

- Mark Schwarzer (goalkeeper, Middlesbrough)
- Mark Viduka (striker, Middlesbrough, has also played for Celtic, Leeds, and Zagreb (Croatia))
- Harry Kewell (midfielder, Liverpool, European Champion in 2005)
- Craig Moore (Captain, defender, Newcastle)

WATCH OUT FOR THIS GUY   TIM CAHILL: This twenty-five-year-old offensive midfielder plays his club ball with Everton in the English First Division. He was the top goalscorer on the team and in the qualifying zone, with seven tallies to his name. He started off with two against Tahiti in a 9–0 Australian rout, and had a hat trick in a 6–1 defeat of Fiji. In his first season in the Premiership, he scored twelve times, proving he can also do it against the big boys!

COMMENTARY   After coming up short for so long, they finally arrived. The journey lasted thirty-two years: the length of time since their last World Cup appearance, at Germany '74. Everyone in the land of kangaroos gives the credit to Coach Hiddink, who took up the reins after the 2005 Confederations Cup, where Australia failed to win a single match. But the truth of the matter is that Australian soccer has been improving steadily over the past several years. In fact, the majority of their top talent plays with English clubs. There is one who plays in Spain (John Aloisi, with Alavés) and another in Italy (Marco Bresciano, with Parma). Hiddink simply instilled them with a sense of confidence and discipline . . . and accuracy from the penalty spot, which they used to defeat Uruguay in their play-off. They have quite a difficult group in Germany, and it will be a true miracle if Hiddink can do for the "Socceroos" what he did for the "Red Devils" four years ago.

NOTE

Before moving on to the next section, I'd like to share a couple of observations with you. The first is that I still harbor the hope that some nation will hire Bora Milutinovic before June 9, 2006. I can't imagine a World Cup without him.

And the second is this photo of a team that, while it will not be going to the World Cup this summer, will be present in my heart. I'm referring to my team from the Golden Years Soccer League, which is made up of a handful of enthusiastic Argentine, Brazilian, Colombian, Uruguayan, Costa Rican, Honduran, Salvadoran, and Mexican players. Some of them will be supporting their teams in Germany (with this

book in hand, of course), while others will be hoping for better luck next time (though still enjoying the book).

Naturally, I cannot forget my lifetime friends from *"La Escuela de Comerció de San Isidro"* in Buenos Aires. They are an important part of my soccer life, and I hope that they too can be there with me in Germany.

Top: *Golden Years Soccer league.* Bottom: *E.N.C.S.I. Champions 2004.*

Two:

Follow the Cup

Okay, then—go get a pen and get ready to record your own version of the events of Germany 2006.

It's very simple. All you have to do is take notes on these pages during the thirty days of the World Cup—and please try to keep any food or beer from spilling on them, okay? During or immediately after every match, jot down the important on-field developments, like the timing of goals and the scorers ... the name of your favorite player from the match ... any yellow or red cards ... most exciting or most important plays ... the final score ... your overall opinion of the match ... and, if you think it's necessary, the influence the referee may have had on the outcome.

After the World Cup, hold on to this book. Every year—or whenever you feel like partaking of a bit of Germany '06 nostalgia—you can take it out again and relive everything that happened.

Sound good?

Let's go. Enjoy the Cup, and wish my team luck—all together now: *Ar-gen-tina! Ar-gen-ti-na!* ...

GROUP A:	GROUP B:	GROUP C:	GROUP D:
Germany	England	Argentina	Mexico
Costa Rica	Paraguay	Ivory Coast	Angola
Poland	Trinidad–Tobago	Serbia–Montenegro	Iran
Ecuador	Sweden	Holland	Portugal

GROUP E:	GROUP F:	GROUP G:	GROUP H:
Italy	Brazil	France	Spain
Ghana	Croatia	Switzerland	Ukraine
United States	Australia	South Korea	Tunisia
Czech Republic	Japan	Togo	Saudi Arabia

THE MUNICH OPENER

GROUP A:
GERMANY • COSTA RICA • POLAND • ECUADOR

GROUP A — GAME #1

INAUGURATION
GERMANY____ vs. COSTA RICA____
Munich, Friday, June 9, 2006

Goals:_____

My Favorite Player: _____

My Favorite Play: _____

Match Quality:
    ❑ Boring   ❑ Uneventful   ❑ Excellent   ❑ Good
    ❑ A Classic   ❑ Best Match I've Ever Seen in My Life

Comments:_____

_____

GROUP A — GAME #2

POLAND___ vs. ECUADOR___
Gelsenkirchen, Friday, June 9, 2006

Goals:_____

My Favorite Player: _____

My Favorite Play: _____

Match Quality:
    ❑ Boring   ❑ Uneventful   ❑ Excellent   ❑ Good
    ❑ A Classic   ❑ Best Match I've Ever Seen in My Life

Comments:_____

_____

GROUP A — GAME #17

GERMANY___ vs. POLAND___
Dortmund, Wednesday, June 14, 2006

Goals:_____

My Favorite Player: _____

My Favorite Play: _____

Match Quality:
    ❏ Boring   ❏ Uneventful   ❏ Excellent   ❏ Good
    ❏ A Classic   ❏ Best Match I've Ever Seen in My Life

Comments:_____
_____

GROUP A — GAME #18

ECUADOR___ vs. COSTA RICA___
Hamburg, Thursday, June 15, 2006

Goals:_____

My Favorite Player: _____

My Favorite Play: _____

Match Quality:
    ❏ Boring   ❏ Uneventful   ❏ Excellent   ❏ Good
    ❏ A Classic   ❏ Best Match I've Ever Seen in My Life

Comments:_____
_____

GROUP A — GAME #33

ECUADOR ___ vs. GERMANY___
Berlin, Tuesday, June 20, 2006

Goals:_____

My Favorite Player: _____

My Favorite Play: _____

Match Quality:
      ❏ Boring   ❏ Uneventful   ❏ Excellent   ❏ Good
      ❏ A Classic   ❏ Best Match I've Ever Seen in My Life

Comments:_____

_____

GROUP A — GAME #34

COSTA RICA___ vs. POLAND___
Hanover, Tuesday, June 20, 2006

Goals:_____

My Favorite Player: _____

My Favorite Play: _____

Match Quality:
      ❏ Boring   ❏ Uneventful   ❏ Excellent   ❏ Good
      ❏ A Classic   ❏ Best Match I've Ever Seen in My Life

Comments:_____

_____

FINAL GROUP A STANDINGS:

POSITION	TEAM	W	L	T	GF	GA	DIFF	Points
1A								
2A								
3A								
4A								

GROUP B:
ENGLAND • PARAGUAY • TRINIDAD AND TOBAGO • SWEDEN

GROUP B — GAME #3

ENGLAND___ vs. PARAGUAY___
Frankfurt, Saturday, June 10, 2006

Goals:_____

My Favorite Player: _____

My Favorite Play: _____

Match Quality:
    ❑ Boring   ❑ Uneventful   ❑ Excellent   ❑ Good
    ❑ A Classic   ❑ Best Match I've Ever Seen in My Life

Comments:_____
_____

GROUP B — GAME #4

TRINIDAD AND TOBAGO___ vs. SWEDEN___
Dortmund, Saturday, June 10, 2006

Goals:_____

My Favorite Player: _____

My Favorite Play: _____

Match Quality:
    ❑ Boring   ❑ Uneventful   ❑ Excellent   ❑ Good
    ❑ A Classic   ❑ Best Match I've Ever Seen in My Life

Comments:_____
_____

GROUP B — GAME #19
ENGLAND___ vs. TRINIDAD AND TOBAGO___
Nuremberg, Thursday, June 15, 2006

Goals:_____

My Favorite Player: _____

My Favorite Play: _____

Match Quality:
    ❏ Boring   ❏ Uneventful   ❏ Excellent   ❏ Good
    ❏ A Classic   ❏ Best Match I've Ever Seen in My Life

Comments:_____

_____

GROUP B — GAME #20
SWEDEN___ vs. PARAGUAY___
Berlin, Thursday, June 15, 2006

Goals:_____

My Favorite Player: _____

My Favorite Play: _____

Match Quality:
    ❏ Boring   ❏ Uneventful   ❏ Excellent   ❏ Good
    ❏ A Classic   ❏ Best Match I've Ever Seen in My Life

Comments:_____

_____

GROUP B — GAME #35
SWEDEN___ vs. ENGLAND___
Cologne, Thursday, June 20, 2006

Goals:_____

My Favorite Player: _____

My Favorite Play: _____

Match Quality:
❏ Boring   ❏ Uneventful   ❏ Excellent   ❏ Good
❏ A Classic   ❏ Best Match I've Ever Seen in My Life

Comments: _____
_____

GROUP B — GAME #36

PARAGUAY___ vs. TRINIDAD AND TOBAGO___
Kaiserslautern, Thursday, June 20, 2006

Goals: _____

My Favorite Player: _____

My Favorite Play: _____

Match Quality:
❏ Boring   ❏ Uneventful   ❏ Excellent   ❏ Good
❏ A Classic   ❏ Best Match I've Ever Seen in My Life

Comments: _____
_____

FINAL GROUP B STANDINGS:

POSITION	TEAM	W	L	T	GF	GA	DIFF	Points
1B								
2B								
3B								
4B								

GROUP C:
ARGENTINA • IVORY COAST
SERBIA AND MONTENEGRO • HOLLAND

GROUP C — GAME #5

ARGENTINA___ vs. IVORY COAST___

Hamburg, Saturday, June 10, 2006

Goals:_____

My Favorite Player: _____

My Favorite Play: _____

Match Quality:
  ❑ Boring ❑ Uneventful ❑ Excellent ❑ Good
  ❑ A Classic ❑ Best Match I've Ever Seen in My Life

Comments:_____
_____

GROUP C — GAME #6

SERBIA AND MONTENEGRO___ vs. HOLLAND___

Leipzig, Sunday, June 11, 2006

Goals:_____

My Favorite Player: _____

My Favorite Play: _____

Match Quality:
  ❑ Boring ❑ Uneventful ❑ Excellent ❑ Good
  ❑ A Classic ❑ Best Match I've Ever Seen in My Life

Comments:_____
_____

GROUP C — GAME #21
ARGINTINA___ vs. SERBIA AND MONTENEGRO___
Gelsenkirchen, Friday, June 16, 2006

Goals:_____

My Favorite Player: _____

My Favorite Play: _____

Match Quality:
  ❏ Boring ❏ Uneventful ❏ Excellent ❏ Good
  ❏ A Classic ❏ Best Match I've Ever Seen in My Life

Comments:_____

_____

GROUP C — GAME #22
HOLLAND___ vs. IVORY COAST___
Stuttgart, Friday, June 16, 2006

Goals:_____

My Favorite Player: _____

My Favorite Play: _____

Match Quality:
  ❏ Boring ❏ Uneventful ❏ Excellent ❏ Good
  ❏ A Classic ❏ Best Match I've Ever Seen in My Life

Comments:_____

_____

GROUP C — GAME #37
HOLLAND___ vs. ARGENTINA___
Frankfurt, Wednesday, June 21, 2006

Goals:_____

My Favorite Player: _____

My Favorite Play: _____

Match Quality:
    ❏ Boring   ❏ Uneventful   ❏ Excellent   ❏ Good
    ❏ A Classic   ❏ Best Match I've Ever Seen in My Life

Comments: _____

_____

GROUP C — GAME #38
IVORY COAST___ vs. SERBIA AND MONTENEGRO___
Munich, Wednesday, June 21, 2006

Goals: _____

My Favorite Player: _____

My Favorite Play: _____

Match Quality:
    ❏ Boring   ❏ Uneventful   ❏ Excellent   ❏ Good
    ❏ A Classic   ❏ Best Match I've Ever Seen in My Life

Comments: _____

_____

FINAL GROUP C STANDINGS:

POSITION	TEAM	W	L	T	GF	GA	DIFF	Points
1C								
2C								
3C								
4C								

GROUP D:
MEXICO • ANGOLA • IRAN • PORTUGAL

GROUP D — GAME #7

MEXICO___ vs. IRAN___
Nuremberg, Sunday, June 11, 2006

Goals:_____

My Favorite Player: _____

My Favorite Play: _____

Match Quality:
  ❏ Boring ❏ Uneventful ❏ Excellent ❏ Good
  ❏ A Classic ❏ Best Match I've Ever Seen in My Life

Comments:_____

_____

GROUP D — GAME #8

ANGOLA___ vs. PORTUGAL___
Cologne, Sunday, June 11, 2006

Goals:_____

My Favorite Player: _____

My Favorite Play: _____

Match Quality:
  ❏ Boring ❏ Uneventful ❏ Excellent ❏ Good
  ❏ A Classic ❏ Best Match I've Ever Seen in My Life

Comments:_____

_____

GROUP D — GAME #23

MEXICO ___ vs. ANGOLA___

Hanover, Friday, June 16, 2006

Goals:_____

My Favorite Player: _____

My Favorite Play: _____

Match Quality:
    ❏ Boring   ❏ Uneventful   ❏ Excellent   ❏ Good
    ❏ A Classic   ❏ Best Match I've Ever Seen in My Life

Comments:_____

_____

GROUP D — GAME #24

PORTUGAL___ vs. IRAN___

Frankfurt, Saturday, June 17, 2006

Goals:_____

My Favorite Player: _____

My Favorite Play: _____

Match Quality:
    ❏ Boring   ❏ Uneventful   ❏ Excellent   ❏ Good
    ❏ A Classic   ❏ Best Match I've Ever Seen in My Life

Comments:_____

_____

GROUP D — GAME #39

PORTUGAL___ vs. MEXICO___

Gelsenkirchen, Wednesday, June 21, 2006

Goals:_____

The World Cup

My Favorite Player: _____

My Favorite Play: _____

Match Quality:
    ❑ Boring   ❑ Uneventful   ❑ Excellent   ❑ Good
    ❑ A Classic   ❑ Best Match I've Ever Seen in My Life

Comments:_____

_____

GROUP D — GAME #40

IRAN___ vs. ANGOLA___

Leipzig, Wednesday, June 21, 2006

Goals:_____

My Favorite Player: _____

My Favorite Play: _____

Match Quality:
    ❑ Boring   ❑ Uneventful   ❑ Excellent   ❑ Good
    ❑ A Classic   ❑ Best Match I've Ever Seen in My Life

Comments:_____

_____

FINAL GROUP D STANDINGS:

POSITION	TEAM	W	L	T	GF	GA	DIFF	Points
1D								
2D								
3D								
4D								

GROUP E:
ITALY • GHANA • UNITED STATES • CZECH REPUBLIC

GROUP E — GAME #9

ITALY___ vs. GHANA___

Hanover, Monday, June 12, 2006

Goals:_____

My Favorite Player: _____

My Favorite Play: _____

Match Quality:
    ❑ Boring   ❑ Uneventful   ❑ Excellent   ❑ Good
    ❑ A Classic   ❑ Best Match I've Ever Seen in My Life

Comments:_____

_____

GROUP E — GAME #10

UNITED STATES ___ vs. CZECH REPUBLIC___

Gelsenkirchen, Monday, June 12, 2006

Goals:_____

My Favorite Player: _____

My Favorite Play: _____

Match Quality:
    ❑ Boring   ❑ Uneventful   ❑ Excellent   ❑ Good
    ❑ A Classic   ❑ Best Match I've Ever Seen in My Life

Comments:_____

_____

GROUP E — GAME #25

ITALY___ vs. UNITED STATES___

Kaiserslautern, Saturday, June 17, 2006

Goals:_____

My Favorite Player: _____

My Favorite Play: _____

Match Quality:
    ❏ Boring   ❏ Uneventful   ❏ Excellent   ❏ Good
    ❏ A Classic   ❏ Best Match I've Ever Seen in My Life

Comments:_____
_____

GROUP E — GAME #26

CZECH REPUBLIC___ vs. GHANA___

Cologne, Saturday, June 17, 2006

Goals:_____

My Favorite Player: _____

My Favorite Play: _____

Match Quality:
    ❏ Boring   ❏ Uneventful   ❏ Excellent   ❏ Good
    ❏ A Classic   ❏ Best Match I've Ever Seen in My Life

Comments:_____
_____

GROUP E — GAME #41

CZECH REPUBLIC___ vs. ITALY___

Hamburg, Thursday, June 21, 2006

Goals:_____

My Favorite Player: _____

My Favorite Play: _____

Match Quality:
  ❏ Boring   ❏ Uneventful   ❏ Excellent   ❏ Good
  ❏ A Classic   ❏ Best Match I've Ever Seen in My Life

Comments: _____
_____

GROUP E — GAME #42

GHANA___ vs. UNITED STATES___
Nuremberg, Thursday, June 22, 2006

Goals: _____

My Favorite Player: _____

My Favorite Play: _____

Match Quality:
  ❏ Boring   ❏ Uneventful   ❏ Excellent   ❏ Good
  ❏ A Classic   ❏ Best Match I've Ever Seen in My Life

Comments: _____
_____

FINAL GROUP E STANDINGS:

POSITION	TEAM	W	L	T	GF	GA	DIFF	Points
1E								
2E								
3E								
4E								

GROUP F:
BRAZIL • CROATIA • AUSTRALIA • JAPAN

GROUP F — GAME #11

BRAZIL___ vs. CROATIA___
Berlin, Tuesday, June 13, 2006

Goals:_____

My Favorite Player: _____

My Favorite Play: _____

Match Quality:
    ❏ Boring   ❏ Uneventful   ❏ Excellent   ❏ Good
    ❏ A Classic   ❏ Best Match I've Ever Seen in My Life

Comments:_____

_____

GROUP F — GAME #12

AUSTRALIA___ vs. JAPAN___
Kaiserslautern, Monday, June 12, 2006
(As the schedule currently stands, Game #12 takes place before Game #11.)

Goals:_____

My Favorite Player: _____

My Favorite Play: _____

Match Quality:
    ❏ Boring   ❏ Uneventful   ❏ Excellent   ❏ Good
    ❏ A Classic   ❏ Best Match I've Ever Seen in My Life

Comments:_____

_____

GROUP F — GAME #27
BRAZIL___ vs. AUSTRALIA___
Munich, Sunday, June 18, 2006

Goals:_____

My Favorite Player: _____

My Favorite Play: _____

Match Quality:
❏ Boring   ❏ Uneventful   ❏ Excellent   ❏ Good
❏ A Classic   ❏ Best Match I've Ever Seen in My Life

Comments:_____

_____

GROUP F — GAME #28
JAPAN___ vs. CROATIA___
Nuremberg, Sunday, June 18, 2006

Goals:_____

My Favorite Player: _____

My Favorite Play: _____

Match Quality:
❏ Boring   ❏ Uneventful   ❏ Excellent   ❏ Good
❏ A Classic   ❏ Best Match I've Ever Seen in My Life

Comments:_____

_____

GROUP F — GAME #43
JAPAN___ vs. BRAZIL___
Dortmund, Thursday, June 22, 2006

Goals:_____

My Favorite Player: _____

My Favorite Play: _____

Match Quality:
- ❏ Boring   ❏ Uneventful   ❏ Excellent   ❏ Good
- ❏ A Classic   ❏ Best Match I've Ever Seen in My Life

Comments: _____
_____

GROUP F — GAME #44

CROATIA___ vs. AUSTRALIA___
Stuttgart, Thursday, June 22, 2006

Goals: _____

My Favorite Player: _____

My Favorite Play: _____

Match Quality:
- ❏ Boring   ❏ Uneventful   ❏ Excellent   ❏ Good
- ❏ A Classic   ❏ Best Match I've Ever Seen in My Life

Comments: _____
_____

FINAL GROUP F STANDINGS:

POSITION	TEAM	W	L	T	GF	GA	DIFF	Points
1F								
2F								
3F								
4F								

GROUP G:
FRANCE • SWITZERLAND • SOUTH KOREA • TOGO

GROUP G — GAME #13

FRANCE___ vs. SWITZERLAND___
Stuttgart, Tuesday, June 13, 2006

Goals:_____

My Favorite Player: _____

My Favorite Play: _____

Match Quality:
- ❏ Boring   ❏ Uneventful   ❏ Excellent   ❏ Good
- ❏ A Classic   ❏ Best Match I've Ever Seen in My Life

Comments:_____

_____

GROUP G — GAME #14

SOUTH KOREA___ vs. TOGO___
Frankfurt, Tuesday, June 13, 2006

Goals:_____

My Favorite Player: _____

My Favorite Play: _____

Match Quality:
- ❏ Boring   ❏ Uneventful   ❏ Excellent   ❏ Good
- ❏ A Classic   ❏ Best Match I've Ever Seen in My Life

Comments:_____

_____

GROUP G — GAME #29
FRANCE___ vs. SOUTH KOREA___
Leipzig, Sunday, June 18, 2006

Goals:_____

My Favorite Player: _____

My Favorite Play: _____

Match Quality:
    ❏ Boring   ❏ Uneventful   ❏ Excellent   ❏ Good
    ❏ A Classic   ❏ Best Match I've Ever Seen in My Life

Comments:_____

_____

GROUP G — GAME #30
TOGO___ vs. SWITZERLAND___
Dortmund, Monday, June 19, 2006

Goals:_____

My Favorite Player: _____

My Favorite Play: _____

Match Quality:
    ❏ Boring   ❏ Uneventful   ❏ Excellent   ❏ Good
    ❏ A Classic   ❏ Best Match I've Ever Seen in My Life

Comments:_____

_____

GROUP G — GAME #45
TOGO___ vs. FRANCE___
Cologne, Friday, June 23, 2006

Goals:_____

My Favorite Player: _____

My Favorite Play: _____

Match Quality:
　　　❏ Boring　　❏ Uneventful　　❏ Excellent　　❏ Good
　　　❏ A Classic　❏ Best Match I've Ever Seen in My Life

Comments:_____
_____

GROUP G — GAME #46
SWITZERLAND__ vs. SOUTH KOREA__
Hanover, Friday, June 23, 2006

Goals:_____

My Favorite Player: _____

My Favorite Play: _____

Match Quality:
　　　❏ Boring　　❏ Uneventful　　❏ Excellent　　❏ Good
　　　❏ A Classic　❏ Best Match I've Ever Seen in My Life

Comments:_____
_____

FINAL GROUP G STANDINGS:

POSITION	TEAM	W	L	T	GF	GA	DIFF	Points
1G								
2G								
3G								
4G								

GROUP H:
SPAIN • UKRAINE • TUNISIA • SAUDI ARABIA

GROUP H — GAME #15

SPAIN___ vs. UKRAINE___

Leipzig, Wednesday, June 14, 2006

Goals:_____

My Favorite Player: _____

My Favorite Play:_____

Match Quality:
    ❏ Boring   ❏ Uneventful   ❏ Excellent   ❏ Good
    ❏ A Classic   ❏ Best Match I've Ever Seen in My Life

Comments:_____

_____

GROUP H — GAME #16

TUNISIA___ vs. SAUDI ARABIA____

Munich, Wednesday, June 14, 2006

Goals:_____

My Favorite Player: _____

My Favorite Play: _____

Match Quality:
    ❏ Boring   ❏ Uneventful   ❏ Excellent   ❏ Good
    ❏ A Classic   ❏ Best Match I've Ever Seen in My Life

Comments:_____

_____

GROUP H — GAME #31

SPAIN___ vs. TUNISIA___

Stuttgart, Monday, June 19, 2006

Goals:_____

My Favorite Player: _____

My Favorite Play: _____

Match Quality:
    ❏ Boring   ❏ Uneventful   ❏ Excellent   ❏ Good
    ❏ A Classic ❏ Best Match I've Ever Seen in My Life

Comments:_____

_____

GROUP H — GAME #32

SAUDI ARABIA___ vs. UKRAINE___

Hamburg, Monday, June 19, 2006

Goals:_____

My Favorite Player: _____

My Favorite Play: _____

Match Quality:
    ❏ Boring   ❏ Uneventful   ❏ Excellent   ❏ Good
    ❏ A Classic ❏ Best Match I've Ever Seen in My Life

Comments:_____

_____

GROUP H — GAME #47

SAUDI ARABIA___ vs. SPAIN___

Kaiserslautern, Friday, June 23, 2006

Goals:_____

My Favorite Player: _____

My Favorite Play: _____

Match Quality:
❏ Boring   ❏ Uneventful   ❏ Excellent   ❏ Good
❏ A Classic   ❏ Best Match I've Ever Seen in My Life

Comments: _____

_____

GROUP H — GAME #48

UKRAINE___ vs. TUNISIA___

Berlin, Friday, June 23, 2006

Goals: _____

My Favorite Player: _____

My Favorite Play: _____

Match Quality:
❏ Boring   ❏ Uneventful   ❏ Excellent   ❏ Good
❏ A Classic   ❏ Best Match I've Ever Seen in My Life

Comments: _____

_____

FINAL GROUP H STANDINGS:

POSITION	TEAM	W	L	T	GF	GA	DIFF	Points
1H								
2H								
3H								
4H								

SECOND ROUND

Teams advancing out of **THE GROUP STAGE**

1. _____   9. _____

2. _____   10. _____

3. _____   11. _____

4. _____   12. _____

5. _____   13. _____

6. _____   14. _____

7. _____   15. _____

8. _____   16. _____

Second-round **MATCHUPS**

_____ vs. _____   _____ vs _____

_____ vs. _____   _____ vs _____

_____ vs. _____   _____ vs _____

_____ vs. _____   _____ vs _____

SECOND ROUND — GAME #49

1A_____ ____ vs. 2B_____ ____

Munich, Saturday, June 24, 2006

Goals:_____

My Favorite Player: _____

My Favorite Play: _____

Match Quality:
  ❑ Boring   ❑ Uneventful   ❑ Excellent   ❑ Good
  ❑ A Classic   ❑ Best Match I've Ever Seen in My Life

Comments:_____

_____

SECOND ROUND — GAME #50

1C_____ ____ vs. 2D_____ ____

Leipzig, Saturday, June 24, 2006

Goals:_____

My Favorite Player: _____

My Favorite Play: _____

Match Quality:
  ❑ Boring   ❑ Uneventful   ❑ Excellent   ❑ Good
  ❑ A Classic   ❑ Best Match I've Ever Seen in My Life

Comments:_____

_____

SECOND ROUND — GAME #51

1B_____ ____ vs. 2B_____ ____
Stuttgart, Sunday, June 25, 2006

Goals:_____

My Favorite Player: _____

My Favorite Play: _____

Match Quality:
    ❏ Boring   ❏ Uneventful   ❏ Excellent   ❏ Good
    ❏ A Classic   ❏ Best Match I've Ever Seen in My Life

Comments:_____
_____

SECOND ROUND — GAME #52

1D_____ ____ vs. 2C_____ ____
Nuremberg, Sunday, June 25, 2006

Goals:_____

My Favorite Player: _____

My Favorite Play: _____

Match Quality:
    ❏ Boring   ❏ Uneventful   ❏ Excellent   ❏ Good
    ❏ A Classic   ❏ Best Match I've Ever Seen in My Life

Comments:_____
_____

SECOND ROUND — GAME #53

1E_____ ____ vs. 2F_____ ____

Kaiserslautern, Monday, June 26, 2006

Goals:_____

My Favorite Player: _____

My Favorite Play: _____

Match Quality:
    ❏ Boring   ❏ Uneventful   ❏ Excellent   ❏ Good
    ❏ A Classic   ❏ Best Match I've Ever Seen in My Life

Comments:_____

_____

SECOND ROUND — GAME #54

1G_____ ____ vs. 2H_____ ____

Cologne, Monday, June 26, 2006

Goals:_____

My Favorite Player: _____

My Favorite Play: _____

Match Quality:
    ❏ Boring   ❏ Uneventful   ❏ Excellent   ❏ Good
    ❏ A Classic   ❏ Best Match I've Ever Seen in My Life

Comments:_____

_____

SECOND ROUND — GAME #55

1F_____ _____ vs. 2E_____ _____

Dortmund, Tuesday, June 27, 2006

Goals:_____

My Favorite Player: _____

My Favorite Play: _____

Match Quality:
    ❏ Boring   ❏ Uneventful   ❏ Excellent   ❏ Good
    ❏ A Classic   ❏ Best Match I've Ever Seen in My Life

Comments:_____

_____

SECOND ROUND — GAME #56

1H_____ _____ vs. 2G_____ _____

Hanover, Tuesday, June 27, 2006

Goals:_____

My Favorite Player: _____

My Favorite Play: _____

Match Quality:
    ❏ Boring   ❏ Uneventful   ❏ Excellent   ❏ Good
    ❏ A Classic   ❏ Best Match I've Ever Seen in My Life

Comments:_____

_____

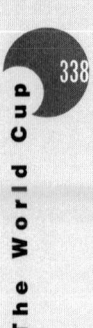
QUARTERFINALS

Teams advancing to **THE QUARTERFINALS**

1. _ARG_

2. _____

3. _GER_

4. _____

5. _____

6. _____

7. _____

8. _____

Quarterfinal **MATCHUPS**

_____ vs. _____

_____ vs. _____

_____ vs. _____

_____ vs. _____

QUARTERFINALS — GAME #57

1 ___ *Re* ___ vs. ___ ___ ___

Berlin, Friday, June 30, 2006

Goals:_____

My Favorite Player: _____

My Favorite Play: _____

Match Quality:
    ❏ Boring   ❏ Uneventful   ❏ Excellent   ❏ Good
    ❏ A Classic   ❏ Best Match I've Ever Seen in My Life

Comments:_____

_____

QUARTERFINALS — GAME #58

5_____ ____ vs. 7_____ ____

Hamburg, Friday, June 30, 2006

Goals:_____

My Favorite Player: _____

My Favorite Play: _____

Match Quality:
    ❏ Boring   ❏ Uneventful   ❏ Excellent   ❏ Good
    ❏ A Classic   ❏ Best Match I've Ever Seen in My Life

Comments:_____

_____

QUARTERFINALS — GAME #59

2_____ ____ vs. 4_____ ____

Gelsenkirchen, Saturday, July 1, 2006

Goals:_____

My Favorite Player: _____

My Favorite Play: _____

Match Quality:
❏ Boring   ❏ Uneventful   ❏ Excellent   ❏ Good
❏ A Classic   ❏ Best Match I've Ever Seen in My Life

Comments:_____

_____

QUARTERFINALS — GAME #60

6_____ ___ vs. 8_____ __

Frankfurt, Saturday, July 1, 2006

Goals:_____

My Favorite Player: _____

My Favorite Play: _____

Match Quality:
❏ Boring   ❏ Uneventful   ❏ Excellent   ❏ Good
❏ A Classic   ❏ Best Match I've Ever Seen in My Life

Comments:_____

_____

SEMIFINALES

Semifinal **MATCHUPS**

_____ vs. _____   _____ vs. _____

SEMIFINAL — GAME #61

A_____ ___ VS. C_____ ___

Dortmund, July 4, 2006

Goals:_____

My Favorite Player: _____

My Favorite Play: _____

Match Quality:
- ❏ Boring ❏ Uneventful ❏ Excellent ❏ Good
- ❏ A Classic ❏ Best Match I've Ever Seen in My Life

Comments:_____

_____

SEMIFINALS — GAME #62

B_____ ___ VS. D_____ ___

Munich, July 5, 2006

Goals:_____

My Favorite Player: _____

My Favorite Play: _____

Match Quality:
- ❏ Boring ❏ Uneventful ❏ Excellent ❏ Good
- ❏ A Classic ❏ Best Match I've Ever Seen in My Life

Comments:_____

_____

THIRD-PLACE MATCH

THIRD PLACE — GAME #63

_____ ___ vs. _____ ___

Stuttgart, Saturday, July 8, 2006

Goals:_____

My Favorite Player: _____

My Favorite Play: _____

Match Quality:
      ❏ Boring   ❏ Uneventful   ❏ Excellent   ❏ Good
      ❏ A Classic ❏ Best Match I've Ever Seen in My Life

Comments:_____

_____

Third-Place Team: _____

THE FINAL MATCH IN BERLIN

THE FINAL MATCH — GAME #64

_____ ____ VS. _____ ____

Berlin, Sunday, July 9, 2006

Goals:_____

My Favorite Player: _____

My Favorite Play: _____

Match Quality:
    ❏ Boring   ❏ Uneventful   ❏ Excellent   ❏ Good
    ❏ A Classic   ❏ Best Match I've Ever Seen in My Life

Comments:_____

_____

World Champions: _____

Runners-up:_____

GERMANY '06 AT A GLANCE

Champions: _____

Winning Coach: _____

Runners-up: _____

Runners-up Coach: _____

Top Goalscorer: _____

Other Standouts: _____

Greatest Goal: _____

Greatest Matches: _____

Best Overall Player: _____

My Favorite Player: _____

All-World Cup Team

Goalkeeper: _____

Defenders: 1. _____   3. _____

             2. _____   4. _____

Midfielders: 1. _____   3. _____

             2. _____   4. _____

Strikers: 1. _____   2. _____

Final Standings

1. _____   17. _____

2. _____   18. _____

3. _____   19. _____

4. _____   20. _____

5. _____   21. _____

6. _____   22. _____

7. _____   23. _____

8. _____   24. _____

9. _____   25. _____

10. _____   26. _____

11. _____   27. _____

12. _____   28. _____

13. _____   29. _____

14. _____   30. _____

15. _____   31. _____

16. _____   32. _____

ORY LAP

The Twelve Host Cities

The Twelve Host Cities

As we say on television, "We've come to the end of our program." But before we say farewell—and in keeping with what I promised back at the start—we're going to conclude our World Cup run with a "Victory lap," with the trophy already in hand (if you'll allow me), through the twelve host cities of the Eighteenth FIFA World Cup, Germany 2006.

We're going to start in the south, where the event itself will start on June 9th, in the beautiful city of Munich, capital of the state of Bavaria. From there, we'll head north, in a west-to-east zigzag, until we reach Berlin, the German capital and the seat of the Grand Finale on July 9th.

Once we get to know Munich, we'll be heading to one of its southern neighbors, the city of Stuttgart. From there, we'll head east, to lovely Nuremberg, and then on into central Germany, where we'll find three very closely-set cities: Frankfurt, Kaiserslautern, and Cologne.

We'll continue with our zigzagging pattern back toward the east, to the heart of the former East Germany, the city of Leipzig. Then we'll make a turn for the west, where we'll find two more host cities, Dortmund and Gelsenkirchen.

The trip will then take us north, toward the cities of Hanover and Hamburg, and then to the northeast and our final destination: Berlin.

So make yourselves comfortable, get your cameras ready, and secure your Cup (however you want to do it), because we're about to embark on our "Victory lap" through all of Deutschland, the beautiful country of Germany.

One:

Munich:
The Heart of Bavaria

We begin our trip on June 9, 2006, in the place where it all kicks off: the beautiful city of Munich. It's the third-largest city in Germany, but it's the most heavily visited, and is itself one of the most important cities in all of Europe.

Here is where the international press center will be situated, the place from which all the World Cup games will be broadcast throughout the world.

The city itself isn't very large. Its population is around a million and a half inhabitants. It's a financial center and the capital of the state of Bavaria, in the south of the country, and the most "German" state of them all. Here is where the "oompah" bands, with their requisite accordions, and which we associate with so much of German folk music, come from, not to mention the famous lederhosen worn by men from the Alps.

And of course, as I've already mentioned, this region produces the best and most popular beer in all of Germany.

Given that it's the home of Bayern Munich, the most popular professional soccer team in the land, Munich has the advantages of being a major sports city as well. The Olympics were celebrated here in 1972, as were several championship finals, such as the 1974 World Cup final, the 1988 European Championship final, the 1997 Champions League final, and several track-and-field competitions and basketball games as well.

Munich was founded on the shores of the Isar River, at the foothills of the Alps, more than seven hundred years ago, but it still retains aspects of a young city. Like other large German cities, Munich was also largely destroyed during the Second World War, and then rebuilt. That's the reason for the luster of its new and contemporary look.

Its historic district, however, includes some ancient buildings and churches restored to all their original splendor. The most beautiful of these surround the Karlsplatz, such as St. Michael's Church and the symbol of Munich, the Cathedral of Our Lady (Frauenkirche).

The other plaza in the historic district is the Marienplatz, the Plaza of the Virgin Mary. It is surrounded by the beautiful Rathaus (city council building), the Church of the Holy Spirit, St. Peter's Church, and the best-known tourist attraction in Munich, the Glockenspiel Tower, with its mechanically rotating figures that represent important episodes of local history.

Don't forget your cameras or camcorders, because the entire city is very photogenic, very German.

NEW MUNICH

The old stadium where the Munich Olympics and the '74 final were held—the Olympiastadion München—still exists, but it will not be in use during this summer's World Cup. It has been made obsolete by a positively spectacular structure, the best stadium in all of Germany, and one of the most modern-looking ones on earth.

It's called the FIFA World Cup Stadium of Munich, and it lies to the north of the city, in the Frottmaning area. It has three decks of stands, holding a total of 66,000 people, all under cover. It cost 280 million euros to construct, and was inaugurated in the summer of 2005. The cost was shared by the local Munich government, Bayern Munich, and the city's other Bundesliga team, TSV 1860 Munich.

From outside, the stadium looks absolutely magical. It's surrounded by a sort of transparent shell that lends it an impressive and futuristic look. Four first-round games will be played here, including the inaugural event, as well as one second-round match and one of the two semifinals.

Of course, in the 1974 World Cup, six matches were played in Munich's old Olympic Stadium: Italy versus Haiti, Haiti versus Poland, and Argentina versus Haiti in the first round, followed by Brazil versus Poland in the third-place match, and of course the final in which the Germans defeated Johan Cruyff and his "Clockwork Orange" two goals to one.

WHO WILL PLAY IN MUNICH?

The four first-round matches that will take place in Munich are as follows (all times are local German time, which is six hours ahead of Eastern Standard Time):

Thursday, June 9th, 6 p.m. (Inauguration): Germany vs.
Costa Rica
Wednesday, June 14th, 6 p.m.: Tunisia vs. Saudi Arabia
Sunday, June 18th, 3 p.m.: Brazil vs. Australia
Wednesday, June 21st, 4 p.m.: Ivory Coast vs.
Serbia and Montenegro

A second-round match will take place on Sunday, June 24th at 5
p.m., between the winners of Group A and the second-place finisher in
Group B. The semifinal will be held on Wednesday, July 5th, at nine in
the evening.

TOURISM IN MUNICH

As we've already seen, the city's historic district is quite attractive
and photogenic, filled with historic plazas and ancient cathedrals.
It is simply a must-see. When you're there, be sure to check out the
Viktualienmarkt, a colorful, open-air market. It's highly recommended
for fruits, vegetables, meats, sausages, and the two breweries that are

located there. It's an ideal place to sample some real Bavarian suds and watch the locals shop for their dinner.

Another nearby spot that is ideal for having lunch is the Bavarian restaurant Weisses Brauhaus. The food and decor are both completely authentic to the region, and you know it's a good restaurant because it's where all the locals go.

Another popular Marienplatz eatery is the Hofbräuhaus, though the majority of its customers are tourists. But since you'll be one yourself, you don't have to feel bad about eating there. It's quite a good restaurant—much more colorful, for example, than the Americanized version that sits in Las Vegas.

The two plazas, the Karlsplatz and the Marienplatz, are also ideal places to go shopping for souvenirs and other such things. There are boutiques, shoe stores, toy shops, and a pair of department stores.

And speaking of plazas, the Königsplatz (to the east of the city) is a must-see for taking in art and culture. It's the most impressive plaza in Munich, and surrounded entirely by museums. There's something for all tastes: Greek, Roman, and Modern art.

And before you leave, you have to visit Leopoldstrasse, which is lined with restaurants, cafés, bars, clubs, and all-around good ambience. It's the center of Munich's buzzing nightlife.

MY FAVORITE CORNER

If you find you need to relax, you should visit my favorite spot in Munich, the city's main park: the Englischer Garten.

It's simply immense, one of the largest parks in all of Europe, and ideal for walking, jogging, or swimming in the tributaries of the Isar River that crisscross it. It was constructed more than two hundred years ago. It's also a nice place to visit at dusk. Within the limits of the park sits one of the oldest and most famous breweries in all of Munich, called the Chinesischer Turm, for its pagoda-style construction, which dates to 1791. I recommend it highly, as do I recommend a climb up the hill where the park's Greek temple, the Monopteros, sits, offering a gorgeous view of the rest of the city.

If the heat is too oppressive (I doubt it will be, for the German summer is generally quite mild), break out your bathing suit and head for the public baths known as the Müllersches Volksbad, situated along the Isar. It's a beautiful setting, with a majestic swimming pool built all the way back in 1900. And as if a refreshing swim weren't enough, the spectacle of seeing so many scantily clad Germans—some of them completely nude—is certainly something worth writing home about!

Two:

Stuttgart:
Germany's Car Capital

In 1926, Stuttgart ceased to be a little village on the edge of the Black Forest in southern Germany to become the car capital of the country.

It was in that year that two great luxury car manufacturers, Mercedes-Benz and Porsche, opened their factories there, changing the face of the city forever.

Today, with nearly 600,000 inhabitants, Stuttgart is one of the most important industrial centers in Germany and all of Europe. It's also the capital of the state of Baden-Württemberg, which boasts the highest per capita income in the entire country, and is located some 200 kilometers (125 miles) to the west of Munich, in the same scenic valley, where it was founded by the Romans almost two thousand years ago.

During the Renaissance, it enjoyed many prosperous years of cultural and commercial development. That's the period from which the two palaces that symbolize the city—the Altes Schloss (the Ancient Palace) and the Neues Schloss (the New Palace)—date. Both are supremely elegant, and both are located right in the heart of Stuttgart, around the Schillerplatz.

STUTTGART'S STADIUM

Stuttgart is the home of a local Bundesliga team. Their home field is the Gottlieb-Daimler stadium, which will be used during this summer's World Cup, and which is also a veteran of the 1974 tournament, where it saw Argentina play both Poland and Italy.

It's one of the most ancient sports stadiums in all of Germany, constructed in 1933 and named Neckar-Stadion. It's where Germany played for the first time after World War II—in 1950, against Switzerland. It was also where they played for the first time as a unified country, in 1990, once again against the Swiss.

Another interesting bit of trivia is that the current coach of the German national team, Jürgen Klinsmann, retired on this very field back in 1999. If his selection finishes second in Group A, they will play here on June 25th against the winner of Group B . . . which could be England. Can you imagine that?

He'll have another opportunity if Germany loses in the semifinals and has to play for third place in Stuttgart on July 8th. (Though I doubt very much that this prospect is of much interest to Klinsmann.)

Since its original construction, Gottlieb-Daimler has undergone a number of expansions and renovations. Today it has a capacity of some 54,000 seats, all situated in comfortable, covered stands.

WHO WILL PLAY IN STUTTGART?

Stuttgart will play host to four first-round matches and two matches in the second round. Here is the schedule (again, with all times local):

Tuesday, June 13th, 6 p.m.: France vs. Switzerland
Friday, June 16th, 6 p.m.: Holland vs. Ivory Coast
Monday, June 19th, 9 p.m.: Spain vs. Tunisia
Thursday, June 22nd, 9 p.m.: Croatia vs. Australia

The second-round matches will take place on Sunday, June 25th, between the winner of Group A and the second-place finisher in Group B, and on the 8th of July, where the third-place team will be decided.

TOURISM IN STUTTGART

The two palaces I mentioned earlier are both worth a visit, but, since this is the capital of the German auto industry—the Detroit of Germany, as it were—the best attractions that Stuttgart has to offer are the Porsche and Mercedes museums.

I recommend both of them, whether you are into cars or not, but especially the Mercedes museum. It's free to enter, and they offer an audio tour in several languages, including English and Spanish. Starting on May 20th, the museum will be moved to a new location, which probably means the introduction of an entrance fee. Some two hundred cars and trucks will be on display. For your shopping requirements, I recommend the Schlossplatz. Among the many other things you can buy there are the cuckoo clocks famous all over the world. If you're looking for a good gift for your mother-in-law, pick one up for her, sit back, and admire the results. And while you're at it, get one for yourself, too!

MY FAVORITE SPOT

It's definitely the Mercedes-Benz Museum—a magnificent opportunity to admire the mechanical works of art produced throughout the years by this industrial giant, one of the most prestigious and influential companies on earth.

And just so you know, the museum's new location is very close to the Gottlieb-Daimler stadium, so you can plan a visit even on a game day.

Three:

Nuremberg:
The Medieval City

The Second World War left it in ruins, but its inhabitants were able to rebuild it and revive its beautiful medieval past. Today, Nuremberg is one of the most picturesque cities in Germany, with its little red-roofed houses and its narrow, winding streets and alleys that hearken back to the Middle Ages. Part of the wall that surrounded it during that period survived the war, and we can still enjoy it today.

Nuremberg is located some 160 kilometers (about 100 miles) to the north of Munich but is still in the state of Bavaria, with a population of half a million people. Its history began toward the end of the first millennium, around the year 1000, when it was founded as a military camp for the Holy Roman Emperor Henry III.

Nuremberg is also known, unfortunately, for its Nazi past. It was one of Hitler's favorite cities, and he tried to turn it into the capital of the Third Reich. The members of Hitler Youth, arrogant in their brown shirts, marched through its streets more than once. It was here that the anti-Jewish racial laws of the Nazi government were written, which is why they carried the name of the city. It was also the seat of the famous tribunal that judged and sentenced the leaders of that same government after the war.

A part of that dark past can be seen in a museum located in the immense stadium that the Nazis constructed on the city's south side. The exhibition is called "Fascination and Terror" (*Faszination und Gewalt*). All that remains of the stadium are the ruins that the war left and the podium from which Hitler made his speeches.

NUREMBERG'S "FRANKENSTADION"

This new stadium was built in 1991 and remodeled in 2005, just in time for the Confederations Cup. Three games were played here: Argentina–Australia, Argentina–Germany, and, in the semifinals, Brazil–Germany. It was also the scene of the European Champions Cup final in 1997. The 2006 World Cup will mark the Frankenstadion's first participation in this event.

Its design is very modern and it is constructed in the form of an octagon, that is, it's neither oval-shaped nor round or square; instead, it has eight sides.

Its capacity is more than 37,000 people and it's home to the local team, FC Nuremberg, nine times the German champion.

WHAT TEAMS WILL PLAY AT NUREMBERG?

No less than Mexico and the United States. The Mexicans will open the first round of the competition in Nuremberg, and the Americans will close it. In total, five games will be played on this site. Here is the schedule (local time):

Sunday, June 11th, 6 p.m.: Mexico vs. Iran
Thursday, June 15th, 6 p.m.: England vs. Trinidad and Tobago
Sunday, June 18th, 3 p.m.: Japan vs. Croatia
Thursday, June 22nd, 4 p.m.: United States vs. Ghana

In the second round, there will be only one game in the Frankenstadion, on Tuesday, June 25, at 9 p.m., between the winner of Group D and the second-place finisher of Group C (which means Mexico could return here to play again, as could Argentina).

TOURISM IN NUREMBERG

The heart of the city is the Main Market Square (the Hauptmarkt), where there's a beautiful church, the Church of Our Lady (Frauenkirche). This is where you feel Nuremberg's daily life and energy. It's also the best place to buy arts and crafts and souvenirs of the city.

Next to the church is one of the chief symbols of Nuremberg, an immense Gothic-style fountain that, more than a fountain, seems like an altar in the form of an obelisk. It's called the Schöner Fountain (Schöner Brunnen). It was built more than five hundred years ago and measures some twenty meters (sixty-two feet) in height. It's decorated with forty statues of biblical figures and people prominent in local history. It's impressive. Don't fail to visit it and take pictures.

On Burgstrasse, as you leave the Market Square, I also recommend you go to the Fembohaus, a mansion built in the sixteenth century. Take the elevator to the top floor and you'll have a good view of all of Nuremberg. Upon leaving the mansion, continue going up the same street until you arrive at the top of a little hill, where you'll find the city's most beautiful building, the emperor's castle, the famous Kaiserburg. If you've got any strength left in your legs, climb the 113 steps of the tower so you can enjoy the best panoramic view of the city.

You also shouldn't fail to visit the bridges that cross the city's river, the Pegnitz, and especially the Museum Bridge (the Museumsbrücke). From there, one can take in another of the city's important symbols, the Holy Spirit Hospital (the Heilig-Geist-Spital). The building is constructed on an island in the river and was partially destroyed during the war. But in 1950 it was restored to its original medieval form and style. Today it's a restaurant (very good and very expensive).

MY FAVORITE SPOT

It's an Italian restaurant called C'era Una Volta da Luigi, better known as the "Hosteria de Luigi." You can find it on Johannisgasse, very near the main train station. The charming owner is a tall, slim, long-haired, and very sociable Italian fellow named Luigi Fusaro. He speaks a little Spanish and in his best years was a professional soccer player. The food is delicious—especially the pasta—and very reasonably priced. I recommend it in the most enthusiastic terms.

Four:

Frankfurt:
The Financial Center

Like New York, Frankfurt is a great international financial center made up of big buildings. And since it's found along the banks of the Main River in western Germany, they sometimes call it "Mainhattan." In truth, it's one of the most modern and important of all German cities. It's a modern city of skyscrapers and many, many banks and financial institutions, and it's the home of the Federal Bank and the Frankfurt Stock Exchange. For all these reasons, it's a metropolis made up of young, energetic people who live a fast-paced and competitive lifestyle.

It's the fifth-largest German city (with some 700,000 inhabitants) and the most important in the state of Hesse, but it's not the state capital (which is Wiesbaden). Besides all the money that moves through it, Frankfurt is also famous in the world of literature because it's here that was born the "German Shakespeare," the famous writer Johann Wolfgang von Goethe. The house where he was born and raised is today a museum, the Goethehaus, and is located in the city's historic center. (More on him when we get to Leipzig.)

Frankfurt's modernity masks the fact that it's also one of Germany's oldest cities. Its history goes back all the way to the first century before Christ and the days of the Roman Empire. Historical names like Frederick I (a.k.a. Barbarossa), Charlemagne, and Napoléon are linked to Frankfurt's past. For many years, it was the city where German kings and emperors were elected and crowned (thirty-six kings and ten emperors).

FRANKFURT'S STADIUM

It's called the Waldstadion and it has room for 48,000 spectators. It was constructed in 2005, on the same location as the original stadium, which was put up in the 1920s and where several games of the 1974 World Cup were played (Brazil played all its first-round games there). The old Waldstadion was also the site of the final for the UEFA Cup, the Europeans Champions Cup, and Eurocup 1988, and it was where the fight between Muhammad Ali and the German heavyweight Karl Mildenberger took place in 1966.

The new stadium was inaugurated with the Confederations Cup in 2005. It was here that Mexico played Greece and, in the final, Brazil met Argentina. Today, it's the home of the local Bundesliga team, Eintracht Frankfurt. The great novelty of its design is the stadium's retractable roof, which is made of a transparent fabric.

WHAT TEAMS WILL PLAY HERE?

Four first-round games will be played at Frankfort and one second-round game. These are the teams and times (local time) they will meet:

Saturday, June 10th, 3 p.m.: England vs. Paraguay
Tuesday, June 13th, 3 p.m.: South Korea vs. Togo
Saturday, June 17th, 3 p.m.: Portugal vs. Iran
Wednesday, June 21st, 9 p.m.: Holland vs. Argentina

In the second phase, one of the quarterfinal games will be played here on Saturday, July 1.

TOURISM IN FRANKFURT

In spite of its modern skyscrapers, the city of Frankfurt has a historical center, also rebuilt after the Second World War. The Romerberg Square is the very heart of the city's most ancient section. There you will find a lovely fountain called the Fountain of Justice (which, in German, is called—take note!—Gerechtigkeitsbrunnen) and the building that houses the old city's mayoral residence, which is called the Romer. Here is where the kings and emperors of the past had their coronations. This square is the city's only place where the architecture is typically German, since the rest is totally modern and contemporary. About a block from the square is the river Main. Go there and cross a bridge to the other side in order to admire the city from its best perspective and to take some good photos of its skyline.

And while you're on the banks of the Main, take advantage of your time to absorb a little of the culture and information in a district called the Museumsufer, which encompasses the most eclectic mix of museums in the entire country. This is where you'll find the Museum of Communication, the Museum of German Cinema, the Museum of Ethnology, Museum of Icons, and the favorite of the kids, the Museum of Natural Science, where many dinosaur fossils and skeletons are exhibited.

To go shopping and to satisfy your cravings for a bite to eat (for something both German and international), you'll need to cross the river again and visit Zeil Street, just to the north of the Römerberg Square, which is Germany's longest street of shops and restaurants. Finally, if your nostalgia for Latin music consumes you (or if you simply wish to move your bones), get yourself over to the Latin Palace Changó, in Münchenerstrasse and close to Frankfurt's Central Train Station. It's the city's mecca for the *merengue*, the *salsa*, the *bachata*, the *vallenatos*, and the *regaetton*. Some of the biggest names in tropical music, like ToZo Rosario, have played at this club. For the World Cup, it will probably have a super program of invited artists. Get loose and let go (or as we say in Spanish: *"Dame más gasolina"*).

MY FAVORITE SPOT

In Frankfurt, it's the Restaurant Buenos Aires, located next to the river on Dreieichstrasse. It's a very *porteño* (Buenos Aires) place in terms of its decoration, food, and Argentine music from the 1980s (Soda, Baglietto, Charlie García). The menu includes roasted meats, *empanadas, matambre, provoleta*, and, of course, Argentine wine and beer. The owner is L. A. Cocinamo; he tends to the place personally and loves to talk *fútbol*. Don't fail to go there.

Five:
Kaiserslautern:
The Great Military Base

Germans know Kaiserslautern for two reasons: first, for being the largest U.S. military base in their whole country (or outside of North America, for that matter), and, second, because it's the home of the brothers Fritz and Ottmar Walter, stars of the World Champion 1954 team, and authors of *The Battle of Bern*.

For this latter reason, Kaiserslautern has one of the most fanatical soccer populations in all of Germany. In deference to their passions, FIFA rewarded them with the opportunity to be a host city this summer.

That's the deal with this small city of soccer and U.S. soldiers, founded more than twelve hundred years ago in the middle of a forest near the border with France, some 100 kilometers (60 miles) southwest of Frankfurt.

It's not what you'd call a center of tourism, being known primarily as a place where textiles, machinery, and steel are produced. Nor is it very big, with a population of only around 100,000, some 40,000 of which are U.S. military families.

FRITZ WALTER STADIUM

After its construction in 1926, it was known as Betzenbergstadion, but in 1959, after the retirement of 1954 World Cup champion and Kaiserslautern native Fritz Walter, the stadium was renamed in his honor.

Built atop scenic Betzenberg, the hill that overlooks the city, it has a capacity of 41,000 spectators and is also the home field of the Bundesliga's Kaiserslautern. The team had five players on the '54

squad, the Walter brothers being its primary stars. Kaiserslautern has won four German league titles, quite a feat for such a small city.

Fritz Walter stadium underwent a complete renovation in 2003.

WHO WILL PLAY IN KAISERSLAUTERN?

In order to make them feel more at home, FIFA will let the United States play a match in Kaiserslautern. Also en route are Italy, Spain, and Paraguay, among others. Here is the calendar of matchups:

Monday, June 12th, 3 p.m.: Australia vs. Japan
Saturday, June 17th, 9 p.m.: Italy vs. United States
Tuesday, June 20th, 9 p.m.: Paraguay vs. Trinidad and Tobago
Friday, June 23rd, 4 p.m.: Saudi Arabia vs. Spain

Monday, June 26, will see the second-round match between the Group E winner and the second-place finisher in Group F. In other words, it could be the Americans playing "at home" if they win their group. And their opponent could be the Brazilians, if they finish second in theirs.

TOURISM IN KAISERSLAUTERN

The city's historic center is quite attractive and worth a visit. It doesn't quite have the splendor of some other German cities, simplicity being its greatest virtue.

The main area is the Martinsplatz, covered with leafy trees and a lovely fountain that makes the place perfect for a relaxing stroll.

Nearby lies the township of Kaiserslautern, first built in 1745, and the Zum Donnersberg hotel, where Napoléon once ate breakfast. And you can do the same in the neighborhood of the hotel, taking advantage of any of the smallish restaurants that are located around there. You'll also find clothing, crafts, and souvenir shops.

Also not far from the plaza is the only wood structure remaining in the city, Spinnradl Inn, which was built over 260 years ago.

Other Kaiserslautern attractions can be found on the outskirts of the city, like the zoo, the Betzenberg Deer Park, a cozy Japanese garden, and on the way to the stadium you'll find a replica of the structure itself, only fashioned out of hundreds of thousands of LEGOS and called the "Mini-Betzen."

MY FAVORITE SPOT

It also lies along the road to Fritz Walter Stadium. It's a statue called *Elf Freunde*, which in German means "Eleven Friends," in reference to a soccer team, of course. It's one of the most lovely monuments to the sport that I've ever seen in my world travels. When I visited it in December 2005 I couldn't help but take a picture at the foot of the statue.

We'll see how many tourists do the same during the World Cup this summer. You, of course, should be no exception!

Six:

Cologne:
The Rome of the Rhine

Now we've come to the Rhine River valley and the most ancient city in all of Germany: Cologne.

It was founded by the Romans some fifty years after the death of Christ. The name is one hundred percent Latin in origin and stems from the "colony" that the Romans founded along the banks of the river. Then they brought Christianity, and with it, its art. It was here that the wife of the emperor Claudius was born.

Today, the city's ancient Roman past is preserved in the layout of the streets in the old town, and in its many museums. Perhaps for that reason Cologne (or, in German, Köln) is the capital of German art and the German art industry.

After the museums, the main tourist attraction in Cologne is its cathedral, which stands as one of the highest in the world and also as one of the best examples of Gothic architecture in all of Europe. It's imposing and beautiful at the same time and is one of the very lucky few historic structures in Germany that managed to survive the bombings of World War II.

The rest of the city wasn't quite as lucky. The destruction was extensive, but so was the reconstruction. The old part of town still retains its medieval charm, and stands in harmonious contrast with the modern high-rise buildings that sprang up after the war.

During the Middle Ages, Cologne experienced its greatest period of development, becoming one of the most prosperous and populous cities in the world, after Paris and Constantinople.

Today it is home to a population of around a million inhabitants, many of whom are from other parts of Europe and the Middle East who have decided to put down roots here. As a result, the city boasts

restaurants purveying all types of international cuisine, from Italian to Arabic.

And a Carnival famous throughout Germany!

That's why people say that folks from Cologne are happy, kind, and good drinkers. You can see this latter fact in the hundreds of pubs and breweries that dot the city. Here they aren't called biergartens but rather *Kölschen Weestchaff*, where they serve the local fare, known throughout the world as *Kölsch*. Don't forget to try a glass!

The Cologners also love their soccer. FC Köln is their local Bundesliga club, and their home field was formerly known as the Müngersdorfer.

COLOGNE'S NEW STADIUM

The old Müngersdorfer no longer exists. The city decided to raze it and build a new, larger, more modern structure. It cost a total of 26 million euros and has a capacity of forty thousand.

It was inaugurated in March of 2004, and rebaptized, à la Hamburg and Munich, the FIFA World Cup Stadium–Cologne. All the seats are covered, and the roof is "convertible" in case of inclement weather.

It was the site of several 2005 Confederations Cup matches, including the debut between Argentina and Tunisia.

WHO'S PLAYING IN COLOGNE?

Cologne will be seeing World Cup matches for the first time in its lengthy history, since it didn't play host to any games during the 1974 event. So you can imagine how excited the organizers are to see the teams arrive and start kicking the ball around.

This city will also play host to five matches: four in the first round, and one to open the second. Here are the dates:

> **Sunday, June 11th, 9 p.m.:** Angola vs. Portugal
> **Saturday, June 17th, 9 p.m.:** Czech Republic vs. Ghana
> **Tuesday, June 20th, 4 p.m.:** Sweden vs. England
> **Friday, June 23rd, 9 p.m.:** Togo vs. France

The second-round match will take place on Monday, June 26th, at 9 p.m., between the winner of Group G and the runner-up team in Group H.

TOURISM IN COLOGNE

The best way to admire Cologne is to arrive via train at their main station just off to one side of the big cathedral. As you arrive, you cross over the Hohenzollernbrücke, from which bridge you will enjoy a majestic view of the river, the spectacular cathedral, and the pointed spires of the old medieval district.

When you exit the old Hauptbahnhof (main train station), a set of stairs will take you up to the little Domplatte, the plaza right there in front of the cathedral. This has an interesting history. Construction began in 1248 but was never completed. One hundred years later, they picked back up with the work, adding the chorus and one of the towers, but once again the building was halted, this time in 1560. Another two hundred years would pass before it was finally completed in 1880.

And don't fail to go inside the structure, which contains a museum relating the history of the church. I recommend it.

I also suggest you visit the most important museum in the entire city, situated to one side of the cathedral: the German-Roman Museum of Cologne. There you can see a perfectly preserved thermal bath built by the Romans some two thousand years ago. You'll also come across an extraordinary ancient mosaic floor, the famous Dionysus Mosaic, which was discovered during the Second World War, during the construction of an underground bomb shelter. It measures over seventy square meters and was the floor of an ancient Roman villa. It's simply a gem. You have to see it.

Standing in stark contrast with all this ancient history is a much more modern museum, the Ludwig. It is home to the best collection of twentieth-century art in the country.

There are many more things to see and do, but those two are the most important items on the agenda, and more than sufficient to balance your diet of soccer and tourism.

MY FAVORITE SPOT

The best way to enjoy the beautiful historic downtown area of Cologne is from along the opposite bank of the Rhine.

The same view that you enjoy when arriving at the city by train can be yours from the terrace of the Hilton Hotel. From there, the majestic cathedral and the historic neighborhoods around it dominate the scene, along with the nearby museums and the many spans across the river.

From the terrace, a boulevard extends the full length of the Rhine. I highly recommend it for a nice evening walk, or one in the early morning. Make plans to visit it, and, as always, take your camera.

Seven:

Leipzig:
Music and Liturature

Its reputation as a cultural center dates from the Middle Ages, when Leipzig was the university and publishing capital of all Europe. It was here that the University of Leipzig was founded in 1409, and here that the most books anywhere on the continent were printed and published. Years later, it was the residence of two towering German intellects, the influential philosopher Friedrich Nietzsche, and the great poet and writer Johann Wolfgang von Goethe, the most

illustrious figure in German letters and the man who dubbed the city the "Little Paris." It was also in Leipzig that the glorious German musician and composer Johann Sebastian Bach lived and worked.

The cultural industry still exists, but it's not the same as it was in those times. It's been replaced by gymnastics. Since its Communist period (1945–89), Leipzig was the world capital of gymnastics, a tradition that continues today in Germany's national physical education program, which is the finest in the world.

Leipzig dates back to the sixth century of the modern era, when it was founded by Sorbian merchants. Situated in the eastern part of Germany, some 200 kilometers (125 miles) to the south of Berlin, in

the state of Saxony, Leipzig was the heart of the former German Democratic Republic. Its population is about half a million people.

The popular movement that ended with the fall of the Berlin Wall began, rightly enough, here in Leipzig, in October of 1989, with the "Monday Protests." Every Monday, tens of thousands of people marched peacefully through the streets of the city demanding liberty and democracy. Since the reunification of the country in 1990, Leipzig has experienced a great urban transformation, with the construction of new buildings, residences, museums, commercial centers, and government offices.

And speaking of the government, the new German chancellor, Angela Merkel, the first woman to direct Germany's government, lived for a long time in Leipzig. She studied physics at the city's famous university and worked at the Academy of Science's Institute of Physics and Chemistry.

THE LEIPZIG STADIUM

For many years it was Germany's largest stadium, with a capacity of 100,000. But after its reconfiguration in 2004, its capacity was reduced to 44,000 rather more comfortable seats. It's called the Zentralstadion and was built in 1956 by the old Communist govern-

ment. It was the home ground of East Germany's national soccer team.

The first important tournament held in the new Zentralstadion, following its reconfiguration, was the Confederations Cup in 2005. It was there that Brazil faced Greece, and Australia faced Tunisia in the first round, and that Mexico and Germany battled for third place.

No team from the Bundesliga plays in this stadium since Leipzig doesn't have a professional soccer team at this time, which is a great irony when you consider that it was in this very city that the league was founded in 1900.

WHAT TEAMS WILL PLAY IN LEIPZIG?

Five games will be played in Leipzig stadium, four in the first phase and one opening match of the second round. Here is the schedule (again, all times are local) and the participants:

Sunday, June 11th, 3 p.m.: Serbia and Montenegro vs. Holland
Wednesday, June 14th, 3 p.m.: Spain vs. Ukraine
Sunday, June 18th, 9 p.m.: France vs. Korea
Wednesday, June 21st, 4 p.m.: Iran vs. Angola

On Saturday, June 24th, in the Cup's second phase, the winner of Group C will meet the second-place finisher of Group D. Because of this arrangement, it's possible that Argentina and Mexico will play here.

TOURISM IN LEIPZIG

If you arrive in Leipzig by train, you'll find yourself in a very imposing train station, the Hauptbahnhof, which is the largest in Europe. This is a good place from which to explore the city on foot, but before heading out to the street, take some time to shop, as the terminal houses a huge commercial center with more than 140 shops.

Once you're out of the station, the first thing you have to do is walk some ten minutes to the Market Plaza in the center of the city. The buildings that surround it exhibit the best architecture in all of Leipzig, the little that was saved from the bombs of the war. It's here that you will see, and surely take pictures of, the Museum of History and the Old Mayoral Building, which was built more than five hundred years ago. You'll also be able to admire the Stadtisches Kaufhaus store to the south of the plaza.

Not far from here, two blocks to the north, on Katharinenstrasse, you'll find two other fabulous buildings that will evoke the city's glorious cultural past: the Romanushaus and the Fregehaus.

If the shops in the station don't interest you, in the outlying buildings of the Market Plaza you'll find two covered commercial arcades, both elegantly decorated and called "passages": the Mädlerpassage and the Handwerkerpassage. Here you'll find boutiques, jewelry stores, and galleries, as well as cafés, restaurants, and pubs.

And speaking of pubs, in the basement of the Mädlerpassage you'll find the most famous pub in the city, and possibly in all of Germany, the Auerbach's Keller. It was included by Goethe in his celebrated dramatic poem *Faust*. Don't fail to visit it so that you can relive scenes from Goethe's famous epic (in case you haven't read it, don't worry—I haven't either) and in order to sample some good Saxony wine, served directly from the barrel.

And to the west of the Market Plaza one finds the famous church that I mentioned earlier—the church of St. Thomas—where Bach was the music director and principal organist. It's also the home of the Thomaner Choir, the most famous children's choir in the world, and also the oldest. It's been in existence for more than eight hundred years! The choir still exists and performs regularly in the church, where the Bach Museum is located. Here you can learn more about the life and magnificent work of the composer. I recommend it most enthusiastically. Another architectural attraction, albeit one of a more modern, even revolutionary bent, that I also recommend you visit is the tallest building in Leipzig, the Universitätshochhaus, which was constructed in the form of a giant open book.

MY FAVORITE SPOT

Very near the book building is the best spot in Leipzig to have a good time—dance, dine, drink in a pub, or enjoy a coffee—at a place called Moritzbastei, where you can find the ruins of the wall that at one time surrounded the city. It's the favorite spot of young people, students, and, of course, tourists.

Another place I recommend you go, especially if you need a haircut, is the "Super Cuts," in the train station. First, because there's a very pretty and really excellent young woman hairstylist there named Gesine. And, second, because, as she herself told me, the barbershop will be open every day during the Cup until midnight.

Now you know: if you need a trim for less than $20, go visit Gesine and tell her hello from me.

Eight:

Dortmund:
The Beer Capital of Germany

Technically, Munich is the beer capital of Germany, but Dortmund is where most of it is made. There are more breweries here than in the Bavarian capital—more, even, than in any other European city—and so the title really belongs to Dortmund.

Ironically enough, for many years it was the capital of the German coal and steel industry. In fact, Dortmund is known the world over for those two products, which provided jobs and salaries not only for German citizens but also for thousands of Italian, Turkish, Greek, and Spanish immigrants. This international flow makes Dortmund one of the most cosmopolitan and tolerant cities in all of Germany.

The city was founded in the ninth century, but its golden age was the nineteenth, when coal and steel reigned supreme. And its prosperity continued on into the twentieth, despite (or perhaps thanks to) the onset of the two world wars. Part of this history is preserved to this day in the Museum of Industry. Dortmund's era of steel and coal faded into history in the 1980s. Unemployment ran rampant, and the city was forced to reinvent itself in order to survive. The plan was to invest in technology and service industries, and that plan yielded results. Today, Dortmund is one of Germany's most important technological centers.

Since it was one of the most prominent industrial centers under the Nazi regime, Dortmund was heavily targeted by Allied bombing runs during the Second World War. Its reconstruction took decades, and wasn't fully realized until the 1970s, and today you'll find it a modern city laced with a few restored historical structures.

It's located in the state of North Rhine-Westfalia, to the northeast

of Cologne, in one of the most important industrial regions in either Germany or Europe at large: the Ruhr valley. Its population numbers some 700,000 people, about on a par with San Francisco.

DORTMUND'S STADIUM

The Westfalenstadion is the home of the popular local team Borussia Dortmund. The south end of the stands is famous throughout the entire Bundesliga for being the home of 25,000 screaming, rabid fans who congregate there to support their local team.

It was built specifically to host games during the 1974 World Cup. It's where Johan Cruyff and his "Clockwork Orange" eliminated Brazil 2–0. The Dutch also faced Sweden and Bulgaria on that same pitch.

In 2001, it was remodeled and expanded to accommodate a capacity of 70,000. For the World Cup, however, it will max out at 66,000.

WHICH TEAMS WILL PLAY IN DORTMUND?

Brazil will be playing here once again, this time against Japan in the first round. Also appearing will be the Trinidadians and the Germans, among others. Here's the complete calendar:

Saturday, June 10th, 6 p.m.: Trinidad and Tobago vs. Sweden
Wednesday, June 14th, 9 p.m.: Germany vs. Poland
Monday, June 19th, 3 p.m.: Togo vs. Switzerland
Thursday, June 22nd, 9 p.m.: Brazil vs. Japan

Two second-round matches are also slated for the Westfalenstadion. One will be the quarterfinals on June 27th, between the winner of Group F and the runners-up in Group E. In other words, it could easily be Brazil returning to Dortmund to face either Italy or the United States. What do you think?

The other matchup will be a semifinal match on July 4th.

TOURISM IN DORTMUND

As I mentioned before, Dortmund's iron and steel mines attracted thousands of European immigrants in the twentieth century. And we all know what tends to crop up in cities full of immigrants: restaurants! You'll find that dining will be a joy in Dortmund. The selection of international cuisines—from the most simple to the most elegant of all—is virtually unlimited. There's always something good.

Beer—the city's new industry—also comes in a wide range of varieties. Pubs and biergartens abound. And if you'd like to learn more about brewing and the history of this popular beverage, there's even a museum for you: the Brauerei Museum.

Another museum that could be of interest is the museum of industry—the Westfalisches Industriemuseum. It's located in an old coal mine, and in it you can follow along with Dortmund's industrial past and see up close what it was like to work in the mines and steel factories.

For musical spectacles—both classic and rock—or bicycle racing, equestrian shows, or ice-skating competitions, check out the schedule of events at the Westfalenhalle concert hall. It has a 16,000 seat capacity and is one of the largest and most popular venues of its kind in all of Germany. More than three million people visit it annually.

MY FAVORITE SPOT

I t's the giant park in the neighborhood where the Westfalenhalle is located. It's called Westfalenpark, and it's the best place I found in all of Germany for burning off a little bit of soccer fever.

The park is simply immense, and it reminds me quite a bit of the parks along the Avenida General Paz in Buenos Aires, where anyone driving by can look out their car window and see groups of friends playing pickup games almost any time of day.

So take your ball, and prove to those Germans that you've got the moves. Who knows . . . maybe they'll sign you to a Bundesliga team.

Nine:
Gelsenkirchen:
Soccer and Coal

The one has nothing to do with the other, but both made Gelsenkirchen well known throughout Germany.

First, let's talk about the soccer.

The partisans of the local Bundesliga team, FC Schalke 04, seven times the German champions, form the most fervent and scandalous fan base in the entire country. The club itself boasts 48,000 members.

The coal isn't being extracted anymore, but for many years it was the city's primary industry. Gelsenkirchen was called "the city of a thousand lights" because of the fires of the ovens that processed the mineral and glowed throughout the night.

Many of those old mines are today museums, theaters, and cabarets. In other words, coal continues to play a part in the life of this city of 300,000 inhabitants located in the heart of the industrial zone of the Ruhr River valley.

Now, though, what rules is the sun. Instead of coal, the city began, gradually, to invest in solar energy, to the point of converting itself into Germany's most important research center for this type of energy and the production of solar panels and generators.

At the same time, Gelsenkirchen moved away from its polluted mineral past and toward the development of green areas, creating parks and protecting forests. In essence, it's the greenest city in the entire country, with more than a third of its area covered by parks, forests, and gardens. The city, located in the state of North Rhine-Westphalia, is very near the border with Belgium and Holland and only half an hour from Dortmund and an hour from Cologne.

GELSENKIRCHEN'S COVERED STADIUM

This is, without a doubt, the most spectacular stadium of this World Cup. The president of FIFA, Sepp Blatter, said once that the Arena AufSchalke of Gelsenkirchen is "a pilot project for the entire world."

Built at a cost of 115 million euros ($140 million), it is the most expensive of all such stadiums. It was inaugurated in 2001.

Its great novelty lies in its having a field that is completely covered with a retractable roof. Like the field in Sapporo, Japan, that was used in the World Cup of 2002, the covering over Gelsenkirchen's pitch can also be retracted so that the grass gets sun and water. The process takes four hours, and there is a tour of the stadium that explains it all very well. I recommend you take it. I had an opportunity to do just that when I visited the city in December of 2005 and it's definitely worth the effort.

The AufSchalke seats 53,000 people comfortably and offers an excellent view of the field from each and every seat. The stadium, which, strictly speaking, is a multipurpose arena, is also utilized for concerts, basketball games, American football games, cycling, track and field, exhibitions of all sorts, and conventions.

WHO'S PLAYING IN GELSENKIRCHEN?

The honor of playing on this revolutionary field will go to, among others, Mexico, the United States, and Argentina, the latter, coincidentally, having been tabbed to play on Sapporo's covered field in the South Korea/Japan World Cup (against England). This is the complete schedule for the five games that will be played in Gelsenkirchen's Arena AufSchalke:

Friday, June 9th, 9 p.m.: Poland vs. Ecuador
Monday, June 12th, 6 p.m.: United States vs. Czech Republic
Thursday, June 16th, 3 p.m.: Argentina vs. Serbia and Montenegro
Wednesday, June 21st, 4 p.m.: Portugal vs. Mexico

There will also be a quarterfinal game on Saturday, July 1st, at five in the afternoon.

TOURISM IN GELSENKIRCHEN

With so much green in the city, you have to enjoy it from close up. Try to get out and exercise a bit, whether it's a matter of walking, running, or kicking a ball around in any one of Gelsenkirchen's

many parks. And there are a lot to pick from: the Nordsternpark, the Rivierpark Nienhausen, the Schloss Berge park, and the Resser-Mark forest park. If you don't want to sweat much but you desire to stay in contact with nature and its creatures, you can visit the city's zoological park, the Erlebniswelt "Zoom."

To better understand Gelsenkirchen's technological contribution to the development of solar energy, and to learn at the same time how it functions, you have to go to the excellent solar exposition at the Science Park. If you're traveling with your children, don't fail to take them to this park.

MY FAVORITE SPOT

If you want to see how it was that the city transformed its coal mines into tourist centers, visit the old Consol and Bergehalde Rungeberg coal mines, whose nighttime illumination is sensational. In both, you'll be able to see German creativity in action. What in the past was the motor of a dangerous and polluting industry is today a fountain of clean, healthful work. The mines have been reconditioned to house museums, exhibitions, bars, and restaurants. What's been done here is truly incredible, an example for all the nations of our world.

Ten:

Hanover:
The Convention Center

For much of the seventeenth century, Hanover was one of the most influential cities in all of northern Europe. It even got to become a kingdom—the Kingdom of Hanover—headed by a family so powerful that one of the sons, George I, was later crowned as king of England.

From that age, only a single spectacular garden remains. Nothing more. The city was completely destroyed in the Second World War. Worse still, the reconstruction proceeded so quickly that today there are no modern buildings even worth mentioning.

The only spectacular feature about the city is its convention center. It's not just any convention center . . . but the largest convention center on earth. The Hanover Messe. The place is simply immense.

It has its own train station, and a parking lot with a 45,000-vehicle capacity. Thanks to Hanover Messe, the city is the German capital of industrial fairs and expositions.

The Expo 2000, at the end of the past millennium, was the last major international fair of the twentieth century, and it was dedicated to the latest humanistic, technological, and ecological developments. Hanover Messe also plays host to an annual fair celebrating the biggest computers on earth, known as the CeBit.

Hanover, which is the capital of the state of Lower Saxony, in northern Germany, lies about 150 kilometers (90 miles) south of Hamburg, and has a population of approximately half a million inhabitants, comparable to Tucson, Arizona.

HANOVER'S STADIUM

I t goes by a name similar to that of Munich's stadium: the FIFA World Cup Stadium of Hanover. Originally (back in 1954), it was called the Niedersachsenstadion.

Since 1959, it housed the local Bundesliga team, Hanover 96. It also played a part in the first World Cup to be held in Germany, back in 1974. It was here that Brazil faced both Argentina and East Germany in the second round. Uruguay also played here against Holland and Bulgaria, in the earlier stage of that tournament.

For the 2005 Confederations Cup, the city decided to renovate the stadium, thanks to an investment of 63 million euros ($76 million). A roof was installed, and the seating capacity was increased to some 45,000 people.

That was where Mexico opened the Confederations Cup against Japan, and went on to their historic 1–0 win over Brazil. Later, they would lose to Argentina in the semifinals, on penalties.

WHAT COUNTRIES ARE PLAYING IN HANOVER?

Mexico will be back, and they hope Hanover will bring them continued success. Other nations appearing here include Italy, making their debut.

All told, five matches will be played out upon the Hanover grass. Here's the complete schedule:

Monday, June 12th, 9 p.m.: Italy vs. Ghana
Thursday, June 16th, 9 p.m.: Mexico vs. Angola
Tuesday, June 20th, 4 p.m.: Croatia vs. Poland
Friday, June 23rd, 9 p.m.: Switzerland vs. South Korea

There will only be one second-round match played here, on June 27th, between the Group H winner and the runners-up from Group G—and that very well could mean France and Spain coming face-to-face . . .

TOURISM IN HANOVER

Getting back to those royal gardens from the seventeenth century that I mentioned earlier—the Herrenhäuser Gardens have retained all the majesty of their days of old. They occupy quite an extensive area, four soccer fields arranged in a square. Through its center runs a breezy parkway covered by leafy trees.

I recommend it highly if you ever feel like spending a relaxing

hour or so among the meticulously landscaped flowers, trees, and shrubs in their perfect and intricate geometric patterns. Before the war, the Gardens adorned the entrance to a palace, but that was completely destroyed by the Allied bombing.

One palace that is still standing in Hanover is the official residence of the city's mayor. It's a majestic structure built over a century ago in the Renaissance style, and it sits along the banks of a river surrounded by a forest. Today it is a symbol of Hanover, and one of the best places for catching a view of the city from up on high. It even sports a cable car that will carry you to the top of an observation tower.

Not far from there, and quite near to the stadium itself, sits Germany's largest artificial lake, called the Maschsee. It was constructed in 1933, and along one of its shores rises a statue very much in the Nazi style that commemorates its inauguration and honors the thousands of workers who worked on it. Rent a rowboat or a paddleboat and spend an afternoon enjoying the peace and tranquility of its waters.

Along the opposite shore sits a small artificial beach that is frequented by the occasional nudist. Don't forget your camera!

If it's shopping you want, you can either walk or take a taxi to Hauptbahnhof, the city's main train station. All the streets south of the station are closed to vehicular traffic, forming an immense pedestrian mall. There you'll find all the shops and stores that you could ever need.

MY FAVORITE SPOT

I'm not much of a dancer, as you know, but there are places that, by virtue of their ambience, can motivate anyone to move their body, regardless of their personality. And that's exactly what happened to me when I visited the only salsa club in Hanover.

Owned by a very genial Colombian man, it's called El Diablo Rojo and it's situated underneath the city's main train station. It's not a huge place, but they throw quite a party!

I've never danced so much salsa in my life, much less with so many surprising and exotic girls, all of whom were very talented—especially so considering their diverse origins. I danced without restraint with Russians, Croatians, Romanians, Iranians, Turks, and—of course—Germans. They were all incredibly skillful dancers.

I recommend the place as well. And don't worry if your inhibitions as a dancer are similar to my own. That place will get you moving, whether you like salsa or not!

Eleven:

Hamburg:
The Great Port City

The first thing I have to tell you about Hamburg is that "hamburgers" do *not* come from here. More than that, the people of Hamburg don't even eat them. Here, as in the rest of Germany, the sausage is king.

That said, I should also tell you that we're dealing here with Germany's second-largest city, and that it's located in the north. Hamburg has nearly two million inhabitants, and it's the German capital of international commerce, owing mainly to the fact that it is Europe's largest port and one of the world's seven most important ports. The port is so big that more than 80,000 people work there. All those Mercedes-Benzes, Porsches, BMWs, Audis, and Volkswagens that you see left Germany by boat from Hamburg's harbor.

Its history dates back to the Middle Ages, when the city was founded along the banks of the Elbe River and quickly grew to become Europe's chief commercial center. For many, many years, it was an independent republic, until Germany itself was formed as a nation and Hamburg became one of its sixteen states.

Besides being a maritime and commercial center, Hamburg is also the capital of the German press. This is where the most important German magazines and daily newspapers are published. It's also Germany's theater and musical theater capital, rather like a German Broadway.

The "Hamburgers," the people of Hamburg, are great lovers of soccer and fervent followers of Hamburg SV, the city's Bundesliga team. Hamburg is also renowned for its international success in cycling, tennis, hockey, and aquatic sports on the Elbe.

HAMBURG'S STADIUM

During Germany's first World Cup, three games were played in Hamburg, one of them being the historic match between the two

Germanys, which West Germany won, 1–0. Those matches were played in Hamburg's old Volksparkstadion, which no longer exists. It was demolished and replaced by a new one at a cost of 97 million euros.

It was inaugurated in 2000 and is called, like the ones in Munich and Hanover, the FIFA World Cup Stadium of Hamburg. It has a seating capacity of 51,000 and is also the home field of the local team.

WHO PLAYS IN HAMBURG?

During the Cup, five games will be played in Hamburg, four in the first round and one of the quarterfinals. These are the first-round games:

Saturday, June 10th, 9 p.m.: Argentina vs. Ivory Coast
Thursday, June 15th, 3 p.m.: Ecuador vs. Costa Rica
Monday, June 19th, 9 p.m.: Saudi Arabia vs. Ukraine
Friday, June 22nd, 4 p.m.: Czech Republic vs. Italy

The quarterfinal match, set for 9 p.m. on Thursday, June 30th, will bring together the winners of the opening second-round games in Cologne and Kaiserslautern.

TOURISM IN HAMBURG

Your stroll through Hamburg must begin on the banks of Lake Binnenalster, which is located right in the center of the city. It's surrounded by beautiful commercial districts built in a variety of architectural periods and styles. The lake is encircled also by all kinds of specialty shops, restaurants, boutiques, cafés, and department stores. The most popular shopping venues are the Alsterpavillion, the Jungfernstieg, and, especially, the Hanseviertel, a mall with glass-covered pathways that's ideal for walking around in on a rainy afternoon without out losing sight of the lake.

From the same Lake Binnenalster you can take a boat tour, via the canals that crisscross the city, to the other of Hamburg's lakes, Lake Aussenalster, located only a few blocks from here. On the northern edge of the lake, there's a lovely park that I recommend, the Stadtpark, from which you can enjoy a lovely view of the city and its skyline. Bring your camera.

If you prefer, instead of climbing into a vessel, you can walk over to the Market Plaza. There, you'll find the Hamburg town hall (the Rathaus), the city's best museums, and its famous and historic theater, the Schauspielhaus.

Another spot that's excellent for panoramic photos of the city is the tower of the St. Michael's Church, on Ludwig-Erhard-Strasse. Climb its 449 steps and you'll be able to see all of Hamburg and its port. The "Michel" tower is the principal symbol of the city and it boasts the largest clock in all of Germany.

Quite nearby you'll find the city's most important commercial street, the Mönckebergstrasse, which I recommend for shopping. Either before shopping or after, be sure to ask how you get to the Chilehaus (just say "Chile House). Built in 1920 by a merchant who made his fortune importing salt from Chile, it has a very interesting structure in that it's shaped like a boat.

For lunch, I recommend you visit the sailing-ship restaurant, the *Rickmer Rickmers*, which is anchored on the banks of the Elbe. The ship is beautiful and more than one hundred years old. The food is expensive but quite varied. While you're eating, you can admire from close at hand the ceaseless activity of Hamburg's port, with its immense cranes loading and unloading cargo from ships bound for and arriving from all parts of the world.

When night comes to Hamburg, you'll note that everyone, tourists and natives alike, makes their way down to St. Pauli, the city's most famous district and possibly the most famous *barrio* in all of Germany. If I tell you how its fame began, you'll begin to understand what kind of *barrio* it is: it was where the sailors would go for entertainment when they dropped anchor in Hamburg. There's something else, too; one of its streets, the Reeperbahn, also known as "The Mile of Sin," is famous for its sex shops and erotic shows.

MY FAVORITE SPOT

But St. Pauli also has bars, beer halls, pubs, clubs, and restaurants for other tastes as well. At dawn, if you're not too sleepy, I recommend you do what the locals do after a long night of excess: go have breakfast at the Fishermen's Market, the *Fischmarkt*, down on the docks. Originally, it was a market for fish and shellfish, but these days it's that and much more. There's everything from vegetables, fruits, meats, and fish to curios and various used items—not to mention live music. The Fishermen's Market is at its most colorful and engaging on Sunday morning. Be sure to visit it.

Twelve:

Berlin:
The Great Capital

They've destroyed it, divided it, and rebuilt it—and then done it all over again—several times. Perhaps because of this, Berlin is Germany's most fascinating and enigmatic city. It's located in the eastern part of the nation, and it's one of my favorite cities, not just in Germany but in the entire world. It's here that the Grand Finale, the championship, of the World Cup will be played. And I'll celebrate my birthday on the very day of the game, July 9, 2006.

Following Germany's reunification in 1990, Berlin has once again regained its status as capital and principal cultural center. Today the city is Germany's largest, and it's where its more than three million inhabitants live, work, and play. It's as large as Houston.

Berlin was founded seven hundred fifty years ago. Toward the end of the 1800s, it became the capital of Imperial Germany. It prospered rapidly and converted itself into one of the most important cities in Europe. Its history, that of a city that's seen it all, has been torrid and full of unexpected turns of fate, but it's also been prosperous and happy. The twentieth century's two world wars were quite punishing on Berlin. After the war, Berlin was divided into four sectors, each one controlled by a different Allied military power: England, the United States, France, and the Soviet Union. In 1961, the Soviets erected a wall around their sector so that people could not escape from it. The wall served as the symbol of the Cold War for twenty-eight years, until it was brought tumbling down in 1989. In that same year, communism in Eastern Europe also came to an end.

Today, Berlin is a dynamic, booming metropolis, a place bursting with life and creativity. By virtue of being a rebuilt city, all of its new buildings, plazas, and avenues are modern. Its old structures have been majestically renovated, and they seem now as if nothing had ever disturbed them. Some examples of this process are the Reichstag (the palace of the German parliament), the Berlin cathedral, the New Synagogue, and the beautiful theater, the Schauspielhaus.

THE HISTORICAL OLYMPIC STADIUM

The city's stadium, the Olympic Stadium of Berlin, the Olympiastadion, is one of the most famous such structures in the world. It's where the glorious African-American athlete Jesse Owens won four gold medals in the 1936 Olympics, proving for the benefit of Hitler, who was in attendance, that the "Aryans" were not the superior race he imagined them to be. It was, in fact, Hitler, who, in 1934, ordered that the stadium be built. He personally directed the work and was present, on his stage of honor (which still exists), for the opening of the 1936 Olympiad.

During the Second World War, the Olympic Stadium was hit by Allied bombs, but it was not destroyed. After being repaired, it became

the home of Hertha Berlin, the city's Bundesliga professional soccer team. In 1974, it was one of the World Cup venues—it's where Chile played its three games (against Australia and the two Germanys). Recently, the Olympiastadion was exhaustively remodeled and modernized, making it one of the sites for the present World Cup.

WHO GETS TO PLAY IN BERLIN?

Four first-round games will be played here, as well as one quarterfinal match and, as I already noted, the championship game itself, the Grand Finale. The four first-round games will all be played at 9 p.m. (local time) and are follows:

> **Tuesday, June 13th:** Brazil vs. Croatia
> **Thursday, June 15th:** Sweden vs. Paraguay
> **Tuesday, June 20th:** Ecuador vs. Germany
> **Friday, June 23rd:** Ukraine vs. Tunisia

The quarterfinal game, to be played on Friday, June 30th, at 5 p.m., brings together the winners of the opening second-round games at Munich and Leipzig. The Grand Finale is Sunday, July 9th, at 8 p.m.

TOURISM IN BERLIN

Berlin boasts a cultural life that's very active and a nightlife that's very upbeat. They've got everything here. Theaters, cinemas, concerts, ballet, opera, discotheques, cabarets, jazz, rock, heavy metal, and rap. Even *salsa* and *merengue*!

The best place to go for shopping (or to grab a bite to eat and watch Berliners come and go) is on Kurfürstemdamm Avenue, better known as "Ku'damm." In the days when Berlin was divided, the "Ku'damm" was the center of West Berlin. It's full of boutiques, all kinds of stores and shops, restaurants, cafés, and beer halls. This is also where you'll find one of the most iconic images of the city, the ruins of the bell tower from the old Kaiser Wilhelm Church, which was destroyed during the war and never rebuilt. You'll want to get some pictures of this.

If you prefer to go to a "mall," or commercial center, I recommend the Potsdamer Platz Arkaden, which, located in Potsdamer Platz, is full of international stores. And if you want to buy something fine and elegant (and if you want to spend a lot of money), you should go to the

Kaufhaus des Westens, known locally as the "KaDeWe." It's like a German Macy's or Bloomingdale's, where they've got everything, and it's all suitably pricey. Even if you don't buy anything, visit it anyway because it's so colorful and festive.

But since neither man nor woman lives by shopping alone, the best dose of culture that one can absorb in Berlin is on Museum Island, in what was East Berlin. The "island" is an impressive grouping of six very important museums dedicated to all the great masters of cultural and artistic expression throughout history.

The best photos of Berlin can be taken at the glorious Brandenburg Gate, the single greatest symbol of the city and one of the world's most recognized monuments. It serves as the entrance to the historic center of the old Soviet sector of divided Berlin. The wall the Russians put up was squarely in front of the Gate. Visit it and you breathe in its history, for one can easily imagine Napoléon's troops, or Hitler's, or Stalin's, marching through its columns. Of the wall, all that's left is a yellow line painted on the ground indicating its location and a museum, the Gallery of the East, on Mühlenstrasse.

And speaking of photos, don't fail to visit the television tower at the famous Alexanderplatz, located at the very heart of what was once

Communist Berlin. The tower measures 365 meters in height and at its pinnacle is perched a rotating café, the Tele-Café, which offers the best view of the city.

To burn a few calories and to engage with nature a bit, I recommend a walk, or a morning jog, in the marvelous Tiergarten park. It's immense and heavily forested and it's located right in the center of the city. You can enter it through the Brandenburg Gate. It's also where you'll find the largest zoo in all of Europe. I recommend it to you as an inexpensive alternative to shopping some morning before the games.

MY FAVORITE SPOT

Finally (and if you're in a romantic or introspective mood), I recommend you go to the Hotel Adlon, which is located in the Plaza Parisien (the Pariser Platz), which itself is right in front of the Brandenburg Gate. The hotel is the most famous and historic in all of Berlin, but the reason I'm recommending it to you is its restaurant, and not so much for its food (which is both excellent and expensive) but for its excellent ambience. In the summer, the tables are set up out on the hotel's sidewalk, where the view of the Gate is simply splendid. The best time to go is after nine o'clock in the evening, when the sun is beginning to hide behind the monument. The experience of seeing the colors of the sunset while contemplating Berlin's past is simply unforgettable.

If we're fortunate, perhaps we'll see each other there. And if you bring this book, I'll be delighted to sign it for you—and maybe I'll pay for dinner!

BIBLIOGRAPHY

Books and Publications:

Calderón Cardozo, Carlos. *Por Amor a la Camiseta* (México: Clio, 1998).

Cantor, Andrés. *¡Goool!* (New York: Simon & Schuster, 1996).

"El Libro de Oro del Mundial," Clarín (Argentina: Diario Clarín, 1998).

Douglas, Geoffrey. *The Game of Their Lives* (New York: HarperCollins Publishers, 2005).

El Gráfico, "Los Maravillosos Mundiales de Fútbol," *El Gráfico* (Argentina: El Gráfico, 1996).

Etchandy, Alfredo. *Memorias de la Pelota* (Uruguay: Ediciones del Caballo Perdido, 2002).

Fernández, Ángel. *Esto es Fútbol Soccer* (México: Aguilar, 1994).

Fernández, Claudia y Andrew Paxman. *El Tigre* (México: Grijalbo, 2000).

Galeano, Eduardo. *Soccer in Sun and Shadow* (New York: Verso, 2003).

García Pimentel, Roberto; Francisco Forastieri Monasterio; Francisco Javier Sánchez. *Triunfos y Tristezas del Equipo Tricolor* (México: Edamex, 1995).

Ghiggia, Alcides. *El Gol del Siglo* (Uruguay: El País y Tendfield, 2000).

Hernández, Panchito. *América, El Mejor de la Historia* (México: Edamex, 1998).

"Germany," *Insight Guides* (Discovery Channel, 2005).

Kohn Hinestrosa, Alfonso. *El Fútbol, su Historia y los Mundiales* (Alkohn Productions, 1994).

Kraunze, León. *Moneda en el Aire* (México: Clio, 1998).

Maradona, Diego Armando. *Yo Soy el Diego* (España: Planeta, 2000).

"Traveler Germany," *National Geographic* (National Geographic, 2004).

Radnedge, Karl, Editor. *The Ultimate Encyclopedia of Soccer* (UK: Carlton Books, 2003).

Seyde, Manuel. *La Fiesta del Alarido* (México: Excelsior, 1970).

Snyder, John. *Soccer Most Wanted* (Brassey's Inc, 2001).

Sotelo, Greco. *Chivas, La Construcción de un Orgullo* (Clio, 1999).

Sotelo, Greco. *El Oficio de las Canchas* (Clio, 1998).

Tirelli Gatti, Enrique. *El Libro de Oro de las 15 Copas del Mundo* (Soccer Golden Book Inc, 1993).

Yallop, David. *Cómo se Robaron la Copa* (Oveja Negra, 2001).

Zenteno Cervantes, Armando and Francisco G. Sánchez. *Los 14 Mundiales* (México: Ediciones Castillo, 1994).

Internet:

www.concacaf.com	www.futbolfactory.futbolweb.net
www.conmebol.com	www.soccerhall.org
www.ESPNsoccernet.com	www.soccertimes.com
www.fifa.com	www.todoslosmundiales.com.ar
www.footballdatabase.com	

I'd like to thank all my passionate friends and soccer fans who show me their unconditional love no matter where I go.

PHOTO CREDITS

Page ii: Diether Endlicher/AP Wide World; page vi: Dusan Vranic/AP Wide World; page viii: Darko Bandic/AP Wide World; pages x, 261, 262: Petr David Josek/AP Wide World; page xiv: Martial/Trezzini/Keystone/AP Wide World; page 2: ©Congress- und Tourismus-Zentrale Nürnberg; pages 4, 361: ©Tourismus + Congress GmbH Frankfurt am Main; page 10: Koji Sasahara/AP Wide World; page 12: Fabrizio Giovannozzi/AP Wide World; pages 18, 26, 29, 33, 44, 247, 263, 289, 301: AP Wide World; pages 54, 65, 79, 94, 108, 121, 138, 155, 173, 191, 205, 221: Carlo Fumagalli/AP Wide World; pages 234, 276, 288: Armando Franca/AP Wide World; pages 236, 275, 282, 283, 287: Paulo Duarte/AP Wide World; page 243: Michael Probst/AP Wide World; page 244: Fred Ernst/AP Wide World; page 245: Andre Penner/AP Wide World; page 246: Luca Bruno/AP Wide World; page 248: Roberto Candia/AP Wide World; page 249: Fernando Llano/AP Wide World; page 250: Jorge Saenz/AP Wide World; page 251: Moises Castillo/AP Wide World; page 252: Yun Jai-Hyoung/AP Wide World; page 253: Daniel P. Derella/AP Wide World; pages 254, 346: Will Shilling/AP Wide World; page 255: Thomas Kienzle/AP Wide World; pages 256, 283: Michael Sohn/AP Wide World; page 257: Andres Leighton/AP Wide World; page 258: Hasan Jamali/AP Wide World; page 259: Christof Stache/AP Wide World; page 260: Joerg Sarbach/AP Wide World; pages 261, 262: Steven Governo/AP Wide World; page 263: Paul White/AP Wide World; page 264: Antonio Calanni/AP Wide World; pages 265, 294: Lionel Cironneau/AP Wide World; pages 265, 274, 295: Martin Meissner/AP Wide World; pages 266, 269: Peter Dejong/AP Wide World; page 267: Kai-Uwe Knoth/AP Wide World; page 268: Nick Potts/PA/AP Wide World; page 270: Maxim Malinovsky/AP Wide World; page 271: Alik Keplicz/AP Wide World; pages 277, 303, 304: Lee Jin-man/AP Wide World; page 277: Mindaugas Kulbis/AP Wide World; page 278: Ahn Young-joon/AP Wide World; pages 285, 286: Efrem Lukatsky/AP Wide World; page 291: Anja Niedringhaus/AP Wide World; page 292: Martial Trezzini/Keystone/AP Wide World; page 294: Sang Tan/AP Wide World; pages 293, 297, 298: Hasan Sarbakhshian/AP Wide World; pages 296, 299: Frank Augstein/AP Wide World; page 302: Anvar Ilyasov/AP Wide World; page 300: Jesus Dominguez/AP Wide World; page 305: Matilde Campodonico/AP Wide World; page 306: Paul Ellis/AP Wide World; page 350: ©Christl Reiter/ The Munich City Tourist Office; page 352: ©Rudolf Sterflinger/The Munich City Tourist Office; page 354: ©Stuttgart-Marketing GmbH; page 368: ©Günther Ventur/City of Cologne; page 371: Leipzig Tourist Service-Schmidt; page 378: Bildarchiv Monheim GmbH/Alamy; page 382: ©Jens Klages/Landeshauptstadt Hannover; page 385: ©Fachbereich Umwelt und Stadtgrün/Landeshauptstadt Hannover; page 388: ©Michael Zapf/Hamburg Tourismus GmbH; page 393: ©www.berlin-tourist-information.de/Berlin Tourismus Marketing GmbH.